PRAISE FOR A PREVIOUS EDITION OF *WITHDRAWN*

Wyoming
Off the Beaten Path ®

"*Wyoming Off the Bea...*
cowpoke into the Old...
This painstakingly researched guide is a
well-deserved companion."

—*Boise Magazine*

DATE DUE

Help Us Keep This Guide Up to Date

Every effort has been made by the author and editors to make this guide as accurate and useful as possible. However, many changes can occur after a guide is published—establishments close, phone numbers change, hiking trails are rerouted, facilities come under new management, etc.

We would love to hear from you concerning your experiences with this guide and how you feel it could be improved and be kept up to date. While we may not be able to respond to all comments and suggestions, we'll take them to heart, and we'll make certain to share them with the author. Please send your comments and suggestions to the following address:

The Globe Pequot Press
Reader Response/Editorial Department
P.O. Box 480
Guilford, CT 06437

Or you may e-mail us at: editorial@GlobePequot.com

Thanks for your input, and happy travels!

INSIDERS' GUIDE®

OFF THE BEATEN PATH® SERIES

Off the Beaten Path®

FIFTH EDITION

wyoming

A GUIDE TO UNIQUE PLACES

MICHAEL McCOY

INSIDERS' GUIDE®

GUILFORD, CONNECTICUT
AN IMPRINT OF THE GLOBE PEQUOT PRESS

The prices, rates, and hours listed in this guidebook
were confirmed at press time. We recommend,
however, that you call establishments to obtain
current information before traveling.

To buy books in quantity for corporate use
or incentives, call **(800) 962–0973, ext. 4551,**
or e-mail **premiums@GlobePequot.com.**

INSIDERS' GUIDE®

Text design by Linda Loiewski
Maps created by Equator Graphics © The Globe Pequot Press
Illustrations by Carole Drong
Spot photography throughout © Daryl Benson/Masterfile

ISSN 1542-6262
ISBN 0-7627-3541-4

Manufactured in the United States of America
Fifth Edition/First Printing

To Wyoming, "the way the West was . . ."

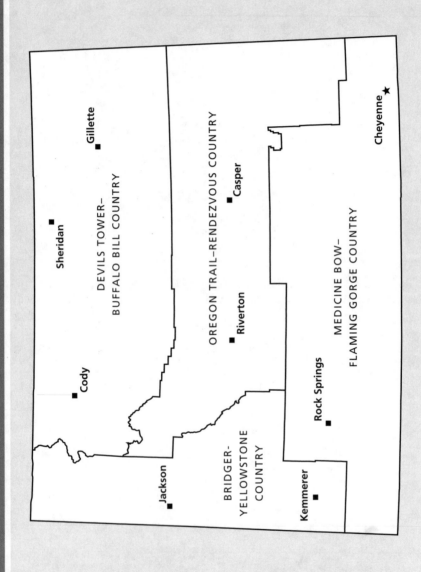

Contents

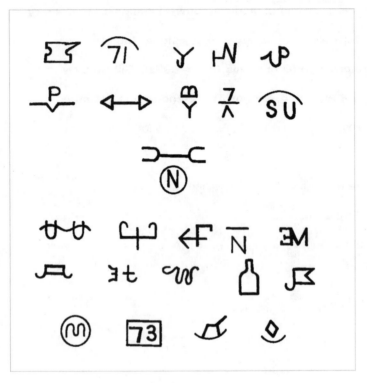

A Few Wyoming Brands

Introduction

The original edition of *Wyoming Off the Beaten Path* was written by another team of authors, but when the offer to update the book came my way, I jumped at it. Wyoming, you see, is in my blood.

I was raised in Iowa where I always felt special because I was born in Wyoming. Among the wannabe cowpokes in my neighborhood—which included just about every boy under the age of eleven—saying you were from Wyoming was rather like saying Roy Rogers was your uncle. Don't ask me how or why, but for a while there, when I was three or four, I even believed I was the cowboy gracing the Wyoming license plate. Today, although my mailing address reads "Idaho," the first thing I see every morning when looking out my east-facing windows is the Wyoming Tetons.

My time actually residing in Wyoming doesn't add up to much—a grand total of six or seven years—but I've worked and/or lived in virtually every corner of the state. I was born in Wheatland, I graduated from the university in Laramie, and I got married in Grand Teton National Park. I've spent time as a National Park Ranger at Devils Tower, cooked shrimp and steaks at Grand Targhee Ski Resort, and worked archaeological projects out of Rock Springs, Worland, Rawlins, Casper, and other towns. I've hiked, bicycled, and/or cross-country skied in Yellowstone, the Great Divide Basin, the Wind Rivers, the Tetons, the Absarokas, the Wyoming and Salt River Ranges, the Medicine Bows, the Laramie Range, the Big Horns, the Gros Ventres, the Black Hills, and lesser-known ranges like the Owl Creek and Green Mountains and the Rattlesnake Range. I've played pool or horseshoes and drunk beer with cowboys in places you've heard of and others you probably haven't, including lone-pony towns like Hyattville, Jeffrey City, Woods Landing, Hulett, Bondurant, Savery, and Manderson.

If I've learned one thing about Wyoming during my ramblings, it is this: The state-line greeting signs weren't stretching the truth when they told you it's LIKE NO PLACE ON EARTH. Thanks to the sparsity of vegetation covering much of the state, passersby actually have opportunities to study the earth instead of a bunch of grass and trees. Wyoming reveals more about its inner self than just about any state of the Union, which explains why in the Tetons, the Big Horns, Wind River Canyon, and other locations you'll see camps and buses teeming with geology students from colleges throughout the United States. The long list of critters you can see afoot and on wing in Yellowstone and other parts of Wyoming makes the state one of the great wildlife viewing areas of the world. Then there's the sky: endless, and unfathomably blue. Even the mindset of

Wyoming's human residents is different. Difficult as it is to believe in this era of contracts, litigation, scams, and red tape, in Wyoming there really are folks who still seal business deals with a handshake. Those involved know—corny as it may sound—that a promise from a fellow honest man or woman is worth more than a bunch of words on a piece of paper, any day.

Wyomingites tend to be plainspoken, straightforward, and politically conservative, yet the first-time visitor might find the populace more complicated than expected. You might meet a rancher who adamantly opposes wolf reintroduction and despises grizzly bears, yet who has chosen to preserve his ranch lands in perpetuity under a conservation easement. He loves and respects that land more than anyone can understand, and he doesn't want subdivisions made of it; the man is a conservationist to his very soul. You may meet a one-time confirmed vegetarian from New York who now religiously hunts elk come fall because in Wyoming, living with nature is a fact of life and not something experienced only on television. He's learned that few food items in this world are tastier and less tainted than wild elk meat. You might participate in a whitewater float trip guided by a California-trained lawyer who, after a summer spent in the Tetons, couldn't bear the thought of returning to the bar and the smog, discovering instead that she prefers the outdoors, the oars, and the crisp high-country air.

Today's traveler can still capture a sense of the hardy individualism and its bipolar companion, spirit of community, which hand in hand built the West as we know it. In Wyoming you can ferret out and follow historic trails penetrating a countryside little changed in the last 150 years: the Oregon-Mormon, California, Bridger, Bozeman, Nez Perce, and Pony Express Trails, for starters. These pioneer Wyoming paths, some of which hosted tens of thousands of travelers in the 1800s, have largely reverted to "unbeaten" status, and by following them you will experience a wild sort of country visited by few pilgrims today.

Wyoming by its very nature is off the beaten path. That's obvious. Therefore, many of the attractions featured in this guide are *really* off the beaten path. Be aware when traveling through broad-shouldered Wyoming that services are often few and far between. Prepare accordingly, by always carrying plenty of food and water; by going equipped for minor emergencies, such as a flat tire, so that they don't become major problems; and by always topping off your gas tank before leaving a town for the wide-open spaces. Know, too, that the weather is unpredictable; it can be fierce in a dozen different ways and can change in less than a moment's notice. In winter, take along a sleeping bag for each person, a snow shovel, snacks, and water. And if you get stranded in the snow somewhere, *stay with your car.* The climate can be extremely pleasant, too, but take precautions even then: Because of the intense, high-elevation sunshine, you should always apply a high-SPF sunscreen to your exposed skin and wear a hat and sunglasses to protect your head and eyes.

The Wyoming Division of Tourism has done a logical job of dividing the state into six travel regions, three of which I've borrowed for use in this book: Medicine Bow–Flaming Gorge Country (southern Wyoming), Devils Tower–Buffalo Bill Country (northern Wyoming), and Oregon Trail–Rendezvous Country (central Wyoming). The other three Division of Tourism regions—Jackson Hole–Jim Bridger Country, Grand Teton Country, and Yellowstone Country—I've combined into one region called Bridger-Yellowstone Country, which comprises most of western Wyoming.

After experiencing the grandeur and emptiness of Wyoming's landscapes and the forthright qualities of her people, don't be surprised to find yourself changed on returning home. And please, don't resist it: The world would be a lot better off if everyone added even a small piece of Wyoming to their character.

Wyoming at a Glance

- *Nicknames:* Cowboy State, Equality State
- *Capital:* Cheyenne
- *Motto:* Equal Rights
- *Highest Elevation:* 13,804' (Gannett Peak, Wind River Range)
- *Lowest Elevation:* 3,125' (where the Belle Fourche River flows into South Dakota)
- *Land Area:* 97,914 square miles (ranked 9th in U.S.)
- *Population:* 501,242 (ranked 50th in U.S.)
- *Statehood:* July 10, 1890 (44th state)
- *State Bird:* Western meadowlark
- *State Flower:* Indian paintbrush
- *State Tree:* Plains cottonwood
- *State Mammal:* Bison
- *State Gemstone:* Jade
- *State Fish:* Cutthroat trout
- *State Reptile:* Horned toad
- *State Dinosaur:* Triceratops
- *State Fossil: Knightia* fish
- *Average Annual Precipitation:* 14.5 inches
- *A Sampling of Radio Stations:* Casper: KTWO-AM, 1030 kHz (the Voice of Wyoming); Cheyenne: KFBC-AM, 1240 kHz; Cody: KODI-AM, 1400 kHz; Evanston: KEVA-AM, 1240 kHz; Gillette: KIML-AM, 1270 kHz; Green River: KUGR-AM, 1490 kHz; Jackson: KMTN-FM, 96.9 MHz; Kemmerer:

KMER-AM, 950 kHz; Laramie: KUWR-FM, 91.9 MHz (National Public Radio, available throughout the state); Rawlins: KRAL-AM, 1240 kHz; Riverton: KVOW-AM, 1450 kHz; Rock Springs: KRKK-AM, 1360 kHz; Sheridan: KWYO-AM, 1410 kHz; Worland: KWOR-AM, 1340 kHz

- *Major Newspapers:* Casper Star Tribune, Daily Boomerang (Laramie), Jackson Hole News & Guide, News-Record (Gillette), Northern Wyoming Daily News (Worland), Rocket-Miner (Rock Springs), Sheridan Press, Wyoming Tribune-Eagle (Cheyenne)

- *Travel Information:* The Wyoming Vacation Guide and the Wyoming Vacation Planner are both available through the Wyoming Division of Tourism, (307) 777–7777. On the Internet, information can be found at http://wyoming.gov or www.wyomingtourism.org.

- *Area Code:* There is one area code for the entire state of Wyoming, 307.

Southern Wyoming: Medicine Bow–Flaming Gorge Country

Southern Wyoming is the region responsible for the state's reputation as a windblown, God-forsaken desert. Even here, however, impressive mountains occasionally jut out of the dry land, offering surprisingly verdant, protected havens, teeming with wildlife and forests of aspen and pine. And the deserts themselves hold a host of surprises that will delight those intrepid souls willing to spend the time and effort required to earn a closer look.

Your journey begins in the southeastern corner of the state, then leads along the Interstate 80 corridor, with plenty of side trips taking you off that major thoroughfare. As you cross the state from east to west, you'll visit cities and settlements with names and appearances that bring to mind the Wild West: places like Cheyenne and Laramie, Rock River and Medicine Bow, Green River City and Fort Bridger. Finally, at Evanston, near the Utah border, you'll turn north to continue on to Bridger-Yellowstone Country.

Laramie County

Entering southeast Wyoming from the east, you'll intersect prehistoric Native American trails and newer trails, too, such as the nineteenth-century Texas Cattle Trail. Consider forsaking

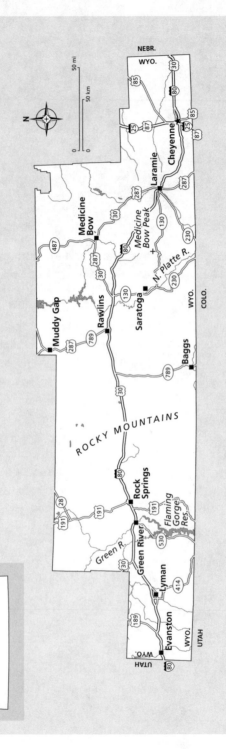

I–80 and crossing the Nebraska-Wyoming border on Highway 30, the old Lincoln Highway (it's located just north of I–80). An abandoned wooden service station, like a symbol of the forgotten old highway itself, with "neb/wyo" painted in the middle of the dilapidated structure, will greet you.

The area around the border town of Pine Bluffs served as a crossroads for prehistoric peoples, pioneer sodbusters, and cattle drovers early on the scene. The nearby pine hills provided the Native American inhabitants excellent campsites with plentiful water, firewood, and small game. More than 600,000 cattle were driven through the Pine Bluffs crossroads area during the heyday of the Texas Cattle Trail in 1871, and the Pine Bluffs rail station served as an important cattle-shipping center for many years. The *Texas Trail Museum* (housed in Pine Bluffs' original 1915 power plant) at Third and Market Streets illustrates the important role played by the town in the development of the West, with its numerous displays on the area's cattle ranches and homesteads, early firefighting techniques, cowgirls of the West, Native American cultures, and the Lincoln Highway. The museum is located in the *Texas Trail Park,* where you can investigate a caboose, railroad boardinghouse, blacksmith shop, homesteader's log cabin, bunkhouse, and the first schoolhouse in Laramie County. The Texas Trail Park and Texas Trail Museum are open from 11:00

BEST ATTRACTIONS IN MEDICINE BOW–FLAMING GORGE COUNTRY

Aspen Alley,
south of Rawlins;
(307) 327–5481

Cheyenne Botanic Gardens,
Cheyenne;
(307) 637–6458

Flaming Gorge National Recreation Area,
south of Green River;
(307) 875–2871

Hobo Pool,
Saratoga;
(307) 326–8855

Little Snake River Valley Museum,
Savery;
(307) 383–7262

Natural History Museum at WWCC,
Rock Springs;
(307) 382–1666

Rose's Lariat,
Rawlins;
(307) 324–5261

Snowy Range Scenic Byway,
outside Laramie;
(307) 745–8971

The Old Corral,
Centennial;
(307) 745–5918

Vedauwoo,
outside Laramie;
(307) 745–8971

The Lincoln Highway

The idea for the Lincoln Highway originated at a dinner meeting of automobile industry tycoons in Indianapolis in 1912. At the time, the nation's two million miles of roads were largely unconnected, and railroads represented the only practical means of coast-to-coast travel. Within three years of the meeting, a patchwork made from existing roads wound its way across the country from Times Square in New York City to Lincoln Park in San Francisco, creating the first transcontinental highway. Wyoming residents lit bonfires along the route across the state on November 13, 1913, to signal the opening of the new Lincoln Highway.

Later improvements made the Lincoln Highway one of the premier roads of its day. The federal government took over the road system in the late 1920s; to mark the event, on September 1, 1928, the Boy Scouts of America installed more than three thousand Lincoln Highway markers along the route.

For the most part the Lincoln Highway ran parallel to the Union Pacific Railroad, which preceded the highway west. Today, fiber-optic cables transport modern-day telecommunications along this historic travel corridor.

A.M. to 4:00 P.M., Monday through Saturday (closed Sunday) from Memorial Day through Labor Day, or by appointment. Call 245–3713 for information.

The **High Plains Archaeology Labs**—with a museum in town at Second and Pine Streets and nearby excavation sites and interpretive center—are open to summer visitors on weekdays and most weekends. The University of Wyoming conducts the archaeological dig; crews of students under the direction of Charles Reher have discovered artifacts dating back 10,000 years, many of which are included in dozens of displays at the museum. The excavation site and new interpretive center can be reached by a five-minute walk along a cement path from the Pine Bluffs information center and rest area south of I–80—or you can drive into town and park at the center.

The new **Windows on the Past** interpretive center has been built over the excavations to allow easy access for the public. The excavations go down 20 feet and have revealed twenty distinct cultural levels occupied by ancient peoples over a span of 100 centuries. For more information, and directions to the site and museum, stop at the chamber of commerce's information center on the south side of I–80, call the chamber at 245–3695, or call the archaeology museum in town at 245–9372. During the off-season, Reher welcomes queries at his university office in Laramie at 766–5136 or by e-mail at arrow@uwyo.edu.

Take time to enjoy a trail walk around the archaeological dig and rest area with the aid of a brochure (available at the visitor center). Interpretive trail signs point out wildlife habitat areas, bird sites, and native grasses and other vegetation found in the *Pine Bluffs Nature Area.*

If you're in the area during the first weekend of August, check out the *Texas Trail Days,* replete with wagon trains, cowboy poetry readings, melodramas, parade, rodeo, street dance, and western barbecues. For information call the Pine Bluffs Area Chamber of Commerce at 245–3695. Alternatively, on any Friday evening from early June through mid-August, you can take in the Outlaw Saloon Summer Rodeo series (632–3626), with its full slate of bull riding, barrel racing, team roping, bareback riding, and more.

Forty-five miles west of Pine Bluffs, after passing through high plains that roll away in every direction from I–80, you will arrive at the capital city of Cheyenne and catch your first glimpse of the Rocky Mountains rising from the plains to the west. Cheyenne derives its name from the *Shey'an'nah,* an Algonquin Indian tribe. The city's wild early days began with the arrival of the Union Pacific Railroad and the establishment of Fort D. A. Russell (now F. E. Warren Air Force Base), built for the protection of the railroaders in 1867. Maj. Gen. Grenville M. Dodge, a Union Pacific surveyor, plotted the city as a major rail terminus situated just east of the long pull over the Laramie Range.

BEST ANNUAL EVENTS IN MEDICINE BOW–FLAMING GORGE COUNTRY

Sierra Madre Winter Carnival,
Encampment; February;
(307) 326–8855

**Don E. Erickson Memorial
Cutter Races,**
Saratoga; February;
(307) 326–8855

**Woodchoppers Jamboree
and Rodeo,**
Saratoga/Encampment; June;
(307) 326–8855

Flaming Gorge Days,
Green River; late June;
(307) 362–3771

Jubilee Days,
Laramie; early July;
(800) 445–5303

Stock Car Races and Fireworks,
Rock Springs; Fourth of July;
(307) 362–3771

Annual Fiesta Days,
Rawlins; July;
(800) 228–3547

Cheyenne Frontier Days,
Cheyenne; July;
(307) 778–7200 or (800) 227–6336

Carbon County Fair & Rodeo,
Rawlins; August;
(800) 228–3547

Hams Fork River Rendezvous,
Granger; August;
(307) 875–5711

In addition to the railroaders, early residents included mule skinners, soldiers, rustlers, stagecoach hands, outlaws, and other opportunists. The railhead made Cheyenne a natural base for numerous cattle barons, who established the elaborate Cheyenne Club, where they conducted cattle business and hosted lavish parties. A marker for the Cheyenne Club stands at the corner of Warren Avenue and Seventeenth Street.

In the 1870s, Cheyenne also became an important center for outfitting miners headed to the goldfields of the Black Hills, and a stagecoach line soon ran between the two areas. The Cheyenne–Fort Laramie–Deadwood Trail started at the corner of Capital Avenue and Sixteenth Street and ended in Deadwood, South Dakota. A trail marker can be visited at the corner of Capital Avenue and Twenty-second Street.

There's plenty to see and do around Cheyenne. The city is home to the rodeo known as the "Daddy of 'em All," ***Cheyenne Frontier Days,*** in July. Most visitors to Cheyenne flock in to see the world's oldest and largest outdoor rodeo—and you should too if it fits your schedule—but be sure also to visit the excellent ***Cheyenne Frontier Days Old West Museum,*** located in Frontier Park at 4501 North Carey Avenue.

This fine museum is a must stop for those interested in exploring the essence of the Old West. An extensive collection of horse-drawn vehicles includes stagecoaches, a hearse, and a range chuck wagon. Native American clothing, rodeo memorabilia dating back to the first Cheyenne rodeo in 1897, a rustic saloon, a Union Pacific exhibit, exhibits on Cheyenne history, and a wonderful collection of Western art make up additional displays. Among other tidbits, you'll

High-Tech Scratching Post

"The first issue of N. A. Baker's *Daily Leader* appeared [in Cheyenne] on September 16, 1867, and on October 25 the telegraph line came in from Laporte, Colorado. Difficulties encountered by the telegraph line crews have a place in Wyoming folklore. Indolent buffalo still roamed the treeless prairie between Omaha and the Laramie Mountains in great herds. They regarded the newly set poles as scratching posts, and several bison could rub a pole out of the ground in a few hours. The line boss decided to spike the poles, points out, to discourage them. This, from the buffalo's point of view, added greatly to their value. Within a few hours, according to the legend, a waiting line of thirty buffalo had formed at every telegraph pole between Cheyenne and Omaha. And when a lone bison lumbered east from Cheyenne, oldsters allowed they had heard of a vacant pole 'somewhere this side of Omaha.'" (From *Wyoming: A Guide to Its Highways, History, and People,* published as part of the Federal Writers' Project in 1941.)

learn about Will Pickett, the African-American cowboy who invented bulldog-ging by throwing a steer using only his teeth. Year-round the museum is open weekdays from 9:00 A.M. to 5:00 P.M. and weekends from 10:00 A.M. to 5:00 P.M., longer hours in summer. Call 778–7290 or visit www.oldwestmuseum.org for additional information.

Another fun diversion that's part of Cheyenne Frontier Days is *The Indian Village,* located near the entrance to Frontier Park at Eighth Street and Carey Avenue. Award-winning Native American dancers give free dance performances several times

southern
wyomingtrivia

The Cheyenne Frontier Days Rodeo, the "Daddy of 'em All," was first held in 1897.

daily during the week's celebration. Also, authentic Native American jewelry, clothing, and other items are available for sale. Frontier Days runs in late July for ten days. For information call (800) 227–6336 or visit the Web site www.cfdrodeo.com.

Nearby, the *Cheyenne Botanic Gardens*—"where sustainability is not just a buzzword"—offer a pleasant contrast to the loud, dusty grounds of Frontier Park. Sit outside among the flowers, take a stroll along the garden pathways, or investigate the exotic plants in the 6,800-square-foot greenhouse conservatory, which constitutes one of the West's most unusual solar energy demonstrations. See, smell, and touch; the inviting oasis is truly a feast of the senses—particularly during the often bleak, blustery Wyoming winter. Not simply for show, the botanic gardens offer social services, education, and therapy to seniors, youths at risk, and handicapped individuals, and grow food year-round for distribution to the gardens' volunteers and for low-income programs. The Cheyenne Botanic Gardens are located at 710 South Lions Park Drive. The gardens are open 365 days a year during daylight hours. The conservatory hours are Monday through Friday from 8:00 A.M. to 4:30 P.M., weekends from 11:00 A.M. to 3:30 P.M., closed most holidays. Admission is free, but donations are welcome. The phone number is 637–6458, and the e-mail address is info@botanic.org. Online you can learn more at www.botanic.org.

For such a sparsely populated state, Wyoming showcases a surprisingly grand *state capitol.* Its twenty-four-carat gold-leaf dome commands the skyline from all entrances to the city. Built between 1887 and 1890, the capitol features Corinthian columns and sandstone quarried at Rawlins and in Colorado. A statue commemorating Esther Hobart Morris, America's first woman justice of the peace, graces the entrance to the capitol. (A replica of the statue is also located in Statuary Hall in the U.S. Capitol in Washington, D.C., along with a statue of Chief Washakie, added in 2000.)

Tom Horn

Tom Horn, one of the last of an ultra-independent breed, was a free agent hired gun, a man who would do just about anything to earn his keep. Among other things, he was a highly skilled stock detective, working for the Wyoming Stock Growers Association. Raised by Apache Indians for part of his youth, Horn later served as an Indian scout, did a stint with Teddy Roosevelt's Rough Riders in the Spanish-American War, and worked for the Pinkerton Agency as an investigator. He was also a murderer . . . or was he?

After being found guilty of killing fourteen-year-old Willie Nickell, Horn was hanged in Cheyenne on November 20, 1903. The debate about whether he was guilty of murder, however, continues to this day. A lot of folks believe that Nickell was actually shot and killed by a feuding neighbor who mistook young Nickell for his father. The pro-Horn faction maintains that Tom Horn never was the bloodthirsty murderer he was made out to be.

At a recent reenactment of Horn's trial in Cheyenne, using evidence that has surfaced since his execution, he was found not guilty of murder. And still, the debate continues.

Partly thanks to Morris, a true pioneer of women's rights, Wyoming has been designated the Equality State. Its first territorial legislature granted women the right to vote in 1869, and later the legislature required that women be allowed to vote in Wyoming as a condition of Wyoming's entrance into the Union in 1890. (The Nineteenth Amendment to the Constitution, giving all women citizens of the United States the right to vote, would not be passed for another twenty-nine years.) Wyoming also swore in the country's first all-female jury and elected the first female governor, Nellie Tayloe Ross, in a 1924 special election held to replace her husband, Governor William B. Ross, who had died in office. In 1933 Franklin D. Roosevelt appointed Nellie Tayloe Ross director of the U.S. Mint, a post she held until her retirement in 1953.

The Spirit of Wyoming, a bronze statue on the plaza between the capitol and the Herschler Building, stands more than 18 feet high and depicts a cowboy and his horse seemingly at odds with the elements. The statue is the work of international award-winning sculptor Edward J. Fraughton.

Inside, note the eight large murals in the Senate and House of Representatives chambers. Illustrating early Wyoming life, they're titled *Chief Cheyenne, Frontier Cavalry Officers, Pony Express Rider, Railroad/Builders/Surveyors, Cattlemen, Trappers, Homesteaders,* and *Stagecoach.* The ceilings of both chambers are inlaid with striking Tiffany stained glass, crafted with the Wyoming state seal as the focal point. From there proceed to Room 302 where a 1982 mural, *Wyoming: the Land, the People,* by Mike Kopriva depicts Wyoming's past and present culture and lifestyles. Before exiting the capitol, have a look at the mounted elk and bison to get an up-close perspective of the size of some of Wyoming's common wildlife. The capitol is open to the public Monday through Friday from 8:00 A.M. to 5:00 P.M. It is closed on weekends. Tours are available year-round. For information on access and in-session activities, call 777–7220 or visit www.state.wy.us. The capitol is located on Capitol Avenue and Twenty-second Street.

Now that you've seen where the legislature works, take a short walk over to the 1904 **Historic Governors' Mansion** at 300 East Twenty-first Street. The mansion housed nineteen Wyoming first families until being replaced by a new residence in 1976. Designed by an Omaha architect, Charles Mudrock, the building features Colonial Revival architecture, with a portico supported by four Corinthian columns flanking the main entrance. A tour video is available for viewing. The Historic Governors' Mansion is open year-round Tuesday through Saturday from 9:00 A.M. to 5:00 P.M., but it closes at noon during the winter months. Call 777–7878 for more information.

The **Wyoming State Museum,** which celebrated its centennial in 1995, houses major collections covering territorial days, Wyoming's first families, Native Americans, Western art, Hollywood Westerns featuring movie star Tim McCoy (once an adjutant general of the Wyoming National Guard and no relation to the author of this book, so far as he knows), and Wyoming fossils and petroglyphs. One of the museum's treasures is the Historic Photographic Collection, comprising some 250,000 images dating back to the 1860s, from such legendary photographers as Joseph E. Stimson and W. H. Jackson. Photo subjects range from cattle brands to stagecoach robberies and from the Teapot Dome to Yellowstone National Park. Located in the Barrett Building at 2301 Central Avenue (just south of the capitol), the Wyoming State Museum is open Tuesday through Friday from 9:00 A.M. to 4:30 P.M. Saturday hours vary with the season; closed Sundays, Mondays, and holidays. Admission is free. For more information call 777–7022, e-mail wsm@state.wy.us, or visit http://wyomuseum.state.wy.us.

A visit to Cheyenne would not be complete without a trip to **Lakeview Cemetery,** in operation for 120 years. Among the more interesting and unusual fatalities recorded in cemetery records are an 1887 death attributed to drinking ice water, an 1892 execution of a seventeen-year-old, and a 1902 death from flypaper poisoning. More common were deaths caused by railroad-related accidents, shootings, and flu epidemics. The first documented hanging by a mob occurred in 1883, the first streetcar death in 1903, the first automobile death in

1915, and the first airplane death in 1923. Wander among the tombstones to discover your own historical oddities. Lakeview Cemetery is still an operational cemetery, so take care not to interfere with funeral services. It is located at 2501 Seymour Avenue. The cemetery gates are always open, but the office is only open Monday through Friday from 8:00 A.M. to 5:00 P.M.

If you're a fan of unique architecture, take the *Historic Downtown Walking Tour,* featured on the city map available at the visitors bureau (778–3133). Three popular favorites are the 1886 Union Pacific Depot, the Tivoli Building, and the Dineen automobile dealership, with its imposing lions hanging out near the roof. Another must-see is the newly renovated Plains Hotel at 1600 Central Avenue. Cheyenne also boasts several top-notch art galleries and western clothing stores, which you'll pass during the walking tour.

By now the digestive juices should be flowing. You can't beat the *Cheyenne Cattle Company* for substantial evening fare, such as steaks, seafood, and other favorites. The Cheyenne Cattle Company, located within the Best Western Hitching Post Inn at 1700 West Lincolnway, opens for evening meals at 5:30 P.M. Food prices are moderate to expensive. Call 775–7303 for further information.

The *Terry Bison Ranch* was formerly the southern headquarters of the huge land holdings of Wyoming's first governor, F. E. Warren. Presidents, generals, and senators were among those who found it a pleasant retreat. Early visitors to Warren's Terry Ranch included Pres. Theodore Roosevelt and Warren's son-in-law, Gen. John "Black Jack" Pershing. Today you can bunk in a log cabin or park your RV and enjoy horseback riding, fishing on a private lake, and motorized tours to view a bison herd of roughly 2,500 head roaming 30,000 acres—all within minutes of downtown Cheyenne. Other facilities on the Terry Bison Ranch include the Senator's Steakhouse and Brass Buffalo Saloon—with live entertainment on weekends—and Terry Ranch Cellars, Wyoming's first winery. Take the Terry Ranch exit off I–25, 7 miles south of Cheyenne, and follow the signs. The season runs from Memorial Day to Labor Day, but the cabins and RV facilities are available year-round. Cabins rent for around $80 per night. Food prices are moderate. For more information call 634–4171 or visit www.terrybisonranch.com.

Another item to add to your Cheyenne "to-do" list is a guided tour for groups of ten or more of *F. E. Warren Air Force Base,* conducted by appointment. (You can make one by calling 773–3381.) To get there, at the west end of town take Randall Avenue to the base main entrance. The tour includes an excellent museum depicting the fort's early military history. Many of the older buildings, some dating back to 1885, are constructed in the Colonial style, with red brick and imposing white columns. Also of interest is the new Archaeology

Prairie Kilotons

Until recently, the 90th Space Wing at Fort Warren commanded 200 intercontinental ballistic missiles, based in underground silos in southeast Wyoming and nearby parts of Colorado and Nebraska. Dismantling of fifty of the most powerful missiles—MX or "Peacekeeper" missiles, each armed with up to ten 300-kiloton warheads—began in the fall of 2002 and is expected to take three years. (The atom bomb dropped on Hiroshima in 1945 yielded thirteen kilotons.) The decommissioning is part of President Bush's decision to reduce the nation's nuclear arsenal from 6,000 warheads to around 2,000. Once the reduction is complete, the base will still command 150 one-warhead Minuteman III missiles.

Interpretive Center, which showcases Native American artifacts uncovered by the base's excavation program.

Originally a frontier army outpost, the base now controls a dwindling arsenal of intercontinental ballistic missiles. In 1930 President Hoover renamed Fort Russell in honor of Francis Emory Warren, Wyoming's first governor and a U.S. senator for thirty-seven years. Warren came to Wyoming in 1868 at age twenty-three, taking a job with A. R. Converse, owner of a mercantile store. The two became partners in the mercantile business and later in livestock operations. The Warren Mercantile Company grew into the largest supplier of furniture and hardware in Wyoming, and Warren's livestock holdings grew to 3,000 cattle and more than 60,000 sheep. By 1909 Warren was the richest person in Wyoming.

During Frontier Days, the base hosts Fort D. A. Russell Days, with living history demonstrations, footraces, and an ice-cream social, followed by a dance where you may—if you are able—do the Virginia reel under lantern light. Guests are asked to come attired in Victorian period costumes or western wear. Other activities include artillery demonstrations and infantry and cavalry horse drills of the 1800s.

For a delightfully nostalgic night's rest, step back in time and check in to the historically renovated ***Rainsford Inn Bed and Breakfast,*** listed on the National Register of Historic Places as part of the Rainsford Historic District. The place is named for George D. Rainsford, an architect and horse .breeder, who came to Wyoming in the late 1870s.

Antiques, heirlooms, and works of local artists fill the Rainsford, where you have your choice of seven rooms, one of which is handicapped accessible and four of which boast whirlpool tubs. The Cattle Baron Room features a western flavor, while for romantic occasions, it's hard to beat the Moonlight and Roses Room. Rooms are between $50 and $90.

In the morning you have your choice of several delectable breakfasts. The Rainsford Inn is located at 219 East Eighteenth Street. For reservations call 638–2337 or e-mail tobeds@sisna.com.

From Cheyenne take Missile Drive to **Happy Jack Road** (Highway 210) heading west. This scenic back road to Laramie rises from Cheyenne's elevation of 6,062 feet to more than 8,640 feet, before beginning the descent into Laramie. The terrain changes dramatically as rolling grasslands give way to the craggy outcroppings of the Laramie Range foothills, and the scent of pine supplants the smell of grass and sage. Keep alert for antelope, coyotes, deer, elk, and other critters.

Happy Jack Road derives its name from Happy Jack Hollinsworth, who started ranching in the foothills of the Laramie Range in 1884. Hollinsworth was said to be always singing and whistling while working his ranch and hauling wood for sale in Cheyenne.

Twenty-six miles out of Cheyenne you'll come upon the entrance to 1,645-acre **Curt Gowdy State Park,** a great spot for camping, hiking, and fishing. The park encompasses Crystal and Granite Reservoirs, the water supply for Cheyenne. There's a $2.00 day-use fee per vehicle ($5.00 for out-of-state vehicles), or you can secure a campsite for $4.00 per night ($9.00 for out of staters). The park is named after native son and renowned sportscaster Curt Gowdy. Long before radio, television, baseball, and football, however, the area was a favorite campground for Native Americans, including the Crow, Cheyenne, Arapaho, and Sioux. Towering granite formations provide a beautiful backdrop for a night under the stars.

Coyote, an Omnivore with Few Peers

Coyotes inhabit both the basin and the range country throughout Wyoming. Certainly a diverse diet is one thing that helps the crafty canid adapt to different environments. A biological study conducted in Yellowstone in the late 1930s documented the following "miscellaneous food and nonfood items" found in a sampling of more than 5,000 coyote droppings, in addition to the more common remains of large and small mammals, birds, cold-blooded vertebrates, invertebrates, and vegetable matter: horse manure, garbage, trash, muskmelon, corn refuse, paper, rag, canvas-leather glove, butter wrapper, twine, banana peel, orange peel, leather (one piece containing a rivet), cellophane, steak bone, grape seeds, mouse nest material, 7 inches of curtain, pear, prune seed, match, 2 square inches of rubber, tinfoil, shoestring, mud, paint-covered rag, 8 inches of rope, 3 square inches of towel, lemon rind, bacon rind, two pieces of shirt, canvas, gunny sack, isinglass, and botfly larvae.

Across Happy Jack Road to the north and less than a mile west is ***Hynds Lodge,*** built by Cheyenne business executive and philanthropist Harry P. Hynds and donated to the Boy Scouts of America in 1922. The building is open to groups large and small on a reservation-only basis from June 1 through October 1. (The reservations office is open beginning the first work day of January each year.) The lodge includes sleeping accommodations for thirty; a large kitchen complete with appliances, pots and pans, and dishes; a dining area; and recreational facilities. For information on Hynds Lodge call Curt Gowdy State Park headquarters at 632–7946.

You may want to stay and poke around this uncommonly beautiful area for a day or two. If you prefer relaxing in style to roughing it, for an outstanding base of operations check into ***A. Drummond's Ranch Bed and Breakfast.*** Meals are a celebration of living art, with fresh herbs garnishing delicious homemade food, served on china with fresh linen and pearl-handled silverware. The living room invites you to gaze at mountain scenery and the establishment's gardens of perennial flowers.

In the rooms terry-cloth robes await your use, as do Jacuzzi tubs adjacent to two of the four guest rooms. The Carriage House loft provides the ultimate getaway, with grand views, a gas fireplace, a private dining area complete with a miniature chandelier, and a deck with a gas cooking grill and a private Jacuzzi. You set your own pace and choose your favorite activity from options that include hiking, horseback riding, mountain biking, cross-country skiing in winter, or simple quiet relaxation. The variety of resident animals, from llamas and horses to geese and goats, will bring out the "kid" in almost anyone.

Rates range from $60 to $175 per night and include a full breakfast. Personalized tour packages are also available, as is boarding for horses. For reservations call 634–6042 or e-mail adrummond@juno.com. Drummond's is located at 399 Happy Jack Road, several miles east of the entrance to Curt Gowdy State Park. To learn more, visit the ranch's Web sites via the bed-and-breakfast links at www.virtualcities.com and www.cruising-america.com.

Albany County

Continuing west on Happy Jack Road, you'll soon be greeted by the otherworldly rock formations of the ***Vedauwoo*** (pronounced *VEE-dah-voo*) area. The name means "earthborn spirits" in Arapaho, and Native Americans regard the area as a particularly sacred place. With a little imagination, you can have a lot of fun transforming the rocks sculpted by eons of water and weather into familiar objects. Seal Rock, for instance—just north of the highway and a few hundred yards before you reach the large Medicine Bow National Forest sign—

Vedauwoo

quickly reveals the source of its name. A few hundred yards beyond the forest sign, turn left (south) to find other intriguing rock formations and to reach the Vedauwoo picnic area. (From there, Happy Jack Road continues on to the Lincoln Monument.)

Try to discover Bison, Loaf of Bread, Hawk, and Dinosaur Bone Rocks on your own. Be sure also to look to the west for the precariously balanced cube as you head south on the winding dirt road. Take your time or the often washboarded road will bounce you right out of your seat. The long-range vista encompasses Twin Mountain, Green Mountain to the east, and Pole Mountain to the west. Vedauwoo offers a refuge in which simply to relax and contemplate your place in the universe (or something less weighty if the mood dictates). The nimble and properly equipped can scale Potato Chip Rock, located near the picnic area, with difficulty ratings ranging from an easy 5.00 to an experts-only 5.14.

You can time your visit to Vedauwoo to join in on a ***Walk When the Moon Is Full*** interpretive hike on the nights of the full moon. Each month a guide focuses on a special theme, such as the Spirit Moon at Vedauwoo or the Pika Moon in the alpine mountains. (Some of these walks take place at locations other than Vedauwoo.) To confirm moonlight walk dates, times, and meeting places, call the Medicine Bow National Forest office at 745–2398 or stop in at the headquarters at 2468 Jackson Street in Laramie.

Continue on the Vedauwoo road until you encounter I–80, but before joining the rush of traffic westward, take a brief detour to the altogether surprising ***Ames Monument.*** Proceed through the underpass and bear left; a 2-mile trip beyond will take you to a 60-foot pyramid of native granite created in 1882 for $65,000 as a monument to Oliver and Oakes Ames, who helped finance the construction of the first transcontinental railroad.

The monument demonstrates the heavy stonework characteristic of the Romanesque-influenced style made famous by its designer, the noted architect

Henry Hobson Richardson. The pyramid appears to have been intentionally placed in the middle of nowhere. That's because originally it stood next to the Union Pacific tracks and the now-abandoned town of Sherman, where the trains were safety inspected before the steep descent into Laramie from Sherman Hill. Around the turn of the century, the railroad moved the tracks a few miles south in order to follow a more desirable grade. As a result, Sherman died a ghost town's death. U.S. Senator Oakes Ames did not fare much better: He was indicted for bribery in connection with the infamous Credit Mobilier Scandal, dying before he could be brought to justice.

Some years after the monument was finished, an enterprising local politician discovered it was in the wrong place. A certain Murphy, justice of the peace in Laramie, found the pyramid was located not on Union Pacific land but on federal land—not a surprising mistake given the strange pattern of railroad land grants in the West. (Railroads were granted land along their routes in a 40-mile-wide strip of alternating square-mile sections. Each railroad section lies next to a government section in a checkerboard pattern that continues to plague land managers today.) When Mr. Murphy discovered the monument was in fact on a government section, he promptly filed a homestead claim on it and told the railroad to get its big stone pile off his land. Railroad lawyers threatened him with impeachment for conspiracy, however, and he backed off.

The Ames brothers may have helped link the country by rail, but the next monument on the tour commemorates the man who kept the nation united and who posthumously gave his name to the country's first transcontinental highway, Abraham Lincoln. To find it, complete the loop back to I–80 and proceed to the summit of Sherman Hill, the highest spot on the coast-to-coast highway, at an elevation of 8,640 feet. Built in 1959, the **Lincoln Monument** originally stood alongside the Lincoln Highway but was moved in 1969 to its present site. University of Wyoming art professor and sculptor Robert Russin

southern wyomingtrivia

Jesse James was incarcerated in Laramie for suspected stage robbery in 1877, but he was freed before his dastardly identity was revealed.

crafted the 12½-foot bronze bust, which rises 42½-feet on a granite pedestal built with stone from the Vedauwoo area. At the summit you'll find a visitor center, rest area, and picnic sites. Happy Jack Road also terminates here, joining I–80 at the summit. (Backtracking about a mile on Happy Jack Road takes you to **Tie City,** where tie hackers once fashioned railroad ties out of logs. Today it is a trailhead for cross-country skiers in the winter and hikers the rest of the year.)

southern
wyoming trivia

Laramie, Fort Laramie, Laramie Peak, the Laramie Range, Laramie County, and the Laramie River all were named after Jacques LaRamie, a legendary free trapper of the 1820s who was reportedly killed by Indians along his namesake river.

Prepare for a spectacular descent into the notoriously windy, mountain-ringed Laramie Basin through a canyon lined on both sides by gloriously red rock. Ancient tepee rings, buffalo kill sites, and unearthed artifacts in the basin indicate that nomadic peoples frequented this area for at least 10,000 years, but it was not until the Union Pacific Railroad arrived in 1868 that a permanent settlement took hold.

Named after Jacques LaRamie, a French Canadian fur trapper and the first white man thought to have visited the area (LaRamie shipped out furs from 1815 to 1827), the city was selected by the Wyoming Territorial Legislature as the site of the Wyoming Territorial Prison and the University of Wyoming.

The *Overland Trail* traversed the Laramie Basin, where it was served by a large station complete with blacksmith shop, roadhouse, and toll bridge crossing the Laramie River. Westbound travelers used the trail heavily between 1862 and 1868 before the Union Pacific Railroad made the journey more convenient and less treacherous. Overland Trail ruts can still be seen stretching out across the prairie along Highway 130 at a point approximately 11 miles west of Laramie.

An "end of the tracks" town, Laramie garnered a reputation as one rough place. In October 1868, for example, a fierce gun battle broke out in town between outlaws and vigilantes. The criminals fled, but not before four were caught and hanged: Asa Moore, Con Wager, "Big Ed," and "Big Steve," a foursome suspected of some fifty murders combined.

The first all-woman jury in the nation sat in Laramie in 1870, an event that moved King William of Prussia to send President Grant a congratulatory message. The breakthrough proved short lived, however, and women did not serve on juries in Wyoming again until 1950. On another suffrage front, Laramie's Grandma Eliza Swain went to the polls in 1870 and earned the distinction of being the first woman in the United States to vote in a general election.

Restored to its original 1890s condition, the Wyoming Territorial Prison lives on as a State Historical Site under the name of *Wyoming Territorial Park.* Although in operation for just a few years, the park has earned the reputation as a class attraction. The prison here once incarcerated notables such as Wild Bunch leader Butch Cassidy (Robert Leroy Parker), who did time for horse thievery. Gov. William A. Richards pardoned Cassidy in January 1896, before he'd served out his two-year sentence—but not before Butch gave his oath as a gentleman that he would do no more thievin' of horses or cattle or banks in Wyoming. (Butch kept his word, but unfortunately the governor forgot to include train robberies in the bargain.) Here you'll also learn about infamous prisoners, such as Clark "The Kid" Pelton, Minnie Snyder, and other evildoers of nearly every imaginable sort.

There's a re-created Wyoming Frontier Town on-site where you can grab a sarsaparilla and listen to storytelling by "Calamity Jane" (a great-great niece of the authentic item), or you can sit back and take a stagecoach ride. The park is also home to a full ranchland exhibit and the Happy Jack Gift Shop.

The performers at the Horse Barn Dinner Theatre entertain with top-quality, rip-roaring dinner shows, June through August. Special events continue throughout the year, including the Beerfest in fall and the Lumberjack Competition in summer. For park and dinner theater information, call (800) 845–2287, or visit the park Web site at www.wyoprisonpark.org. The Wyoming Territorial Park is located at the west end of Laramie at 975 Snowy Range Road.

Besides featuring a gorgeous, tree-lined campus, the **University of Wyoming** (founded in 1886, four years before Wyoming became a state) holds some real treasures tucked away in its buildings of native sandstone. Your first stop should be the visitor information center at 1408 Ivinson Avenue, where you can pick up a campus map and obtain a parking permit. Next, find your way to the **Geological Museum** in the east wing of the S. H. Knight Geology Building. It is one of few such museums in the Rocky Mountains, and its fossils exhibit rivals the best found in the country. In the 1960s Samuel H. Knight hand-hammered copper sheets into a life-size *Tyrannosaurus rex* that now guards the entrance to the museum. Inside, the museum is dominated by two dinosaurs: a 70-foot-long skeleton of a *Brontosaurus* (more properly, *Apatosaurus excelsus*) discovered about 75 miles northwest of Laramie in 1901, and a cast of a skeleton of a juvenile *Allosaurus* discovered in northern Wyoming in 1991. Both date from the Jurassic period, around 145 million years ago. The *Apatosaurus* is one of only six on display in the world. Roughly fifty types of dinosaurs have been unearthed in Wyoming, and new varieties still turn up from time to time. The museum has dozens of displays that tell the dinosaur story and interpret the state's geology. Other highlights include the skeleton of a fifty-million-year-old garfish, the largest complete freshwater fossil fish on display in the world. The museum is easy to recognize: Just look for the life-size statue of *Tyrannosaurus rex* in front. It's open Monday through Friday from 8:00 A.M. to 5:00 P.M., Saturday and Sunday from 10:00 A.M. to 3:00 P.M. Call 766–2646 or visit the Web site www.uwyo.edu/geomuseum for information.

True fossil buffs, who might want closer contact with ancient bones than any museum can offer, should consider spending a week digging fossils on a tour arranged by Laramie-based **Western Paleo Safaris.** Owner-operator J. P. Cavigelli offers weeklong fossil-hunting and camping trips during June, July, and August to groups of no more than seven people; shorter, custom-designed trips are also available. Customers generally fly in to Laramie, Rock Springs, or Casper, Wyoming; Scottsbluff, Nebraska; or Dickinson, North Dakota, and are met at the airport by Cavigelli and an assistant. Bone hunters stay in motels the first and last nights and camp the four nights in between. During the day they visit and dig at a variety of sites, looking for fossils of everything from insects to dinosaurs. All sites are on private land, so participants get to keep nearly everything they find. Western Paleo provides transportation, meals, lodging, and all camping equipment except sleeping bags. Cost for the week is around $1,000 per person. Western Paleo has been in business since 1998; Cavigelli says 30 to 40 percent of his customers are repeats from previous years. For more information call 742–4651 or (888) 875–2233; use PIN 7737.

Moving from fauna to flora, the **Rocky Mountain Herbarium** on the UW campus represents one of the foremost plant collections in the nation. Located on the third floor of the Aven Nelson Memorial Building, the herbarium houses more than 540,000 dried plant specimens, including all of Wyoming's known flowering plants. It is the largest collection of central Rocky Mountain plants in existence. Although the herbarium is primarily a research facility, the public can visit during summer Monday through Friday from 7:30 A.M. to 4:30 P.M., or by special arrangement. Fall, winter, and spring hours are 8:00 A.M. to 5:00 P.M. Monday through Friday. Call 766–2236 for more information or visit the herbarium Web site at www.rmh.uwyo.edu.

Your University of Wyoming tour would not be complete without getting bugged at the **Insect Gallery** in Room 4018 of the Agriculture Building. The collection, started in 1894 by zoology professor Frank Niswander, features live displays of creatures such as hermit crabs, Madagascar hissing cockroaches, and tarantulas, as well as thousands of mounted insects from all over the world. In all, the collection includes more than a quarter of a million insect specimens. The gallery is open Monday through Friday from 9:00 A.M. to noon and 1:00 to 4:00 P.M. To schedule a visit call 766–5338. Other sites not to miss while on campus: the **Anthropology Museum** and the **University of Wyoming American Heritage Center & Art Museum.** One could spend hours at the latter, browsing through the center's extensive collections of printed materials (archives, rare books, and manuscripts) and historic photographs depicting an earlier Yellowstone and other places in Wyoming. The Anthropology Museum (766–5136), open Monday through Friday from 8:00 A.M. to 5:00 P.M. and 7:30 A.M. to 4:30 P.M. summers, is in the Anthropology Building (surprise!); the American Heritage Center and Art Museum (766–4114) is in the UW Centennial

Everybody's

I attended the University of Wyoming in the early 1970s, when Laramie had even more of a Wild West edge to it than it has today. One establishment I vividly recall from those days is a place they called "Everybody's."

Everybody's was housed in a dark old building on the rougher edge of downtown, just yards from the Union Pacific Railroad tracks. It opened its doors when the bars downtown closed, at 2:00 A.M. The proprietor kept the operation within the law, barely I think, by calling it a private club, so on entering you were handed a "membership card." To me, here's the really unexpected part: Most of the clientele was black. Every song on the juke box was by a black performer—Aretha Franklin, the Supremes, Marvin Gaye, the Temptations, and many more. Everybody's was a world unto itself. Where all those black folks came from in Laramie, Wyoming, I never did learn.

I visited Everybody's on only two or three occasions during my days at the university; on one of those, I remember exiting after the sun had risen. Mixed drinks, I recall, such as their high-octane screwdrivers—a glassful of vodka with a shot of orange juice—went for 50 cents.

Complex at the far east end of campus. It's open Monday through Friday from 8:00 A.M. to 5:00 P.M., Saturday from 11:00 A.M. to 5:00 P.M.

Being a university town, Laramie has its share of good restaurants and coffeehouses. A new favorite is the **Altitude Chophouse and Brewery,** downtown at 320 South Second Street. The Altitude is open for lunch and dinner and features good sandwiches, soup, and specials. Prices are moderate; enjoy the pool tables and banquet room and the beer and ale brewed on-site. Call 721–4031 for information.

If you're looking for delicious food at reasonable prices try **Jeffrey's Bistro,** also downtown on the corner of Second Street and Ivinson Avenue, serving lunch and dinner Monday through Saturday. The menu is eclectic, with a number of vegetarian entrees as well as meat and fish—and spectacular desserts. For more information call 742–7046, or visit www.jeffreysbistro.com.

For a jolt of java or mellow cup of hot chocolate, try one of the two coffee shops facing each other across Grand Avenue downtown near the railroad tracks: **Coal Creek Coffee Company** at 110 Grand Avenue or **Muddy Waters** across the street at 113 Grand Avenue. Coal Creek (745–7737), open from 6:00 A.M. to 11:00 P.M. every day, serves great muffins, scones, and soup. On weekends they feature live music and readings. Muddy Waters (742–6982) opens its doors from 7:00 A.M. to 11:00 p.m. Monday through Saturday, 8:00 A.M. to

11:00 P.M. on Sunday. If you're lucky you might catch live music in the evenings, but all the time you can get waffles, breakfast burritos, and bagels for breakfast, sandwiches and soup for lunch, desserts, fresh-squeezed juices and shakes, organic teas—and tons of alternative reading material. You'll see more professors in elbow patches at Coal Creek, more piercings at Muddy Waters.

For western-style nightlife downtown go to **The Buckhorn** or to **The Cowboy Saloon & Dance Hall.** Warning: Both taverns are elbow-to-elbow crowded when the university students are in town, but it's always a great show and you're likely to see things you've never seen before.

By now you may have crisscrossed Ivinson Avenue a dozen times. The street's named for Edward and Jane Ivinson, heads of Laramie's most promi- nent pioneer family. Edward Ivinson was a banker who built an elaborate Queen Anne–style mansion in 1892 with the expectation of using the residence as the Governor's House once he became elected to that office. The gesture was a grand expression of self-importance not matched by public sentiment. In 1973 the abandoned home, situated at 603 Ivinson Avenue, was converted into **The Laramie Plains Museum.** Years of renovation have brought the structure back to its previous level of elegance. Among its treasures are a well-outfitted

Laramie Plains Museum

kitchen with century-old appliances, a one- room schoolhouse located on the property, intricately hand-carved furniture made by prisoners at the Wyoming Territorial Prison, and period clothing ranging from wedding dresses to funeral wear. Docent-guided tours are offered Tuesday through Saturday from 9:00 A.M. to 5:00 P.M. and Sunday from 1:00 to 4:00 P.M.; they last about an hour, and are priced at $4.25 for adults and $2.25 for students; children under age six are free. Call 742–4448 for an update or tap into the history- and photo-packed Web site at www.laramiemuseum.org.

For the architecture buff Laramie reveals a variety of building styles. Tour **Historic Downtown Laramie** between First and Third Streets, extending from University Avenue to Garfield Street, to view landmark buildings dating from the 1800s. It's also a great opportunity to visit

Laramie's several one-of-a-kind shops. A tour brochure may be obtained by visiting the Laramie Area Chamber of Commerce office, 800 South Third Street.

Start at the 1910 **Elks Lodge Building** at 103 South Second Street, which illustrates the Italianate style, with a cornice supported by heavy brackets. **Saint Matthew's Cathedral** at 104 South Fourth Street, meanwhile, introduced a dignified old-English touch to the rough-and-tumble town. Nearby, at Grand Avenue and Sixth Street, the **Albany County Courthouse** exhibits the Depression-era art deco style.

Two styles of houses were characteristic of railroad worker accommodations. In 1883 Theodore Bath constructed a row of seven small stone cottages, **Bath Row,** to rent to employees of the Union Pacific Railroad. They are among the oldest rental properties in Laramie. Several of the Bath Houses have been restored and are listed on the National Register of Historic Places. They are located in the 100 block of Sixth Street on the east side. (The other style is the shotgun house, which we will visit later.)

Notice the mix of masonry styles in the brickwork of the Tudor Revival residence at 156 North Eighth Street. For an example of a pre-1872 Gothic Revival house, with gables decorated with verge boards and finials at the peaks of the roof gables, travel to 310 South Tenth Street. **The University of Wyoming Alumni House,** 214 South Fourteenth Street, is another fine example of Tudor Revival. The 1930s Art Moderne house, 1415 Custer Street, features rounded corners and contrasting yellow and mauve brickwork, which exhibit a frieze effect.

The 1921 **Cooper Mansion,** now the home of the University of Wyoming's American Studies program, at the corner of Grand Avenue and Fifteenth Street, combines the Mission and Pueblo Revival styles popular in southern California. Rich decorations, such as tiled fireplaces, decorative hardwood flooring, a grand staircase with carved balustrade, and cypress beams imported from Europe highlight the interior. Wilbur Hitchcock, a noted Laramie architect and designer of many University of Wyoming buildings, designed the mansion for Arthur F. T. Cooper, a wealthy English rancher who settled in Albany County. The interior of the Cooper Mansion can be viewed Monday through Friday from 8:00 A.M. to 5:00 P.M.

Now travel to West Laramie for an example of the shotgun house, located at 154 Railroad Street. The shotgun style was originally one room wide, one story high, and usually two to four rooms deep. The entrance was on the gable end with the door and a window facing the street. Most Wyoming shotgun houses were built from the 1870s to the 1920s as housing for Union Pacific workers. The name came about because it was said you could fire a shotgun through the front door and the shot would come right out the back door.

Before setting out on a tour of the nearby Snowy Range and historic Centennial, Saratoga, and Encampment, take a short drive to the remains of *Fort Sanders* on the southern outskirts of Laramie. In 1866 the federal government established Fort John Buford 3 miles south of present-day Laramie. The fort was later renamed Fort Sanders, after Brig. Gen. William P. Sanders, and enlarged to provide protection for travelers on the stage lines that ran from Denver to Salt Lake City and on the Overland Trail, both of which passed nearby. The post was abandoned in 1882. In 1886 the Wyoming Territorial Legislature authorized the building of the first fish hatchery in Wyoming at old Fort Sanders. Unfortunately, all that is left is a partial wall and some foundations of the old fort, but you'll also find a marker within the fenced area surrounding the shell of the Fort Sanders guardhouse. To view Fort Sanders take Third Street south out of town until it becomes Highway 287. Continue about 1½ miles and turn right onto South Kiowa Street. The structure is on your left a few hundred yards down the dirt road.

Streams and lakes in southeast Wyoming, many of them teeming with fish, are part of the Platte River drainage system. Lake Hattie, located off Highway 230, is one good place to find rainbow and brown trout. For information on other fishing spots, such as the Miracle Mile, visit the Wyoming Game and Fish office at 528 South Adams in Laramie, or call them at 745–4046.

For your next day's excursion take the Snowy Range Road (Highway 130) headed west out of Laramie toward Centennial. En route you'll view windswept plains, pine- and aspen-forested foothills, lofty mountain basins holding pristine glacial lakes, and plenty of racing pronghorn antelope. Keep your eyes open also for coyote, foxes, and mule deer. The *Snowy Range Scenic Byway* was designated as the second National Forest Service Byway in the nation in 1988. Built as a wagon road in the 1870s, it was widened using horse-drawn equipment in the 1920s. (Note: The portion through the Snowy Range beginning a few miles past Centennial is open only from Memorial Day through October, weather permitting.)

Ten miles out of Laramie, you'll see a marker for the Overland Trail on the north (right) side of the road. In another 11 miles, you'll reach the entrance to the *Vee Bar Guest Ranch* on the right. The original 1893 structure had its roof raised in 1912 when a second story was added. During its 110-year history, this Centennial Valley landmark has served as a working cattle ranch, the Fillmore Stagecoach Stop, a boardinghouse, a buffalo ranch, and a year-round guest ranch.

Carla, Jim, and Kelly Cole own the Vee Bar today, and they've worked long and hard to restore and preserve the Western gem. The showpiece barn is listed on the National Register of Historic Places. Activities include horseback riding, hay wagon rides, skeet shooting, archery, overnight camp-outs, and river tubing. Great catch-and-release trout fishing is available on the ranch, too. Riders of all skill levels will enjoy the horse excursions to surrounding meadows and mountains, and several major cattle drives take place during the season; in addition, some cattle are moved on a weekly basis.

You choose the activities you want to participate in during your stay. Nighttime entertainment takes a variety of forms, from talks by historians and performing ventriloquists to cowboy poets and musicians leading a sing-along. The food is superb, varied, and served family style in the western tradition. Plenty of fresh fruits and vegetables and delicious homemade bread are always there for the enjoying.

For accommodations you can choose among cabins along the Little Laramie River, which meanders the entire length of the ranch, or the more secluded Vee Bar Cabins, built from logs recycled from 1890s homestead buildings at Jim and Carla's Deerwood Ranch in Centennial Valley. From mid-June through August, the Vee Bar offers a variety of accommodation packages, including $1,600 per couple for a three-night stay and $2,895 for six nights, Sunday through Saturday, for two. The rest of the year, guests can avail themselves of daily bed-and-breakfast rates (rooms go from $100 to $150 per night, depending on the month) and enjoy cross-country skiing, horseback riding, snowmobiling, or the nearby Snowy Range ski slopes. You can take advantage of an evening candlelight meal with varied menu items nightly from mid-September through mid-June. For information and reservations call 745–7036 or (800) 4–VEE–BAR, or visit the ranch's Web site: www .vee-bar.com.

Seven miles down Highway 130, at the base of the Snowy Range, you run into the quaint, historic mining town of Centennial (population 100). Founded in 1875, Centennial owes its name to America's centennial year, and its existence to the discovery of gold in the nearby hills. The promising vein soon played out (although gold was recently rediscovered at the top of Centennial Ridge), and only the stalwarts remained to populate what became a rest stop for travelers on their way to the Snowies. The ***Country Junction*** on the eastern edge of town (you can see the whole town from this vantage point) has a good selection of specialty coffees, ice cream, clothing, jewelry, and gifts. It's open in summer from 10:00 A.M. to 5:30 P.M. seven days a week, and in winter on weekends only, same hours. The address is 2742 Highway 130; the telephone number is 745–3318.

Don't let the diminutive size of the 1907 railroad depot housing the ***Nici Self Museum*** discourage you from visiting. It's a great little museum within walking distance of the Country Junction. The structure is the oldest surviving depot of the Laramie, Hahn's Peak, and Pacific Railway Company, which originally was formed to haul the huge amounts of gold anticipated from the mountain mines. Historical collections include exhibits on blacksmithing, lumbering, mining, railroading, and ranching. Outside you'll find a beehive (tipi) burner used to burn sawdust and a 1944 Union Pacific caboose. The museum is open Friday through Monday, mid-June through Labor Day from 1:00 to 4:00 P.M., or by special appointment; closed in winter because there is no heat! For information call 742–7158.

On up the hill on Highway 130, *The Old Corral Hotel and Steak House,* as its name suggests, specializes in steaks. Rooms rent for $59 to $89 on weekdays and $69 to $99 on weekends, all year. Check out the unique woodwork in the bar area. Food prices are moderate and the restaurant is open daily from 7:00 A.M. to 9:00 P.M. For more information and reservations, call 745–5918 or (888) 653–2677, or visit www.oldcorral.com.

The Forest Service Visitor Center a mile west of Centennial provides maps and information on the Snowies and the Medicine Bow National Forest, which you are now reentering. (You were also in part of the same forest near Vedauwoo, between Cheyenne and Laramie.) For information on the Medicine Bow National Forest, call 745–2398.

Located about 32 miles west of Laramie, the *Snowy Range Ski Area* provides affordable skiing for the whole family beginning in mid-November and lasting through mid-April, depending on snow conditions. The facilities include four lifts, twenty-seven downhill trails, a network of cross-country trails, certified ski instruction, and a cafe and lounge. For information call 745–5750 or visit www.snowyrange.com.

The highest point on the Snowy Range Road is at Libby Flats, 10,000 feet above sea level. Medicine Bow Peak, elevation 12,013 feet, towers over the flats. The *Libby Flats Observation Point* scenic outlook offers a stunning vista of alpine meadows and several mountain ranges in Wyoming and Colorado. The area abounds with trails, campgrounds, and lakes stocked with trout, and an incredible variety of wildflowers can be found on the Libby Flats Wildflower Trail. Patches of snow may remain in the area even during the peak temperatures of August. Bring a sweater to ward off the chilling winds common at these lofty elevations.

Carbon County

The best is yet to come. Follow Snowy Range Road as it winds west from the summit at Libby Flats until you come to the mirrored surfaces of *Mirror Lake* and *Lake Marie.* Now is the time to bring out the picnic basket, recline on the rocks at the shore of Lake Marie, and meditate on its crystal-clear waters. The trail leading to Medicine Bow Peak—dramatic, glacier sculpted, reaching sky-ward—originates at Lake Marie.

Push on west until you come to North Brush Creek Road, then turn right. This will lead you to the top of Kennaday Peak (formerly called Bald Mountain or Old Baldy), named after an early homesteader and ranger. A flight of stairs gets you into the 14-foot-square glass observation room of the **Kennaday Peak Lookout.** From this vantage point far above the treeline, you can view a remarkable panorama. The lookout tower is open in summer Friday through Monday from 10:00 A.M. to 5:00 P.M., weather permitting. Slippery road conditions may prevail after a rain or snow. For information call the Brush Creek Visitors Center at 326–5562 or the Medicine Bow National Forest's Saratoga District Office at 326–5258.

Retrace your tracks back to Highway 130 and head west until you reach Highway 230, then go south 10 miles and turn onto Highway 70. Soon you'll arrive at Encampment, population 440. Native Americans gathered at Camp le Grand or Grand Encampment, situated at the base of the Sierra Madre Mountains, to hunt buffalo and other wild game. Later, trappers rendezvoused in the area. In the late 1880s the area grew into a productive copper-mining district after Ed Haggarty made a big strike on the Continental Divide near Bridger Peak. When it held the title of "Copper Capital of the United States," Encampment also boasted the longest aerial tramway in the world. Built in 1902, it conveyed copper ore 16 miles from the famous Rudefeha Mine (named after the four original partners: Rumsey, Deal, Ferris, and Haggarty) or Ferris-Haggarty Mine to the smelter at Encampment. Power was supplied by water running through a 4-foot-wide wooden pipeline. The original partners were bought out by a Chicago promoter, and the name of the mining company changed to North American Copper Company. Millions of dollars worth of copper were shipped out of Encampment before the price of the metal collapsed in 1908. The mines closed and the owner was indicted for overcapitalization and fraudulent stock sales.

The excellent **Grand Encampment Museum,** operational for some thirty years, can keep you roaming around its intriguing displays for hours. The Doc Culleton Interpretive Center and original pioneer town are at the heart of the museum. You'll also see a two-story outhouse that solved the problem of contending with the deep snows of winter. Then there's the folding oak bathtub and dozens of other odd finds. The museum grounds feature numerous historic buildings, such as a tie hack's cabin, livery stable, false-front store, newspaper office, and stage station, and three original towers from the 16-mile aerial tramway. The museum also serves as a national repository of Forest Service memorabilia; among the related artifacts located on the grounds are the old Slash Ridge Guard

Tower and the Webber Springs Guard Station. The Grand Encampment Museum is located at Seventh and Barnett Streets (although it is easier to find the museum than street signs in Encampment). Here you can also pick up a map for the tour of *Historic Homes and Business Buildings.* The museum is open daily from Memorial Day weekend through Labor Day. Hours are 10:00 A.M. to 5:00 P.M. Monday through Saturday and 1:00 to 5:00 P.M. Sunday. The museum stays open in September from 10:00 A.M. to 5:00 P.M. on Saturday and 1:00 to 5:00 P.M. on Sunday, and then closes for the winter. Call 327–5308 for information on the museum or its annual Grand Encampment Cowboy Gathering.

To experience "life on the frontier," time your visit for the annual *Wood-choppers Jamboree and Rodeo,* held at Encampment on the third weekend in June. The two-day event includes lumbering competitions, with lumberjacks arriving from as far away as California and Australia. You can also watch skilled ax throwers whiz axes at a target, while you enjoy a delicious barbecue. Call 326–8855 for information on the jamboree.

Side excursions out of Encampment include those leading to the nearby Sierra Madre copper-mining *Ghost Towns of Dillon and Rudefeha.* Both towns have remnants of buildings and mining equipment from days of old when they bustled with activity. Inquire locally about directions, road conditions, and whether a four-wheel-drive vehicle is required. Many roads that are passable in dry weather turn into quagmires after a rainstorm.

If you're up to an hour-long hike, strike out on the *Indian Bathtubs Trail* to see the natural 4-foot-deep depressions in granite rock formations, which were used by Native Americans for bathing. To reach the area from Riverside, take Highway 230 east 1 mile to Carbon County Road 200. Turn south on that road, also known as Blackhail Mountain Road, and proceed 1 mile to a parking area. Follow the trail southwest as it crosses a sagebrush flat and then proceeds up an incline to a bench at the halfway mark. It then crosses a rocky ridge before making a fairly steep descent to Cottonwood Creek. The round-trip should take about one hour, and good hiking boots are advisable. From the vantage point of the bathtubs, you'll earn good views of the entire Medicine Bow Mountain Range and the Encampment-Riverside Valley.

Eighteen miles north of Encampment, in Saratoga, you can relax your body in hot mineral springs adjacent to the North Platte River. The town, originally called Warm Springs, was rechristened in 1884 after the famed Saratoga Springs resort area in New York State. The average temperature of the mineral waters here is a very hot 114 degrees Fahrenheit. The *Hobo Pool* is free and open twenty-four hours every day of the year; it's located at the east end of Walnut Street.

Stop in at the historic **Hotel Wolf,** built in 1893 and originally used as a stagecoach stop on the Encampment-to-Walcott stage line. The Victorian atmosphere and rooms embellished with antiques transport visitors back a century. The food is good and moderate-to-expensive in price. (The restaurant has earned a double-diamond rating from the American Automobile Association.) Hotel Wolf is listed on the National Register of Historic Places. Room rates range from $47 to $90 (request *not* to be put up in Room No. 1, which is directly above the often noisy bar). The hotel is located at 101 East Bridge Street. Call 326–5525 for information.

For lighter fare stop in at **Lollypops** (326–5020), one door down at 107 East Bridge Street. This charming spot features great croissants, Belgian waffles, soups, sandwiches, ice cream, and nonfat yogurt.

You might also want to spend some time visiting Saratoga's art galleries and Whitney's Platte Valley Mercantile. The **Rustic Bar** at 124 East Bridge Street displays some impressive mounted wildlife, including two mountain lions above the back bar, two bucks with their antlers locked in a life-and-death struggle, and a whimsical scene of chipmunks and prairie dogs drinking at a bar.

The **Saratoga Museum** is located across from the airport at 104 Constitution Avenue in a vintage 1915 Union Pacific Railroad depot. Displays include Native American tools and weapons, railroad memorabilia, and Platte Valley artifacts. The museum is open seven days a week from Memorial Day to Labor Day from 1:00 to 5:00 P.M. For information call 326–5511. The Saratoga Historical and Cultural Association also sponsors guided tours to various local historical landmarks during the summer, which you can join by paying a nominal fee.

Saratoga is known as the town where "trout leap on Main Street." The North Platte River, which flows through town, is designated by the Wyoming Game and Fish Department as a blue-ribbon trout stream for approximately 65 miles—from where the river enters the state to the point at which Sage Creek flows into it. And if the trout ignore your flies, you can still try some of Saratoga's other attractions: an ice fishing derby in mid-January; the **Donald E. Erickson Memorial Cutter Races** in mid-February; or the official **Wyoming State Microbrew Competition** the third Saturday in August, when brewers compete for the coveted Steinley Cup. For information call Saratoga-Platte Valley Chamber of Commerce at 326–8855.

For unique accommodations while in the Saratoga area, consider **Far Out West Bed & Breakfast** (326–5869; e-mail fowbnb@union-tel.com), 304 North Second Street. Here the cost of a room for two ranges from $100 to $130, and $15 more per additional person. Or, heading back toward Laramie on Highway 130, turn south on Carbon County Highway 203 for a week-long stay at **Brush**

Creek Ranch. The ranch entrance is 1 mile down the road on the left side. At Brush Creek, a working cattle ranch encompassing 6,000 acres, you can choose your accommodations from among the many rooms in the 7,000-square-foot main ranch house (built in the early 1900s and expanded in the 1930s). Or perhaps one of the renovated western-decor cabins would suit you better. Whichever you prefer, there's nothing quite like taking a load off on the peaceful veranda of the main house as the setting sun turns the sky tequila-sunset red behind the Sierra Madre Mountains.

You can find plenty of activities to keep yourself occupied, such as horseback riding, hayrides, hiking, campfires and cookouts, and barn dances in the old loft. Kids age eight and under can have a fun and educational time hanging out with the wranglers in the corrals. You're also invited to help out with the ranch chores, such as branding, mending fences, and rounding up cattle. "On Mondays," said a former ranch manager, "we meet with the guests to get them to think like a cow. It readies them for the real cattle moving." If you're more interested in stalking trout than in steering steers, Brush Creek Ranch is an Orvis-endorsed lodge, one of only five in Wyoming. Weekly rates at the peak of the season are $1,275 for adults, $1,025 for kids age eight to fifteen, $750 for kids age five to seven, and $600 for youngsters age three to four. Rates are lower in the early summer and fall. For information call 327–5241 or (800) 726–2499, or write to Brush Creek Ranch, Star Route 10, Saratoga 82331. You can also contact the ranch via e-mail at info@brushcreekranch.com or visit their Web site: www.brushcreekranch.com.

The northern road out of Laramie, Highway 30, is the original Lincoln Highway route to Medicine Bow. About 18 miles northwest of Laramie, Highway 34 angles off to the right (east) to the Wyoming Game and Fish Department's *Sybille Canyon Wildlife Research and Education Center* (about a 26-mile round-trip). It is home to a breeding and reintroduction program for black-footed ferrets, plus a short nature trail and picnic area. The center is open from May 1 through September 15 from 8:30 A.M. to 4:30 P.M., weekdays only. (Call ahead at 307–777–4600, as the center was closed in 2004 due to flash-flood damage.)

The black-footed ferret, once prevalent on Wyoming's prairies, was thought to be extinct until a number were captured in the mid-1980s. The ferrets were separated into three groups to prevent disease from wiping out the remaining population. Seven ferrets were sent to a branch of the National Zoo in Washington, D.C., eight journeyed to the Henry Doorly Zoo in Omaha, Nebraska, and the rest took up residence here at the Sybille Research Center. Since then, several hundred ferrets have been bred in captivity, and a number have been reintroduced into the wild reaches of the nearby Shirley Basin. Other black-footed ferrets have been sent to captive breeding programs at zoos in Arizona, Colorado, Kentucky, Canada, and elsewhere.

Back along Highway 30 the next stop is Rock River, population 175, located 21 miles northwest of Bosler and a few miles outside Carbon County, in Albany County. Be sure to stop in at the ***Rock River Museum.*** There you'll find what is purported to be the actual safe Butch Cassidy and his gang blew up when they robbed the Union Pacific's *Overland Flyer.* Housed in the old First National Bank, two blocks west of Highway 30 at the corner of North Second Street and Avenue C, the museum also displays dinosaur bones, a collection of fluorescent minerals, a section of the wooden water pipe that supplied Rock River for nearly a century, a hand-operated washing machine, and historic

Still At Large

Movie buffs will remember the broad-daylight scene in *Butch Cassidy and the Sundance Kid* where the outlaws explode not just the safe but the entire express car, after Woodcock, the loyal railroad employee, refuses to comply with their demands. Circumstances of the real robbery remain murky; the Wyoming newspapers of the day, telling and retelling the story, seldom told it the same way twice. A few facts are clear: At 2:15 A.M. on June 2, 1899, two bandits with drawn pistols stopped a westbound Union Pacific train near Wilcox, just a few miles north of present-day Rock River. They ordered the engineer to uncouple the front of the train—engine, tender, express and baggage cars—from the rest, pull it across a bridge over a small draw, and stop. Then the outlaws blew up the bridge, so that the next westbound train, due in just ten minutes, wouldn't be able to come to the first train's aid. Again with their pistols they persuaded the engineer to run the shortened train 2 miles further west, then looted the express car, blew up the safe, and supposedly made off with $60,000 in unsigned banknotes—though the railroad never made any public statements about how much was stolen. Or there might have been three men, or six; reports conflict and the names of the suspects kept changing from one report to the next. After six weeks the Laramie *Boomerang* decided the culprits must be George "Flat-Nose" Curry and the quarter-Cherokee Roberts brothers, also known as Dave Putty and Bud Nolan. "The Union Pacific officials and others of the officers think that there were only three in the gang who did the work," the newspaper reported. "It was at first supposed that the three men were Hank O'Day, Bob Taylor, and a Mexican, or, if not the Mexican, then a gambler named Cavanaugh. But this idea seems to have been abandoned and George Curry and the Roberts brothers [were suspected of] the crime." There was a massive chase that summer across wide swatches of Wyoming—one sheriff was killed and a newspaper editor had his horse shot out from under him—but no one was ever caught or charged with the robbery.

photos, glass, stoves, and tools. From Memorial Day to Labor Day they're open Tuesday through Saturday from 10:00 A.M. to 3:00 P.M. In the winter the museum is open by appointment; call 378–2205 or 378–2386.

Probably the best-kept food secret on Highway 30 between Laramie and Rawlins is the little *Longhorn Restaurant* in Rock River. Try a Longhorn Burger and the four-berry pie. It's open Monday through Saturday, 11:00 A.M. to 7:00 P.M.; in summer until 8:00 P.M. For more information call 378–2567.

After continuing along Highway 30 for approximately 9 miles, you'll arrive at the *Como Bluff Museum.* The extraordinary structure, located along the right-hand side of the road, was constructed more than six decades ago by Tom and Gracie Boylan. The museum is made out of dinosaur bones that were taken from a nearby dinosaur "graveyard" first discovered by Union Pacific

A Dinosaur Goes Global

Como Bluff—the hill that rises north of Como Bluff Museum—and the plains farther north have been yielding up dinosaur bones to the museums of the world ever since 1877, when two Union Pacific employees contacted the great Yale paleontologist Othniel Charles Marsh with the news they'd found some mighty big bones. Already, a fierce competition was underway between Marsh and Edward Drinker Cope of the Philadelphia Academy of Sciences to see which scientist's crews could discover more species of extinct vertebrate animals. The crews sabotaged each other's bone diggings at Como, while Marsh and Cope quarreled bitterly in the press. Early diggers found bones "strewn about like logs in a lumbering operation," according to one writer. Bones were still so plentiful in the 1880s that government surveyors used them to mark their section corners.

A second round of dinosaur competition began in 1897, when scientists prospecting north of Como Bluff for New York's American Museum of Natural History found the rich Bone Cabin Quarry—named for a nearby sheepherder's cabin built on a dino-bone foundation. Many of that quarry's treasures are still on display in New York. But the richest find came in 1899, when paleontologists working for the Carnegie Museum of Natural History in Pittsburgh found bones of an 84-foot-long *Diplodocus*— a long-necked, long-tailed plant eater—at a site about 25 miles north of Como. The steel tycoon Andrew Carnegie, only 5 feet 3 inches tall himself, liked the huge dinosaur so much he had copies made as gifts for kings, emperors, and presidents throughout Europe and the Americas. The original may still be seen in Pittsburgh, and the full-sized copies are still on display in national museums in London; Paris; Berlin; Moscow; Vienna, Austria; Bologna, Italy; Madrid, Spain; La Plata, Argentina; and Mexico City. It was the first dinosaur millions of people ever saw. Dinosaur digging stopped around Como after the mid-1960s, but has been revived in recent years thanks largely to the leadership of celebrity paleontologist Dr. Robert Bakker—who first learned his trade at Yale, studying and drawing bones that Marsh's men found at Como 125 years ago.

Railroad employees in 1877. The 5,776 bones composing the building have a combined weight of 102,000 pounds and most of them are around 140 million years old. The museum earned a mention in *Ripley's Believe It or Not* as "the oldest building in the world." Proprietor Jodie Fultz charges $3.00 for adults, $2.00 for seniors over age sixty, and $1.50 for children under age twelve. Inside you'll find a variety of rocks and fossils, including petrified sea life—belemnites, ammonites, baculites, and clams—and more dinosaur bones. Fultz will also let you hunt fossils on her land for $5.00 per day. The museum is open from May 1 through October 1, but hours are irregular; if you find it closed, call 379–2323.

Reenter Carbon County as you approach Medicine Bow (population 355), located 18 miles northwest of Rock River. Along the banks of the river near here, Arapaho and Cheyenne Indians found wood just right for making their bows. They called the wood "good medicine" and named the river Medicine Bow. In the early 1870s the town became a major supply point for forts in Wyoming, and the government established a military post in Medicine Bow to protect the railroad and freight wagons from Indian attack. The sleepy town today is one of the best-known names in all of the West, as it was the setting for Owen Wister's landmark Western novel, *The Virginian,* published in 1902. Wister himself, a young Philadelphian and recent Harvard graduate, oppressed by his boring bank job, first visited Medicine Bow in 1885 on behalf of his host, rancher Frank Wolcott, to pick up some live fish due in on the midnight train. That gave Wister time to eat a meal and prowl the town. He counted twenty-nine buildings including privies, meticulously noted the number down in his diary, and then had time for a snooze on the counter of the dry goods store, just as the narrator does in the opening scene of the novel. The trout, intended for Wolcott's creeks and ponds, died in their big milk cans on the nineteen-hour wagon drive back to Wolcott's ranch. But the bass, accustomed to warmer water, survived.

Despite its small size, Medicine Bow boasts two sites listed on the National Register of Historic Places: the **Virginian Hotel** (opened in 1911, nine years after publication of Wister's novel) and the 1913 Union Pacific Depot, which houses a fine museum: the **Medicine Bow Museum,** located in the 1913 railroad depot across Highway 30 from the Virginian Hotel and open during the summer months from 10:00 A.M. to 5:00 P.M. daily or by appointment; call 379–2383 or e-mail info@medicinebow.org to make one.

The museum contains plenty of interesting local and nonlocal western artifacts, including the blackjack table from the Medicine Bow Casino. The Owen Wister Cabin (used by Wister as a hunting lodge in Jackson Hole) and Owen Wister Monument (made of petrified wood) are located next to the museum. The Owen Wister General Store is the building where the author slept on the counter in 1885. Another interesting exhibit, *"The Brands That Tamed the West,"* is adjacent to the museum.

The Virginian Hotel boasted the first electric lights in Medicine Bow. At the time it was the largest hotel between Denver and Salt Lake City and the site of business dealings, romances, and shootings. A grand reopening in 1984 marked the restoration of the hotel's turn-of-the-century opulence. Inside there's a lunch counter where the locals gather, a grand old Western mural on the wall, and the Owen Wister Dining Room. The hotel's Shilo Saloon is another favorite meeting spot for locals and travelers alike. Rooms range from $20 to $70 per night, with the Owen Wister Suite the most opulent. For additional information call 379–2377 or e-mail virginianhotel@yahoo.com.

If you have more time, stroll over to the *Dip Bar*—which takes its name not from its clientele but from that very *Diplodocus* that ended up in so many of the world's museums. The Dip boasts the *world's largest jade bar,* 40 feet long and cut from a four-and-a-half-ton boulder found near Rock Springs. But you won't find the most remarkable feature until you order a long-necked beer and tip your head back to drink it. On the ceiling, proprietor Bill Bennett has painted scenes from local ranches—some current, some many decades gone— just because he has a long memory and thought it would be a good idea. Bennett's a woodcarver, too; you'll want to check out his carvings, such as a 3-foot-long carved stagecoach with passangers inside and a six-horse team, complete with reins and tack; a Native American on horseback closing in on a galloping buffalo bull; and a freighter with his mule team, jerk lines, freight wagon, and water wagon pulled along behind. Each carving is made from a single piece of wood. For more information call 379–2312.

Follow Highway 30 as it bends southwest. Nineteen miles later you'll find the entrance to Hanna, population 1,076, which has a long history of coal mining. The community was named after Marcus Hanna, the Cleveland, Ohio, industrialist and U.S. senator. The area's vast coal deposits were discovered in 1886, and a *Miners Monument* memorializes the 228 miners who died during mine explosions in 1903 and 1908. To locate the monument follow the signs at the eastern edge of town.

If you're in the mood for a cool swim or a hot workout, the *Hanna Recreation Center,* 8000 Highway 72, is open to the public. The center has an inviting swimming pool, sauna, whirlpool, gyms, and workout facilities for use at a modest fee. A newer Miners Monument and a Union Pacific snowplow engine are located near the center. For information and hours call 325–9402.

From this point, for a real treat follow Highway 72 southeast 12 miles to Elk Mountain. The town of fewer than 200 residents takes its name from nearby Elk Mountain, elevation 11,167 feet. The *Elk Mountain Trading Company,* according to legend, once grubstaked a rancher who later amassed a fortune of $78 million. The trading post, part general store and part liquor store, is open year-round from 9:00 A.M. to 8:00 P.M. Monday through Saturday, closed Sunday. To check ahead to inquire if the Elk Mountain Trading Company and associated Wild Wonder Cafe are open, call 348–7478. If you find yourself enjoying the tiny town, you can hole up at the elegantly renovated *Elk Mountain Hotel* (348–7774 or www.elkmountainhotel.com).

Exit I–80 about 25 miles west of Elk Mountain to view the site of *Fort Fred Steele.* After one look at the deserted, sagebrush-blanketed countryside, you might wonder how a soldier could have maintained his sanity on assignment at this desolate outpost. In addition to the bleak surroundings, the fort sits smack in the middle of what is known as the "Wind Corridor"—a phrase you'll come to understand while driving between Laramie and Rawlins on I–80. Orders were orders, however, and there was little room for negotiation in the role of cavalryman. Not surprisingly, Fort Fred Steele gained the dubious distinction of posting the highest desertion rate of any fort in the West.

Named after a Union Civil War hero, Maj. Gen. Frederick Steele, the post was established in 1868 to protect Overland Trail and Union Pacific Railroad traffic. The 1881 brick powder magazine remains, as do the foundations of many buildings from the original fort. Civilians took over the buildings after the government abandoned the fort in 1886. The railroad tie business kept the fledgling community alive, and it even enjoyed a brief spurt of growth when the original Lincoln Highway route was built right through town. By the 1930s, though, the town had pretty much dried up. The restored 1880s *Bridge Tender House* now serves as an interpretive center for the fort, which is administered by the state of Wyoming as a state historic site. Summer hours are May 1 to September 15 from 9:00 A.M. to 7:00 P.M. There are no overnight camping facilities, but there are picnic areas where you can watch the waters of the North Platte River roil past. For information call 320–3013.

Another 9 miles down the interstate, you'll come upon picturesque *Sinclair,* population 450. The Sinclair oil refinery at the edge of town reveals the derivation of the town's present name. During the oil boom of the 1920s, however, the company town that sprung up was known as Parco, built by and named after the Producers Oil and Refining Company. Designed in Spanish Mission style, Sinclair includes a town square with a large fountain fronting the *Parco Inn.* It once provided shelter to travelers on the bustling Lincoln Highway, which passed in front of the hotel. Amelia Earhart, President Franklin Roosevelt, and union leader John L. Lewis were among the notables who overnighted at the Parco. A renovation of the grand old inn is underway, so stay tuned.

The Sinclair Oil Company purchased the refinery in 1934, and nine years later citizens voted to change the town's name to Sinclair. Although the Parco Inn's doors are closed, there's still plenty of interest to see in town. The First National Bank of Parco operated from 1924 to 1933 in a building that now houses the **Parco/Sinclair Museum,** with its rich collection of town and oil-refining artifacts. The museum is open year-round from 9:00 A.M. to 5:00 P.M. Monday through Friday. If the museum door is locked, inquire about entrance at the Sinclair City Hall next door. Then, if you'd like to sample some of the tastiest Mexican food in the state, follow Lincoln Avenue west until you see the **Su Casa Cafe.** You'll be glad you did. (If you miss it, however, don't despair; there's another Mexican eatery just as good in Rawlins . . . read ahead.) Prices are inexpensive-to-moderate. For more information on Sinclair, call the City Hall at 324–3058.

Twenty-seven miles north of Sinclair on Seminoe Road (Road 351), you'll find **Seminoe State Park,** so designated in 1965. The park's centerpiece is the reservoir that backed up after the 1939 construction of the Seminoe Dam. The sprawling reservoir boasts 180 miles of shoreline, great trout and walleye fishing, and lakeside camping facilities. For park information call 320–3013.

Back in Sinclair, get on I–80 westbound for a couple of miles and exit at Rawlins, home of the **Wyoming Frontier Prison,** constructed in 1898 and active until 1982. A tour through the old cell blocks really sends a chill down one's spine, as does a visit (round-trip, one hopes) to the gas chamber. Among the notable prisoners who served time at the Rawlins facility were Annie Bruce, who murdered her father with a poisoned plum pie; William Carlisle, one of the last great train robbers; Talton Taylor, the last man hanged by the state of Wyoming, in 1933; and Perry H. Carroll, the first man executed by gas in Wyoming, in 1937. The oldest man buried in the old prison cemetery was Jim Best, who died of natural causes at age eighty-nine. After serving his time, it's said, Best was released and given the standard new suit, $15 in cash, and a sack lunch. After enjoying his lunch on the lawn of the prison, he returned to the gate and asked to be readmitted. They obliged and he died shortly thereafter.

Guided tours of the prison are conducted from Memorial Day through Labor Day, seven days a week from 8:30 A.M. to 4:30 P.M. From October through April the museum is open Monday through Friday only, and fewer tours are given per day. The tour costs $5.00 for adults, $4.50 for children and seniors, and $20.00 per family. In the prison gift shop you can find, among other things, an interesting book written by an inmate of the prison, *The Sweet Smell of Sagebrush.* The sandstone, castlesque Wyoming Frontier Prison is located at Fifth and Walnut Streets in Rawlins. For information call 324–4422 or e-mail wfp@trib.com.

Rawlins was named after Gen. John A. Rawlins of the U.S. Army, who discovered a spring at the base of the hills in 1867. The spot was first called Rawlins Springs, then later shortened to Rawlins. The town grew up centered around the point where the Union Pacific Railroad divided 20 miles east of the Continental Divide. The ***Carbon County Museum*** at Ninth and Walnut Streets contains a number of interesting exhibits, including the death mask, skull, and shoes made from the skin of notorious outlaw Big Nose George; sheep wagons; and a fine assortment of Native American art and artifacts.

Big Nose George was a robber and murderer. Asked why he had killed two deputies, Big Nose answered, "On the principle that dead men tell no tales." Sentenced to hang on April 2, 1881, Big Nose attempted an escape from his cell a week before his date with fate. After news of the escape attempt made the rounds in Rawlins, a swarm of armed men broke into the jail, hauled Big Nose George to a telegraph pole, and hanged him. No charges were ever brought against any members of the lynching party, who had worn masks to hide their faces. A doctor newly arrived in town, John Osborne (he was elected governor of Wyoming in 1892), took charge of George's body. Legend

Calamity

Big Nose George was not the only well-known western character to do time, both in and out of jail, in Rawlins. None is more famous—or infamous—than Martha Jane Canary, who whooped her way through the West working as a stagecoach driver, laundress, and at other, less-respectable professions. Calamity Jane, as she came to be called, even did a stint touring with Buffalo Bill's Wild West Show. Jane once spent a month in the Rawlins jailhouse after being arrested while on a drunken binge of legendary proportions, which she was enjoying with one of her many "husbands."

"Jane had a very affectionate nature," wrote Dora Dufran, a friend of Calamity's and a madam in Deadwood, South Dakota. "There were very few preachers around to bother her, so whenever she got tired of one man, she soon selected another." Apparently, she also possessed a prodigious thirst, one that beer wouldn't quench. Her standard barkeep order reportedly was, "Give me a shot of booze and slop her over the brim."

Orphaned as a youngster in Virginia City, Montana, Jane grew up as wild as the frontier surrounding her; DuFran wrote that she wasn't immoral, but simply amoral. And she owned a streak of compassion a country-mile wide: DuFran said that just about the only way to put a halt to one of Jane's big drunks was to tell her a friend needed her help. She would stop drinking at once, spend the night sobering up, and the next morning be ready—if not fresh as a daisy—for whatever was needed of her.

has it that the enterprising doctor removed the outlaw's skin, tanned it, and fashioned a pair of two-tone shoes (mentioned above). Doc Osborne put the rest of George's remains in a whiskey barrel and buried them behind his office on Cedar Street, where they were uncovered in 1950. In recent years his remains have been the subject of study by physical anthropologists at the University of Wyoming.

The Carbon County Museum is open May through September on Monday through Friday from 10:00 A.M. to 5:00 P.M. (closed for the lunch hour), and the rest of the year on Monday through Friday from 1:00 to 5:00 P.M. Call 328–2740 for additional information.

When your internal low-on-fuel buzzer sounds, consider tracking down *The Blake House,* open Tuesday through Saturday for lunch and dinner. The restaurant offers "new American cuisine" in the oldest house in Rawlins (circa 1881), located downtown at 221 West Cedar Street. Call 324–6873 for more information. If it's tortillas, refritos, and chiles relleños you've a hankering for, head to *Rose's Lariat* (324–5261), a minuscule eatery 4 blocks east of downtown at 410 East Cedar Street. Rose caters to loyal locals in Rawlins and across Wyoming; many people time their cross-state trips to land at the Lariat at lunchtime. Here you'll find delicious food and a south-of-the-border intimacy, with just twelve counter stools and one small booth. Try the smothered burritos. The restaurant is open from 11:00 A.M. to 7:00 P.M. Tuesday through Saturday. Finally, for fine dining head to *The Aspen House,* where the management claims they serve the best steak in Wyoming, and says the only complaint they've ever received is that the portions are too large. It's open Monday through Friday from 11:00 A.M. to 2:00 P.M. for lunch, and Monday through Saturday from 5:00 to 9:00 P.M. for dinner. For reservations at the restaurant, located at 318 5th Street, call 324–4787.

southern
wyomingtrivia

In 1874 John C. Friend shipped a railcar load of pigment east from the "Rawlins Red" paint mines outside Rawlins. It was used to paint the Brooklyn Bridge.

A 55-mile side trip south from Rawlins on State Highway 71 and dirt county roads will take you into the Medicine Bow National Forest and the spectacular, timbered highlands of the Sierra Madre Range. The *Rawlins Uplift,* which you can't miss as you drive along, marks the eastern edge of the Great Divide Basin and the beginning of the state's southwestern desert basins. Precambrian rocks are exposed in the core of the uplift, while its flanks are composed of younger, outwardly dipping Paleozoic and Mesozoic strata. After driving through several miles of forest lands, prior to encountering State Highway 70, you'll drive beneath a mile-long canopy of aspen trees. Known locally as *Aspen Alley,* the groves put on a colorful show in autumn that attracts Sunday-driving locals by the dozens.

A left turn onto State Highway 70 will take you back to Encampment, whereas a turn west (right) leads to Baggs, Wyoming, via Slater, Colorado, through the pastoral, little-visited valley of the Little Snake River. In microscopic Savery, Wyoming, don't miss the old ranch buildings and pioneer artifacts at the *Little Snake River Valley Museum* (383–7262), quite possibly the least-visited repository of old things in the entire Cowboy State. Exhibits, housed in and around the former Savery School, include the Sundance Kid's rifle, a one-room schoolhouse, and mountain man Jim Baker's cabin. It's open from 11:00 A.M. to 5:00 P.M. seven days a week from Memorial Day through the end of October, and is closed in the winter.

Sweetwater County

I–80 leaving Rawlins penetrates a starkly beautiful red desert region, teeming with wild horses and steaming with their "stud piles"; the horses employ those poetically named mounds of manure to mark their territories. Take the Continental Divide exit west of Creston Junction and cross under I–80 to find the secluded *Henry B. Joy Monument.* Joy was president of the Packard Motor Company and a major force in the Lincoln Highway movement as the first president of the Lincoln Highway Association. The 1939 monument is surrounded by a fence anchored by four concrete Lincoln Highway markers.

Journey another 51 miles down the road, and you'll find the *Point of Rocks Monument* and ruins of the *Almond Overland Stage Station* south of the highway. This station also served as a jumping-off point for the South Pass City goldfields in the 1860s. The sandstone structure was built in 1862 when "Stagecoach King" Ben Holladay moved his line south from the Oregon Trail to the Overland Trail because of Indian hostilities. For a time the infamous Jack Slade served as stationmaster. His violent temper resulted in the deaths of several men, and Slade eventually met his end at the end of a rope supplied by a Montana lynch mob. Ultimately, the railroad replaced the stage line, and the station was abandoned in 1868.

Desert Beauty

Any time I hear someone talking about how bleak the terrain surrounding Rock Springs is, I think back to the summer in the mid-1970s that Nancy and I spent working with an archaeological reconnaissance crew a few miles south of Point of Rocks. We became well acquainted with the Red Desert that summer, during which we camped in a canvas tepee that Nancy had sewn by hand.

Until then I, like countless others who make a practice of zipping through southern Wyoming on I–80 as fast as possible, believed the Red Desert country to be largely an empty wasteland, devoid of anything worthwhile other than oil and coal. But after walking and surveying some 16 square miles of that spacious land in preparation for proposed coal-mining activities, my outlook took a 180-degree turn. Our crew from Western Wyoming College eventually identified more than 200 prehistoric Native American campsites. Amid the stabilized sand dunes stretching south from Point of Rocks, we also encountered coyotes, pronghorn antelope, wild horses, golden eagles, and a host of other living things . . . but very few other humans. I came to realize that the desert is very much alive, but it often reveals itself in subtle ways that can't be appreciated from the interstate.

From exit 122 take Highway 371 north 7 miles along the drainage of Horse Thief Creek to the living ghost town of **_Superior._** At its peak, Superior boasted of 3,000 people, brought in by work in the subterranean coal mines. In forty years of mining activity, more than twenty-three million tons of coal were extracted from Superior area mines. The most intriguing site here is the **_1921 Union Hall,_** which once teemed with labor activity and social events. All that remains today is the shell of the building. Built in the shape of a trapezoid, the remaining walls of the once-imposing hall stand as a stark monument to the boom-and-bust cycles of Wyoming's mining economy.

Return to I–80 and exit on Highway 191 North, then continue through Rock Springs 3 miles before turning right onto Reliance Road. Here you'll find another vivid reminder of the volatility of the coal-mining industry and of the hard life of coal miners: the abandoned **_Reliance Tipple._** The Union Pacific Coal Company built the town of Reliance in the first decade of the twentieth century to house workers for the company's nearby mines. The Reliance Tipple, one of only a few historic coal tipples remaining in the state, was one of the largest and most mechanically advanced of its breed. Built in 1936, the steel-and-iron tipple—and the men, women, and children who worked there—sorted millions of tons of coal by size for loading into awaiting railroad cars. Interpretive signs around the tipple site provide a twenty-minute self-guided tour.

Don't miss the *Natural History Museum* at Western Wyoming Community College, which occupies a high blufftop within the city of Rock Springs. The museum's extensive collections include exhibits of Mayapan, Guatemalan, and Peruvian artifacts, such as water gourds, baskets, sling stones, blowguns, poison-dart quivers, and serpentine masks. The major attractions, however, are the full-size skeleton casts of dinosaurs that are located throughout the campus complex. A self-guided tour brochure obtained at the college information desk directs you to each dinosaur and gives a detailed description of the creature's natural history.

A *Triceratops* greets you at the main campus entrance. Looking rather like a gigantic rhinoceros and weighing up to six tons, *Triceratops'* nutrition came primarily from the giant palm fronds and leafy plants growing in then-tropical Wyoming. The original *Triceratops* from which the cast was made was found in eastern Wyoming near Lance Creek in 1889.

Additional exhibits include a miner's coal car, cave art, a replica of a stone statue from Easter Island (where Charles Love, the staff archaeology and geology professor, has conducted research), and a Foucault pendulum. Located in the atrium of the student center, the pendulum continuously swings in the same plane. As the earth rotates, the room in which it resides rotates with it, but the pendulum swings free. Although it appears as if the pendulum moves with each motion, it is actually the room that has changed position. The pendulum swings over a polished slab of white Wind River Range granite that cooled down and solidified from its molten state more than two billion years ago. The green stone surrounding the granite was cut from a giant jade boulder discovered near Jeffrey City.

Western Wyoming Community College is located at 2500 College Drive. The museum is open from 9:00 A.M. to 10:00 P.M. when classes are in session. School vacation periods may affect the schedule. For additional information call 382–1666.

You'll also want to take in the *Historic Downtown Rock Springs* tour, using the self-guiding pamphlet published by the Sweetwater County Joint Travel and Tourism Board. Copies are available at the Rock Springs Chamber of Commerce office, located at 1897 Dewar Drive, a few blocks off I–80. For information call 362–3771 or visit www.rockspringswyoming.net.

The tour begins at the *Rock Springs Historical Museum,* situated at the corner of Broadway and B Streets. The building was constructed in 1894 as the Rock Springs City Hall and used in that capacity until a new City Hall was constructed in 1978. The museum opened in 1988 as part of the Rock Springs centennial celebration. The elaborate Richardson Romanesque stone structure, extensively renovated in 1992, is listed on the National Register of Historic Places and represents the only example of that style of architecture remaining in south-western Wyoming. Museum collections detail Rock Springs history from the early 1880s through the present, and include exhibits on coal mining and the story behind this "City of Fifty-six Nationalities." The Rock Springs Historical Museum, located at 201 B Street, is open year-around, from 10:00 A.M. to 8:00 P.M. on Monday and Wednesday; 10:00 A.M. to 5:00 P.M. on Tuesday, Thursday, and Friday; 11:00 A.M. to 4:00 P.M. Saturday; winter hours are 10:00 A.M. to 5:00 P.M. Wednesday through Saturday. Call 362–3138 for additional information.

Using the guide mentioned earlier, you can locate several additional historic Rock Springs buildings. The structure at 440 South Main Street, for example, is one of the most compelling in town, with its distinctive stonework and extraordinary roofline. The cut-sandstone exterior is just a facade; the building proper is composed of brick. See if you can find the disappearing 1892 date carved into the stone.

Rock Springs got its name from a spring discovered there in the early 1860s, which led to the establishment of an Overland Trail stage station at the site. The town boomed when the Union Pacific tapped the area's extensive coalfields for fuel to run its trains. (Ironically, the spring disappeared with the onset of underground coal mining.) Despite modern residents' pride in the fact that Rock Springs was settled by a rich blend of ethnic groups, the town's history is marred by the 1885 Chinese Massacre, brought on when the Union Pacific introduced Chinese workers to replace white workers. Some thirty Chinese workers were killed in the uprising, which ended only after federal troops were brought in to quell the violence.

For some local flavor go to **Grubs** (362–6634), located at 415 Paulson Street. You may be obliged to stand in line several deep at the horseshoe counter before being served, but the hamburgers (called Shamrocks) and malts are worth the wait. A pair of supper clubs located west of Rock Springs are also worthy of a visit for delicious steaks, seafood, and other entrees: the **Log Inn Supper Club** (362–7166) and **White Mountain Mining Company** (382–5265). Prices at both restaurants are moderate-to-expensive.

Go several miles north of Rock Springs on Highway 191, then turn onto Chilton Road (Road 17) and follow it as it winds amid an intriguing landscape of extinct volcanoes and immense sand dunes. Go prepared with food, water, and emergency gear; these roads penetrate backcountry with no services or human inhabitants. The **Killpecker Dune Field** is the largest group of sand dunes on the North American continent, second in size in the world only to the Sahara Desert. It features an off-road vehicle area for those equipped to take advantage of it. The Killpecker Dune Field is also home to a herd of rare desert elk.

The remains of volcanoes, seen as flat-topped buttes, include Black Rock, the Boars Tusk, and North and South Table Mountains. **White Mountain** to the west of Chilton Road contains carvings dating from the seventeenth to early nineteenth centuries.

After an hour or two in the hot desert, you may be craving something cold, so stop at the **Farson Mercantile,** located at the crossroads of Highways 191 and 28, for one of the best deals in the Cowboy State. For an extremely reasonable price, you'll receive a mammoth scoop of ice cream; order two scoops and you may be compelled to share what you can't eat with the neighboring wild horses and pronghorns.

The California and Oregon-Mormon Trails run through this open country. Just northeast of Farson on Highway 191 is the "Parting of the Ways," where pioneers opted for one of two alternatives on the Oregon Trail. The shorter Sublette Cutoff tackled more treacherous terrain, including the most difficult river crossing on the entire Oregon Trail. The cutoff took its name from mountain man William Sublette, who reportedly became the first white man to travel the route, in 1826. The gentle descent from Steed Canyon on the east bank of the Green River allowed wagons a deceptively easy approach to the river. In June and early July, however, the time at which most emigrant wagons faced the crossing, they were met with high, swift water fed by mountain snowmelt. Sublette's fellow mountain man, Jim Bridger, took advantage of the dangerous situation, establishing a profitable fee-based ferry system. Mormon emigrants also operated a ferry system at nearby Names Hill, so-called because of the many early pioneers, including Bridger, who carved their names into the sandstone rock face.

A trail register kept by emigrant Winfield Scott Espy describes his arrival at the ferry camp in 1854:

southern wyomingtrivia

Near present-day Farson, in the northwest part of Sweetwater County, on June 28, 1847, mountain man Jim Bridger and Mormon leader Brigham Young met and discussed the feasibility of the Salt Lake Valley supporting a large human population. Confident that it never would, Bridger reputedly offered to pay Young one thousand dollars for the first bushel of corn grown there.

Found as the saying is "all sorts of people" American traders, Frenchmen, Mormons, Loafers, Dandies, Gamblers, Idlers, Grog shopkeepers, Half Breeds & whole Breed Snake Indians. . . . Boasting & bragging the order of the day as well as whiskey drinking & an occasional rowe.

Jim Bridger

In 1822 the Rocky Mountain Fur Company announced in the St. Louis *Missouri Republican* that it was seeking "one-hundred young men to ascend the Missouri River to its source, there to be employed for one, two, or three years." Those unable to resist answering the intriguing want ad included an eighteen-year-old former blacksmith's apprentice named James Bridger. During the next forty-five years spent in the West, Jim Bridger evolved first into the king of the mountain men, and then into the greatest guide the region has known. Bridger was among the few beaver trappers who, after skill and luck allowed him to survive the countless perils of two decades in the wilderness, had the temerity and desire to remain in the West after silk supplanted beaver fur as the favored material of the hat-making industry.

After twenty years of negotiating streams flooded with runoff and traipsing through country thick with bears, Bridger "retired" to establish Fort Bridger, which was actually more of a mercantile and smithy than a fort. From his way station Bridger guided emigrants and explorers, including Capt. W. F. Raynolds. Bridger led Raynolds's party of thirty infantrymen and seven scientists into and through Jackson Hole and Pierre's Hole in 1859–60. The party's mission: to explore "the headwaters of the Yellowstone and Missouri rivers, and . . . the mountains in which they rise."

Raynolds employed Bridger because he wanted the best guide living. Ironically, and out of character for him, Bridger never did get the party to its destination. Some allow that it was on purpose and not by chance: Because he was getting paid by the day, Bridger, who by this time had reached the wise old age of fifty-six, probably was in no hurry to get anywhere (and least of all Yellowstone, which he undoubtedly recalled as a mosquito-infested morass in early summer). Rather than bearing north to Yellowstone from the Union Pass area, as had been the intention, the party entered Jackson Hole, where a Corporal Bradley drowned in the Snake River before the party crossed over Teton Pass.

Raynolds was quite impressed by Bridger's imagination and lively story-telling skills. Aubrey Haines, in *The Yellowstone Story,* tells about one of Bridger's more famous tales, as related by Raynolds: "It was claimed that in some locality [thought to be Specimen Ridge in Yellowstone] . . . a large tract of sage is perfectly petrified, with all the leaves and branches in perfect condition, the general appearance of the plain being unlike that of the rest of the country, *but all is stone,* while the rabbits, sage hens, and other animals usually found in such localities are still there, perfectly petrified, and as natural as when they were living; and more wonderful still, these petrified bushes bear the most wonderful fruit—diamonds, rubies, sapphires, emeralds, etc. as large as black walnuts."

The longer Oregon Trail alternative passed southwest to Fort Bridger before swinging northwest to meet the Sublette Cutoff near present-day Cokeville.

Take Highway 191 south out of Rock Springs to discover the scenic and recreational wonders of *Flaming Gorge National Recreation Area,* which reaches south into Utah. The reservoir, created by damming the Green River, extends for 91 miles. The lake and the lands surrounding it provide a range of activities, from camping and fishing to waterskiing and river floating in summer, to cross-country skiing, snowmobiling, and ice fishing in winter. Don't miss taking in the gorgeous view from the Red Canyon Visitor Center at the north end of the dam. From Rock Springs you can travel completely around the reservoir for a 160-mile journey, following Highways 191, 44, and 530, winding up at the town of Green River. Be on the alert for bighorn sheep, elk, moose, mule deer, and pronghorn antelope. (And for the seemingly arbitrary speed limits, particularly in Utah.)

More than 600 camping and picnic sites and hundreds of miles of hiking trails await. The Firehole Canyon recreation site on the east side of the reservoir provides easy access to sublime high-desert vistas. A number of Flaming Gorge interpretive programs are also available; inquire about them at the visitor centers. Most facilities are open from mid-May to mid-September, while the route is open year-round, although travel at the higher elevations in winter can be hazardous. To reserve a camping site at any of the Flaming Gorge National Recreation Area locations, call (877) 444–6777 or go online to www.reserveusa.com.

> ## southern
> ## wyomingtrivia
>
> The flooding of Flaming Gorge Reservoir eradicated most of Wyoming's populations of canyon mice, cliff chipmunks, and piñon mice.

The striking buttes on the northern outskirts of Green River, known as The Palisades, are the remains of a prehistoric sea bottom. The individual buttes called Castle Rock, Teapot Dome, and Sugar Bowl were made famous by nineteenth-century artist Thomas Moran, in his painting of Native Americans and trappers fording the Green River. Moran is best known for his memorable paintings of Yellowstone and the Tetons.

The *Sweetwater County Historical Museum* boasts an excellent collection of Native American clothing and artifacts, informative displays on trona mining, a large collection of historic photographs of Green River, and extensive research materials covering Sweetwater County topics. The free-to-enter museum is located on the ground floor of the County Courthouse, 80 West Flaming Gorge Way. Hours are from 10:00 A.M. to 6:00 P.M., Monday through Saturday. For information call 872–6435 or 352–6715, or visit the museum's Web site, www.sweetwatermuseum.org.

One historic Green River building you should pay a visit to is the *Green River Brewery* (875–5255), now occupied by a bar and lounge fittingly known as The Brewery. Snacks and more serious foods like pizza, sandwiches, and

Expedition Island

By following Highway 530 from Flaming Gorge, you'll land in Green River, home to *Expedition Island,* where Maj. John Wesley Powell set out on his explorations of the Green and Colorado Rivers in 1869 and 1871. A plaque in the center of Expedition Island (Green River Island Park) commemorates the spot where Powell embarked on his journey. Notes from the diaries kept by men on the Powell expeditions are as amusing today as on the day they were written:

"Tried to drink all the whiskey there was in town. The result was a falure, as Jake Field persisted in making it faster than we could drink it."

—Jack Sumner, 1869

"The present 'City' [Green River] consisted of about thirteen houses, and some of these were of such complex construction that one hesitates whether to describe them as houses with canvas roofs, or tents with board sides."

—Frederick Dellenbaugh, 1871

The town, which started as a stage station, today ranks as the largest supplier of trona in the world. Trona contains the raw material for producing soda ash, which is used in the production of dozens of products, including baking soda, laundry detergent, glass, and paper. Ninety percent of domestic and 25 percent of global production of soda ash comes from the Green River area. An estimated one hundred billion tons of trona, laid down as sediments in an ancient landlocked lake, remain below the lands surrounding Green River.

chicken wings are available at the enterprise. Adam Braum built the first brewery in the Wyoming Territory here in 1872, and it changed hands several times over the next several decades. In 1901 the new owner, Hugo Gaensslen, built a new brewery using locally quarried stone, modeling it after the Chicago Water Tower, a Windy City landmark. That brewery, now listed on the National Register of Historic Places, is located on West Railroad Avenue.

For a respite, maybe to enjoy a picnic or simply to take in nature, mosey down to *Scott's Bottom Nature Area.* Here you'll find a wide variety of plant species, from wild licorice to Russian olive; wildlife abounds at the site, too. Interpretive signs lead you on a ½-mile loop trail. For information visit the Green River Parks and Recreation Department at 50 East Second Street, or call them at 872–0511.

The Green River and its tributaries make southwest Wyoming a top destination for anglers. To find cutthroat and lake trout (and probably inadvertently hook a whitefish or two), go to the Green River Pioneer Trails at *Pioneer Trails Park.* Head west on I–80 to the LaBarge Road exit, then travel on

Highway 372 for 10 miles, and, finally, go east on County Road 60. For licenses and detailed fishing information, contact the Wyoming Game and Fish Department at 351 Astle Avenue, Green River 82935, or call 875–3223.

Uinta County

Fort Bridger ranks as one of Wyoming's longest continuously settled sites. In 1843 fur trapper, entrepreneur, and guide Jim Bridger built Fort Bridger with his partner Louis Vasquez, and the Bridger-Vasquez partnership supplied emigrant wagon trains bound for Utah, Oregon, and California. The Mormon Church took over the property in 1855—after building its own Fort Supply in 1853—and two years later the Mormons burned Fort Bridger after a skirmish with the federal government. Fort Bridger was subsequently rebuilt and used by the government until 1890.

Fort Bridger State Historic Site re-creates the post and associated activities of the pioneer days. The fort has many original and reconstructed buildings, including the commanding officer's quarters dating from 1884; the 1843 Bridger & Vasquez trading post; the first schoolhouse in Wyoming (1860); the 1867 commissary storehouse; and the guardhouse, built in 1887. The museum contains a wealth of information and displays on fur trappers, Native Americans, and the early military. You'll also find weapons, uniforms, Native American artifacts, and personal belongings of Jim Bridger. On Labor Day weekend hundreds of modern-day mountain men and their families rendezvous at Fort Bridger to resurrect the past with authentic mountain man demonstrations, clothing, crafts, and encampment. At the celebration you can watch Native American dancing, knife throwing, and muzzle-loader shooting the way they were practiced in the old days. Fort Bridger State Historic Site is located a few miles southeast of I–80 off exit 34. The grounds are open daily year-round from 8:00 A.M. to sunset. From May 1 through September 30, the museum is open daily from 9:00 A.M. to 4:30 P.M. In October, weekend hours are 9:00 A.M. to 4:30 P.M. From November 1 through April 30, the museum is closed. The Bridger & Vasquez trading post—now a gift shop—is open daily from May 1 through September 30, from 9:00 A.M. to 4:30 P.M. Guided tours are available June 1 to just before Labor Day for a small fee. For information call 782–3842.

Take the Piedmont Road exit from I–80 to access the ghost town of Piedmont and the **Piedmont Kilns.** Back in 1869 Moses Byrne built five charcoal kilns north of Piedmont to provide charcoal for smelters in Utah. Three of the beehive-shaped, 30-by-30-foot kilns remain standing in well-preserved condition, as do several buildings at the town site, which was deserted after the railroad

Piedmont Kilns

moved the track farther north in 1901. Hard to imagine it now, but there were once 1,500 people living in Piedmont. Treasure seekers still scour the area for gold that Butch Cassidy and his boys reportedly buried near here.

Evanston is the last major stop in southern Wyoming. Check out **Pete's Rock 'N Rye,** a funky old roadhouse located on the frontage road along I–80 (turn east after you take the Bear River Drive exit). It has a great jukebox and plenty of local flavor.

Like Rock Springs, Evanston emerged as a railroad and mining town. Also like its neighbor to the east, Evanston suffered racial strife when Chinese miners were hired as strikebreakers in 1869. A riot ensued, forcing the evacuation of Chinatown. In 1922 a fire destroyed a sacred Chinese temple, called a **Joss House,** which when built in 1870 was one of only three such temples in the United States. A replica of the temple was completed in the early 1990s and stands on Depot Square, near Tenth and Front Streets. It contains artifacts salvaged from the 1922 fire. For information on this and other area attractions, stop at the chamber of commerce office, located in the 1906 Carnegie Library Building in Depot Square at 36 Tenth Street, or call 783–0307 or (800) 328–9708.

Conveniently, the Old Carnegie Library also houses the **Uinta County Historical Museum.** Curators of the museum, which has been in operation only since 1987, have done an admirable job of collecting and displaying the heritage of southwestern Wyoming. The museum includes fine collections of artifacts and memorabilia of Native American and Chinese history, as well as materials on ranching, railroading, gambling, and bootlegging, all parts of Evanston's past and/or present. The museum is open 9:00 A.M. to 5:00 P.M. on weekdays year-round, and from 10:00 A.M. to 4:00 P.M. on Saturday and Sunday during the summer. The 1901 Gothic **Depot Square** in Evanston is another interesting place to visit, as is Wyoming's lone remaining roundhouse, built in 1912. For information call the chamber of commerce at (800) 328–9708.

Bear River State Park lies within the Evanston city limits. The park facilities are ideal for picnicking, hiking, wildlife viewing, cycling, cross-country skiing, and other summer and winter outdoor activities. Bear River State Park is located just south of I–80 exit 6, the Bear River Drive exit. For more information call the park headquarters at 789–6547, or send an e-mail message to pthomp@state.wy.us.

Evanston features live pari-mutuel horse racing at *Wyoming Downs,* located 8 miles north on Highway 89. Thoroughbred and quarter horse racing takes place on weekends from mid-June through mid-August. For quality accommodations while in town to watch the horses run (or for whatever reason), try the *Pine Gables Inn B&B* at 1049 Center Street. Built in 1883 by Evanston's first merchant, A. V. Quinn, it operated as a European-style boardinghouse in the 1920s and 1930s. Victorian decor and plentiful antiques characterize the four guest rooms, each of which has a private bath. Rates range from $75 to $155 per night for a double. Call 789–2069 or go to www.pinegablesinn.com for information and reservations.

Places to Stay in Medicine Bow– Flaming Gorge Country

BAGGS

Drifters Inn,
Highway 789;
(307) 383–2015

CHEYENNE

Best Western Hitching Post Inn,
1700 West Lincolnway;
(307) 638–3301

Days Inn,
2360 West Lincolnway;
(307) 778–8877 or
(800) 329–7466

Holding's Little America,
2800 West Lincolnway;
(307) 775–8400 or
(800) 445–6945

Motel 6,
1735 Westland Road;
(307) 635–6806

ENCAMPMENT-RIVERSIDE

Olde Depot Bed & Breakfast,
201 1st Street in Riverside;
(307) 327–5277

Riverside Garage & Cabins,
downtown Riverside;
(307) 327–5361

Vacher's Bighorn Lodge,
508 McCaffrey Avenue;
(307) 327–5110

EVANSTON

Best Western Dunmar Inn,
1601 Harrison Drive;
(307) 789–3770 or
(800) 654–6509

Economy Inn,
1710 Harrison Drive;
(307) 789–9610

High Country Inn,
1936 Harrison Drive;
(307) 789–2810

GREEN RIVER

Oak Tree Inn,
1170 West Flaming Gorge Way;
(307) 875–3500

Sweet Dreams Inn,
1410 Uinta Drive;
(307) 875–7554

LARAMIE

Comfort Inn,
3420 Grand Avenue;
(307) 721–8856 or
(800) 228–5150

1st Inn Gold,
421 Boswell Drive;
(307) 742–3721 or
(800) 642–4212

Motel 8,
501 Boswell Drive;
(307) 745–4856

University Inn,
1720 Grand Avenue;
(307) 721–8855

LITTLE AMERICA

Holding's Little America,
I–80 exit 68;
(307) 875–2400 or
(800) 634–2401

PINE BLUFFS

Gator's Travelyn Motel,
515 West 7th;
(307) 245–3226

Sunset Motel,
316 West Third;
(307) 245–3591

RAWLINS

Days Inn,
2222 East Cedar;
(307) 324–6615

Super 8 Motel,
2338 Wagon Circle Road;
(307) 328–0630

ROCK SPRINGS

Comfort Inn,
1670 Sunset Drive;
(307) 382–9490 or
(800) 221–2222

EconoLodge,
1635 North Elk Street;
(307) 382–4217 or
(800) 548–6621

Holiday Inn,
1675 Sunset Drive;
(307) 382–9200 or
(800) HOLIDAY

Motel 8,
108 Gateway Boulevard;
(307) 362–8200

SARATOGA

Sage & Sand Motel,
311 South First;
(307) 326–8339

Hacienda Motel,
Highway 130 South;
(307) 326–5751

**Saratoga Inn Resort and
Hot Springs Spa,**
601 East Pike Road;
(307) 326–5261

Places to Eat in Medicine Bow–Flaming Gorge Country

BAGGS

Drifters Inn,
Highway 789;
(307) 383–2015

CHEYENNE

Avanti Restaurant,
4620 Grandview Avenue;
(307) 634–3432

Lexie's,
216 East 17th Street;
(307) 638–8712

Little Philly,
1121 West Lincolnway;
(307) 632–6824

**ENCAMPMENT-
RIVERSIDE**

Bear Trap Bar and Cafe,
120 East Riverside;
(307) 327–5277

EVANSTON

JB's,
1969 Harrison Drive;
(307) 789–7537

Michael's Bar & Grill,
1011 Front Street;
(307) 789–1088

Old Mill Restaurant,
30 County Road;
(307) 789–4040

Wally's Burgers,
1612 Harrison Drive;
(307) 789–1373

GREEN RIVER

Embers Family Restaurant,
95 East Railroad Avenue;
(307) 875–9983

Green River Rendezvous,
950 West Flaming
Gorge Way;
(307) 875–6455

LARAMIE

**Altitude Chophouse
& Brewery,**
320 South Second Street;
(307) 721–4031

**The Library Restaurant
& Brew Pub,**
1622 East Grand Avenue;
(307) 742–0500

The Overland Fine Eatery,
100 Ivinson Avenue;
(307) 721–2800

Rose Cafe,
410 South Second Street;
(307) 745–4077

LITTLE AMERICA

Holding's Little America,
I–80 exit 68;
(307) 875–2400 or
(800) 634–2401

PINE BLUFFS

Uncle Fred's Place,
701 Parsons Street;
(307) 245–3443

RAWLINS

**Square Shooter's
Eating House,**
311 West Cedar;
(307) 324–4380

ROCK SPRINGS

Golden Corral,
1990 Dewar Drive;
(307) 362–7234

Renegade Cafe,
1610 Elk Street;
(307) 362–3052

Santa Fe Trail,
1635 Elk Street;
(307) 362–5427

SARATOGA

Lazy River Cantina,
110 East Bridge Street;
(307) 326–8472

**Saratoga Inn Resort and
Hot Springs Spa,**
601 East Pic Pike Road;
(307) 326–5261

Western Wyoming: Bridger-Yellowstone Country

Bridger-Yellowstone Country is that portion of Wyoming primarily responsible for the state's well-deserved reputation as a vacationer's paradise. Some three million visitors per year tour the greater Yellowstone-Teton region alone. Most of those millions, however, visit just the well-known and consequently most crowded sites. Little do they realize that wonderful places offering equal beauty and far more solitude typically lie hidden nearby.

From Kemmerer your trail leads north to Pinedale, a classic cowtown and gateway to the marvelous Wind River Range. An alternative route snakes along the Wyoming-Idaho border, through a largely bypassed, mountain-ringed agrarian corner of Wyoming that was initially settled by Mormon pioneers dispatched from the Salt Lake Valley. From Pinedale and/or Star Valley, it is on to Jackson, Grand Teton National Park, and, finally, Yellowstone National Park—where even within one of the world's most popular natural areas, there are plenty of places that will startle and please those averse to taking the well-worn path.

WESTERN WYOMING:
BRIDGER-YELLOWSTONE COUNTRY

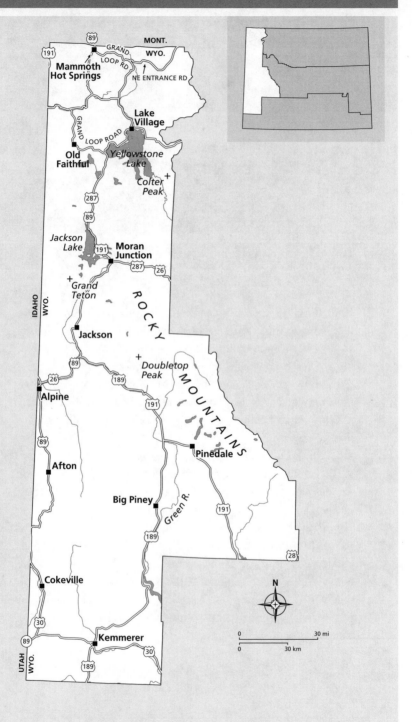

Lincoln County

A fossil of sorts—King Coal, that is—fueled the growth of Kemmerer, population 2,651. Mahlon S. Kemmerer, for whom the town was named, and his partner Patrick J. Quealy opened the area's first coal mine in 1897, establishing the Kemmerer Coal Company. One of the world's largest operational open-pit mines, owned by Pittsburg-Midway, is found here today. Other ventures proved less successful, as numerous mining ghost towns in the hills around Kemmerer attest.

Kemmerer's other primary claim to fame was the opening of the J. C. Penney "Mother Store," under the name of Golden Rule Store, by James Cash Penney in 1902. By 1912 Penney owned thirty-four stores, and he changed the chain's name to J. C. Penney. The Kemmerer store still operates, on the Triangle downtown. Nearby, the restored *J. C. Penney Home* makes for an interesting visit. Located on J. C. Penney Drive across from the Triangle, it is open daily during the summer and in the winter by appointment. Inquire at the chamber of commerce or call 877–9761.

The *Fossil Country Frontier Museum* interprets the region's cultural history. If you have time for only one of the many exhibits, be sure to walk through the replica coal mine for a sense of the dangers Kemmerer's underground

BEST ATTRACTIONS IN BRIDGER-YELLOWSTONE COUNTRY

Darwin Ranch,
miles from nowhere;
(307) 733–5588

Fossil Butte National Monument,
west of Kemmerer;
(307) 877–4455

Half Moon Lake,
outside Pinedale;
(307) 367–4326

Indian Arts Museum at Colter Bay,
Grand Teton National Park;
(307) 739–3300

Lost Horizon Supper Club,
Alta;
(307) 353–8226

Museum of the Mountain Man,
Pinedale;
(307) 367–4101

National Museum of Wildlife Art,
Jackson;
(307) 733–5771

Snake River Brewery,
Jackson;
(307) 739–2337

Star Valley Cheese Factory,
Thayne;
(307) 883–2510

Yellowstone National Park Museum and Archives,
(307) 344–7381

miners faced every workday. A unique summer program involves local citizens presenting Campfire Chats, centering on the area's colorful past. The museum, located at 400 Pine Street, is open Monday through Saturday from 9:00 A.M. to 5:00 P.M. in summer, and 10:00 A.M. to 4:00 P.M., Monday through Friday, in winter. For more information call 877–6551 or e-mail museum@hamsfork.net.

The circa 1925 **Lincoln County Courthouse** has been restored and is worth touring to see the striking American-inspired features. The adjoining jail has been recycled into a display room that houses a respectable collection of fossils. The courthouse and jail are located on Sage Avenue.

Kemmerer's sister city Diamondville is home to delicious Italian food served at **Luigi's Supper Club,** 819 Susie Avenue. Prices are moderate and the choices mouthwatering. It's open Thursdays only from 5:00 to 9:00 P.M. For information call 877–6221.

If you'd like to spend a night in the woods but still want a roof over your head, think about renting the **Kelly Cabin,** the **LaBarge Cabin,** or the **Scaler Cabin** in the Bridger-Teton National Forest. All three are old ranger stations left from when the forest had few serviceable roads and the rangers made their rounds on horseback. They sleep between four and six people and cost only $30 per night, and the Kemmerer District Ranger Office handles reservations. The Kelly Cabin lies about 45 miles north of Kemmerer off Highway 233, or 23 miles northeast of Cokeville off Highway 232. The LaBarge Cabin lies southeast of Afton off the Smith Fork Road, and the Scaler Cabin farther south. Cabin facilities include bunk beds, a wood/gas cookstove, a woodstove for heat, a propane refrigerator, propane lights, and an outhouse. Reservations are required. For reservations, maps, and detailed directions, contact the ranger station at 877–4415, or write P.O. Box 31, Kemmerer 83101. You can also rent cabins in other districts of the Bridger-Teton Forest. Contact the Big Piney District Office in Big Piney, 276–3375, or the Greys River District in Afton, 885–3166, for more information.

Names Hill is one of the three well-known Oregon Trail registers in Wyoming, a place where emigrants carved their names for future travelers to see. Like Register Cliff near Guernsey and Independence Rock southwest of Casper, Names Hill evokes a haunting presence along the historic byway. It is located several miles south of LaBarge off Highway 189. Nearby Fontenelle Reservoir offers camping and picnicking facilities.

Ten miles west of Kemmerer on U.S. Highway 30, you'll see the entrance to **Fossil Butte National Monument.** The road here will take you 3½ miles north to the site where Fossil Butte rises 1,000 feet above Twin Creek Valley to an elevation of 7,500 feet. As its name alludes, the 8,180 acres of rugged topography yield one of the richest freshwater fossil fish deposits in the Western

Hemisphere, preserved in limestone layers between 30 and 300 feet below the surface of the butte. The fossil deposits, laid down fifty million years ago in lake beds, were later thrust upward to become Fossil Butte. The base of Fossil Butte, whose specimens were investigated as early as 1877 and now are show-cased in museums throughout the world, consists of the brightly colored beds of the Wasatch Formation.

The visitor center offers an orientation to the geologic story told in the rocks of Fossil Butte. You can also obtain hiking maps of the area; along the way, trail signs explain the exposed specimens. There are no camping facilities at Fossil Butte, but you can picnic in a small aspen grove about 4 miles from the visitor center. Fossil Butte is open daily from 8:00 A.M. to 7:00 P.M. Memorial Day through Labor Day and 8:00 A.M. to 4:30 P.M. the rest of the year (closed on winter holidays). For information call 877–4455 or visit www.nps.gov/fobu on the Internet.

If simply looking at fossils isn't quite exciting enough, you can dig for your own at **Ulrich's Fossil Quarries.** Three-hour-long excavation outings take place from June through Labor Day, seven days a week, between 9:00 A.M. and 9:00 P.M., weather permitting. You'll be accompanied by an experienced staff member, and Ulrich's furnishes all tools and equipment needed for excavating. Bring your own snacks and liquid refreshments. The $65 fee allows you

The Longest Graveyard in America

Tragedy along the Oregon Trail and other trails leading westward is etched into the Wyoming landscape. Historians estimate that between 6 and 10 percent of the 350,000 emigrants who traveled the Oregon Trail died along the way, approximately ten deaths for each mile of the route. The major danger was cholera, followed by accidents involving livestock, wagons, firearms, and river crossings. Contrary to popular myth, Indians were a minor hazard in terms of the numbers of deaths.

Seventeen miles northwest of Kemmerer on Highway 233 are the graves of two who met their fate along the trail. In 1852 Nancy Jane Hill was traveling with a wagon train that was delayed for more than two weeks by Indian attacks. Although she survived the Indian threat itself, she succumbed to cholera and died on July 5 at age twenty. Her fiancé is said to have returned to her grave site three times over the next fifty-three years.

Alfred Corum and three brothers left Missouri in 1849 to seek their fortunes in the goldfields of California. Their wagon reached Hams Fork Plateau on July 3 and stopped because Alfred had been sick for more than a week. As the brothers tended to his needs, more than 200 wagons passed them on the dusty trail. Alfred died on Independence Day of unknown causes.

BEST ANNUAL EVENTS IN BRIDGER-YELLOWSTONE COUNTRY

Cutter and Chariot Races,
Afton-Thayne; November–March;
(307) 883–2759

**International Stage Stop
Sled Dog Race,**
begins/ends in Jackson;
late January through early February;
(307) 734–1163

**Moose Chase Cross-Country
Ski Race,**
Teton Village; mid-February;
(307) 733–6433

Annual Celebrity Ski Extravaganza,
Jackson Hole; March;
(307) 734–2878

Pole-Pedal-Paddle,
Jackson; April;
(307) 733–6433

**Annual Boy Scouts' Elk
Antler Auction,**
Jackson; May;
(307) 733–3316

Green River Rendezvous,
Pinedale; July;
(307) 367–4101

Oyster Ridge Music Festival,
Kemmerer, July;
(307) 877–6551

Grand Teton Music Festival,
Teton Village; July–August;
(307) 733–1128

Sublette County Fair,
Big Piney; August;
(307) 276–5373

Targhee Bluegrass Festival,
Grand Targhee; August;
(800) 827–4433

to collect and keep specimens other than those designated by the state of Wyoming as "rare and unusual." Winter hours for the associated gallery are 8:00 A.M. to 5:00 P.M., or by appointment. Ulrich's is located off the road to Fossil Butte. For advance reservations, which are required, or for further information call 877–6466 or visit www.ulrichsfossilgallery.com. (No children under ten years of age are permitted.)

Continue on Highway 30/89 to Cokeville, established in 1874, the oldest town in Lincoln County. Keeping up Wyoming's tradition as the Equality State, Cokeville elected a woman mayor and two women council members in 1922. Originally the town was known as Smith's Fork on the Bear River. The Oregon Trail runs right through town and on into Idaho. Many cutoffs converged near Cokeville at the ferry site on the Smith's Fork, considered a primary hub of the Oregon Trail. You'll see an *Oregon Trail Monument* in Cokeville City Park at the corner of East Main Street and Park Street.

Star Valley and *Little Switzerland* are nicknames for a particularly isolated and fertile valley region of Lincoln County located north of Cokeville.

Native Americans long valued the moderate climate and lush valley for grazing their horses and hunting the abundant wildlife. Later, emigrants using the Lander Cutoff between 1840 and 1870 stopped in Star Valley before continuing on toward Oregon. Mormon leader Brigham Young, realizing the potential of the rich farmlands, established the first settlement in the area. Until recently, Star Valley was best known for its dairy products, notably cheese. But since the Summer Olympic Games in Sydney, Australia, it has gained notice as the home of Greco-Roman wrestling gold medalist Rulon Gardner.

With a population of around 1,800, Afton is the hub of Star Valley. Brigham Young disciple Moses Thatcher founded the town in 1885. Boasting the "World's Largest Elk Antler Arch," Afton's arch extends over Main Street at a height of 18 feet and contains more than 3,000 antlers. In contrast, the towering steeple of the original Latter Day Saints "Church of the Valley" lends the town a distinct New England feel. An early Scottish resident named the community after Robert Burns's poem, "Flow Gently, Sweet Afton." On a more raucous note, Butch Cassidy and his gang, favoring the valley's isolation, once wintered here away from the pursuit of the law. Cassidy reportedly papered the local bar with banknotes from one of his gang's many robberies.

western wyomingtrivia

Cokeville, northwest of Kemmerer, once was a multimillion-dollar sheep-shipping site.

A small museum with a big name, the ***Lincoln County Daughters of the Utah Pioneers Museum,*** houses a number of pioneer homesteading items, such as a loom and spinning wheel. The museum is located at 46 East Fifth Street. It is open June through August, Monday through Friday from 1:00 to 5:00 P.M., or by appointment. Also erected by the Daughters of the Utah Pioneers is the ***Star Valley Marker*** at 347 Jefferson Street. The marker commemorates the settling of Star Valley in 1879. An interesting component of the monument is the bell, which originally was housed in an 1892 bell tower and was rung every Sunday morning at 9:30 and 9:50 to aid valley residents in adjusting their clocks.

Afton is home to Aviat Inc., a company that manufactures some of the finest in aerobatic planes. In late June the town hosts the ***CallAir Fly-in,*** with small-craft pilots from throughout the West flying in for airplane-related fun, both on and above the ground. The ***CallAir Museum*** (886–9881) brims with aircraft and displays explaining Star Valley's surprisingly important role in the evolution of small-craft aviation. If the museum's not open, call 883–2759 for more information.

Five miles east of Afton, you'll find the geologically intriguing *Intermittent Spring.* The natural oddity gushes for approximately eighteen minutes, expelling an extraordinary quantity of water; it then ceases to flow for about the same amount of time. It's one of only a handful of intermittent springs in the world, and the only one of its kind in the United States. Like Old Faithful, its cycles are fairly predictable; Intermittent Spring functions for nine months of the year. The best time to view it is during high-water runoff, from the middle of May through the middle of July. To find it, take Second Avenue East to the dirt road leading to Swift Creek Canyon. You'll need to walk a ¾-mile trail to reach the stream from the parking area, but it's a pleasant hike through a beautiful canyon.

Moving north on Highway 89 takes you to Thayne, population 341, where you can stock up on cheese at the *Star Valley Cheese Factory.* The bulk of the cheese produced here is shipped outside the region—some 60,000 pounds annually. You can also grab a bite to eat at the Star Valley Cheese Factory Restaurant. Good sandwiches, great pies, and buffalo burgers. For information call 883–2510.

With the change in the seasons, Thayne and Afton turn to winter and snow to attract visitors, with their *Cutter and Chariot Races.* The All American Cutter Racing Association was organized in Thayne in 1948, but the tradition goes back to the 1920s, when local ranchers and farmers employed horse-drawn sleighs to deliver milk to the creamery, to pick up supplies, and to visit far-flung neighbors and relatives.

Taking a cue from *Ben Hur,* perhaps, the chariot racers have added wheels to their sleighs. The world's first cutter race took place on Thayne's iced-over main drag when, reportedly, a Mormon bishop bested a local rancher in the 1920s competition. Interest in the sport progressively grew over the years, and the first World Cutter and Chariot Racing Championship took place here in 1965. The horse-drawn chariots race a quarter mile on a straight, snow-covered track. The world record for a quarter-mile cutter race, 21.64 seconds, was set in 1994. Cutter and chariot racing takes place in Star Valley beginning the first weekend in November through March. For information call 883–2759.

The *Auburn Rock Church,* one of the oldest buildings in Star Valley, played an important part in local Mormon history. Constructed of striking rough-cut stone in the late nineteenth century, like most LDS churches, in addition to serving a religious role it also operated as a community gathering place.

The tiny town of Freedom, straddling the Wyoming/Idaho border, is the headquarters of the prestigious *Freedom Arms* gun factory. Freedom Arms fashions collector handguns that command a hefty price. Freedom is the oldest settlement in the valley, established by Mormons in 1879. This area of lower

Star Valley is also developing into quite a retirement and golfing mecca. Recommended: beautiful *Cedar Creek Golf Course* (883–2230). The associated Silo Lounge—which looks like . . . well, a silo—reveals the not-too-distant agrarian past of the present links.

Alpine Junction, population 550, is a haven for water sports enthusiasts, thanks to its proximity to the Grand Canyon of the Snake River and Idaho's Palisades Reservoir. Alpine Junction is auspiciously situated at the confluence

Riding the Range—on Two Wheels

In late July 1985 Nancy and I struck out on a backcountry bicycle tour of western Wyoming. Mountain biking was a fairly new sport at the time; touring on mountain bikes with camping gear in tow was almost unheard of. As we quickly discovered, however, there's no better way to become truly acquainted with Wyoming's nonwilderness backcountry than undertaking a tour such as this.

After a friend dropped us and our bikes off at the Tri-Basin Divide, a high saddle separating the Salt River and Wyoming ranges, we followed a gravel byway paralleling the sparkling Greys River. Other than one or two fishermen and a lone Forest Service timber cruiser, we saw no other humans for mile after mile of stunning countryside. A steep climb along Sheep Creek led us to McDougal Gap, then a quick downhill zip delivered us onto the high desert, where we pedaled up and over numerous rimrock ridges before reaching the campground in tiny Daniel.

The most memorable stretch of the five-day trip was from Whiskey Grove Campground, nestled along the upper Green River, to the Horn Ranch, located at the upper, eastern end of the Gros Ventre River Road. After riding over the gnarly Kinky Creek Divide, we stopped in at the exceptionally isolated *Darwin Ranch* for some route-finding advice. "You're going to try and ride what through where?" came the words from an angular, stooped cowboy who, incongruously, spoke with an Australian accent. His incredulous words were delivered as we relaxed with him and three other ranch hands around the kitchen table of the rustic guest ranch, which its amid stunning surroundings at the head of the Gros Ventre River drainage. Collectively they told us, in so many words, that the trail ahead was far too rough, and that trying to cover it on bicycles was a dumb idea.

But we pressed on anyway, soon learning that the cowboys were right. After already having spent eight hours on the bikes that day, the next 5 miles of trail took an additional four hours to cover. Together, up steep hills leading out of countless mud-filled draws, we pushed each bike, then held the bikes back on the equally steep downhills to keep them from turning into runaways. On finally busting out to the main road at the entrance to the Horn Ranch, we immediately set up camp and crashed, too tired even to cook supper.

The next day's trip to Moose in Grand Teton National Park, although long as measured in miles, was a lark compared to the previous day's odyssey.

of the Snake, Greys, and Salt Rivers. With an abundance of hotels and lodges, Alpine makes a great base from which to explore the nearby river and mountain country. The third weekend in June, the community hosts the **Mountain Days** festival, featuring a country music jamboree, various games, a Native American jewelry show, a black powder shoot, a tomahawk throw, and a Pony Express poker ride. For information call 654–7776 or 654–7748.

From Alpine, Highway 26/89 leads through the inspiring 3,000-foot-deep **Grand Canyon of the Snake River,** one of the scenic wonders of Wyoming.

Sublette County

Drive northwest out of LaBarge on Highway 189 to Big Piney (population 408) and stop at the **Green River Valley Museum** for an introduction to the valley's long and colorful history. The museum includes an interesting brand exhibit dating back to 1895, along with the original oil Wardell Buffalo Trap Mural that was featured on the 1995 Wyoming Archaeological Society poster. The museum is located on Highway 189 in Big Piney. It's open Tuesday through Saturday from noon to 4:00 P.M. mid-June to mid-October, or by appointment. Call 276–5343 or visit www.grvm.com for information.

Just before you arrive at Daniel, note the roadside historical marker concerning Father Pierre Jean DeSmet. It's located on the right side of Highway 189. The marker commemorates the one hundredth anniversary of the first Roman Catholic mass held in Wyoming, which occurred on July 5, 1840. To find the actual **DeSmet Monument** and the spot where Father DeSmet delivered the mass, follow the gravel road marked "Daniel Cemetery" for about 3 miles. An added dividend is the wonderful view of the valley and of the Green River you'll savor from this vantage. There's also a small chapel here built of native rock.

Nearby is the grave site of Pinckney Sublette, one of the brothers of William Sublette, the famous fur trader (and discoverer of the Sublette Cutoff), for whom Sublette County was named. Pinckney's extensive travels continued even after his death in 1865: He was exhumed in 1897 as part of a lawsuit to establish the heirs of another brother, Solomon, and shipped off to St. Louis, where he remained until 1935. Then a court ordered his body returned to Sublette County, Wyoming.

If you're interested in enjoying a week or more of top-notch fly fishing—along with horseback trail rides into the mountains, fantastic vistas in the shadow of the Gros Ventre Range, and gourmet meals—then let ranch manager Debbie Hansen and her staff at the **Flying A Ranch** pamper you. Built in 1929, the historic ranch has been completely refurbished, yet it retains its original character. Total comfort in a grand western atmosphere is what the Flying A provides, with its seven spacious handcrafted homestead log cabins, each with a large sitting area, kitchenette, and private bath. Most have a fireplace or wood-burning stove, and each cabin is named after an early valley settler.

For dinner the Flying A features a combination of western fare and continental cuisine, but before you feast on the shrimp scampi, Italian delicacies, or Mexican fare, cocktails (BYOB) are served pondside at the Gilded Moose Saloon. The ranch caters to couples and not to families, so plan to use this as an escape from kids—whether your own or other people's. Rates run from $1,300 to $1,500 per six-day week per person based on double occupancy. The Flying A Ranch season runs from mid-June to late-September. For information during the season, call 367–2385, or write to them at Route 1, Box 7, Pinedale, WY 82941. During the off-season call (888) 833–3348 or write 1701 South First Avenue, Sioux Falls, SD 57105; you can also look them up on the Internet at www.flyinga.com. Call early because the ranch books up fast.

The Flying A, which hosts a maximum of fourteen guests at a time, is located 27 miles northwest of Pinedale and 16 miles southeast of Bondurant off Highway 191. Watch for the ranch sign on the right side of the road as you head northwest. (The gate to the entrance will probably be locked, but on making reservations the staff will give you the lock's combination.)

If it's a working cattle ranch experience you've a hankering for, mosey over to the ***Box "R" Ranch*** near Cora. For more than a century, five generations of the Lozier family have maintained one of the finest cattle/horse and

Early Day Trade Shows

Trappers and hunters used the Green River Valley for a number of their rendezvous, coming here to obtain supplies for the coming season and to sell or trade their bounty. All told there were sixteen major Rocky Mountain rendezvous, with six of them held here in the "Valley of the Green." The first rendezvous occurred in 1825, within 20 miles of the confluence of Henry's Fork and the Green River, near present-day MacKinnon in southwestern Sweetwater County. The event lasted only one day, as trappers traded beaver and other pelts for needed supplies. Later gatherings carried on for more than a week and attracted all sorts of characters, who participated in the revelry of horse racing, skill contests, wrestling bouts, gambling, drinking and fighting, and yarn spinning. By the 1830s dwindling fur supplies and changes in fashion were signaling the end of the once-bustling beaver fur trade. The final rendezvous took place in 1840 along the Seedskeedee (Green River) near present-day Daniel in Sublette County. It had also been the site of the 1833, 1835, 1836, 1837, and 1839 rendezvous.

guest ranches in western Wyoming. The scenery is spectacular at this little slice of heaven: The Box "R" encompasses the only deeded land to border Wyoming's preeminent wilderness area, the Bridger Wilderness of the Wind River Range.

Guests come for a week at a time, during which they have their own designated mount (chosen from more than a hundred head of expertly trained horses and mules) and tack for seven days of riding. You'll even have the opportunity to help round up cattle (early, early in the morning) and move them to new grazing ground. If you have the interest and are handy with tools, you're also welcome to dig in and help Irv Lozier and his son Levi mend fences or perform maintenance work on a guest cabin. Hearty meals are served ranch-style, with wranglers and guests dining side by side. All this, and more, from $1,195 weekly per person, double occupancy and all-inclusive.

The Loziers offer seven different ranch and mountain vacations to suit your fancy, ranging from a week of cattle drives to full-service wilderness pack trips. The Box "R" season runs from late May through September. For complete information call 367–4868 or (800) 822–8466, or see their on-line brochure at www.boxr.com.

Although the fur traders, emigrants, and mounted Indians and cavalry soldiers of yore are all long gone, the pioneer outlook and spirited wildlands of Wyoming live on, little changed over the centuries. And nowhere does the pioneer spirit thrive as it does in and around Pinedale, situated near the site of the last mountain man rendezvous. Famously high in elevation and battered by long, often bitter winters, Pinedale is the doorway to and chief outfitting center for the Wind River Mountains. The Winds encompass some of Wyoming's highest peaks, with Gannett Peak, sitting almost directly north of Pinedale, the state's loftiest at 13,804 feet. In the Winds you can explore 400,000 acres of Bridger-Teton National Forest wilderness. The mountains hold twenty-seven active glaciers, more than 1,300 alpine lakes, and approximately 600 miles of trails, branching out from nine major trailheads. For more information contact the Pinedale Area Chamber of Commerce at 367–2242, or the Pinedale Ranger District of the Bridger-Teton National Forest at 367–4326.

Four miles north of town off Fremont Lake Road, stunning **Fremont Lake** sits at the base of the Wind River Mountains. The lake, named after explorer John C. Fremont, is Wyoming's second-largest natural lake and one of the deepest and purest lakes in the nation. Famous for its large lake trout, Fremont Lake once gave up a record-breaking forty-pounder. Spend a day fishing, wading, or swimming at the sandy beach, or camp overnight at the Forest Service campground. Boat rentals and lake tours are also available.

The Winds in Winter

Having already spent a fair amount of time in the Wind River Range backpacking in the summer months, when the high-country trout bite like crazy, as do the mountain mosquitoes, I decided in the late 1970s that I'd like to visit the fabulous range during the quiet (and bug-free) white of winter. I was also interested in improving my skiing and general outdoor skills, so I signed on for a three-week winter-camping trip with the Lander-based National Outdoor Leadership School (NOLS).

It was late January 1977, midway through an unusually low-snowfall winter. Still, at the higher elevations our group of sixteen managed to find plenty of snow for practicing our telemark turns, for melting down snow to make drinking and cooking water, and for building snowcaves to provide cozy sleeping conditions. (Most of the nights, though, we spent in tents, which weren't nearly as cozy—particularly when the mercury dipped to minus 20, as it did on more than one occasion.)

I was fortunate, because I was already quite practiced at downhill and cross-country skiing. Most of the group members hadn't yet earned their skiing legs, and I remember feeling extremely sorry for them—particularly when one of them would fall over backward while wearing a backpack crammed with eighty pounds of stuff. This made the person so much like a turtle stuck on his back that the rest of us always had to laugh before helping the hapless skier back to his or her feet.

For three weeks we encountered not another soul outside of our tight little group. Not surprisingly, very few folks venture into the Winds in the wild of winter.

Skyline Drive, beginning at the east end of Pinedale, takes you on a 26-mile, hour-long excursion amid a scenic collection of lakes, mountains, and valleys. Along the way you'll come to Elkhart Park, where you can detour on a hike to ***Photographer's Point*** in the Bridger Wilderness. The trail is well marked and delivers a fantastic view of Fremont Peak and the Continental Divide country across a deep glacial valley. The round-trip covers about 8 miles.

A longer drive takes you on a 100-mile trip featuring postcard images of wildlife, mountain walls, and alpine lakes. The highlight of the trip, a gigantic glacier-sculpted monolith known as ***Square Top Mountain,*** towers over the headwaters of the Green River at 11,679 feet. An added bonus is the beautiful ***Green River Lakes.*** Take Highway 191 west 6 miles from Pinedale, and then head north on Highway 352. After the road turns to gravel, travel another 20 miles to reach Green River Lakes and Square Top Mountain. Along the way you'll pass Kendall Warm Springs, home to the rare Kendall dace, a 2-inch-long mini-fish. The remains of Wyoming's first dude ranch, the Billy Wells Ranch, also lie along this stretch of road. Be alert for moose, elk, and deer. The Green

River Lakes parking area marks the jumping-off spot for day hikes and longer trips. You can camp overnight at the Green River Lakes Campground or nearby Whiskey Grove.

Bridger Wilderness Outfitters offers summer and winter wilderness survival courses; youth camps teaching first aid, horseback riding, and leadership skills; fly-fishing pack trips; a seven-day, 120-mile "Ride the Winds" horse packing trip along the Continental Divide; guided big-game hunts; guided snowmobiling in winter; and stays at the historic DC Bar Guest Ranch, one of the oldest dude ranches in the area. For more information contact owner-operator Tim Singewald at 367–2268, (888) 803–7316, or visit www.bwo.com.

Make a point of spending a few hours in Pinedale's *Museum of the Mountain Man.* It's located on the east edge of town just off Highway 191 at the top of the hill as you head north on Fremont Lake Road. You'll be treated to an excellent presentation on the fur-trading era and the life of the mountain men. Look for Jim Bridger's own .40 caliber half-stock rifle, a rare "sight," indeed. The kids will especially enjoy the hands-on exhibits, such as the beaver fur that invites you to PLEASE TOUCH ME. Special programs and living-history demonstrations are scheduled during the summer season, and additional exhibits on the Plains Indians, tie hacking, and pioneer ranching life are featured. The museum is vibrant and spacious, a delightful start or end to any day, and guaranteed to leave a mark on the landscape of your imagination. The museum is open May 1 through September 30 daily from 9:00 A.M. to 5:00 P.M., and in winter by appointment only. The entrance fee is $5.00 for adults and $3.00 for children. Call 367–4101 or visit www.museumofthemountainman.com for additional information.

In early July, Pinedale hosts the *Green River Rendezvous,* with a reenactment of the 1830s rendezvous, when trappers, traders, and Native Americans gathered at the Green River. Events include a two-hour award-winning pageant, rodeos, concerts, historic demonstrations, a discussion of Plains Indian culture, and a pit-roasted buffalo feed. For information call 367–4101.

The 1929 *Log Cabin Hotel,* a National Historic Landmark, rents nine cabins and two rooms in the main building. Many have cooking facilities. It's said that ownership of the motel once changed hands in a poker game, but it's no gamble staying at the Log Cabin today. Rates are $85 to $120 and cabins are available June 1 through September 30; for more information visit www.thelog cabin motel.com or call 367–4579. Farther off the beaten track is *Half Moon Lake Resort* (367–6373, www.halfmoonlake.com), located a few miles northeast of town, 2 miles off the Fremont Lake Road. Cabins, dining, and boat and mountain-bike rentals are among the options at this beautifully situated getaway. Open all year.

McGregor's Pub, at 21 North Franklin Avenue in Pinedale, serves a variety of excellent dishes, from prime rib to fresh fish, at moderate-to-expensive prices. It's considered *the* place in town for a special dinner out. For reservations call 367–4443.

Teton County

From Pinedale travel northwest on U.S. Highway 189/191, soon crossing the Hoback Rim. Sort of a minicontinental divide, the rim marks the watershed divide separating the Columbia and Colorado River systems. After reaching Hoback Junction, where the Hoback River joins the Snake, you'll notice the traffic beginning to pick up. By the time you reach ***Jackson,*** it's nearly bumper to bumper.

That's because there's lots to see and do in Jackson, the southern jumping-off point for Grand Teton and Yellowstone National Parks. In keeping with Wyoming's reputation as the Equality State, in 1920 the town of Jackson became the first town in the United States to be governed entirely by women, when voters elected Grace Miller as mayor and chose other women for the four council positions, as well for city clerk, treasurer, and town marshal. The women remained in office until 1923.

Stop in at the historic Wort Hotel at the corner of Glenwood and Broadway and belly up to the ***Silver Dollar Bar,*** which is inlaid with 2,032 silver dollars. Also check out the display of cattle brands in the lobby near the big old fireplace. JJ's Silver Dollar Bar and Grill serves (arguably) the best prime rib in town, as well as other great entrees. Prices are moderate-to-expensive. For information call 733–2190.

The dining possibilities in and around Jackson are nearly endless. At the ***Sweetwater Restaurant*** (733–3553), located at the corner of King and Pearl Streets, you can eat indoors or dine on the deck. The lamb and trout are real crowd pleasers. Prices are moderate-to-expensive. ***Jedediah's Original House***

western wyomingtrivia

From the 1941 *Wyoming: A Guide to Its Highways, History, and People:* "[Yellowstone] Park hotels are first-class; rates range from $2.75 a day without meals, to $9 a day with meals."

western wyomingtrivia

Effie Jane Wilson, born 1891, was the first white child born in Jackson Hole. Rose Park Marshall, who preceded Effie Jane by ten years, was the first white baby born in Yellowstone National Park.

of Sourdough (733–5671) at 135 East Broadway has great pancakes and other sourdough specialties. It's a good choice for breakfast, as is **Nora's Fish Creek Inn** (733–8288), located west of Jackson at 5600 West Highway 22 in the little town of Wilson. For exotic supper fare, including wild game, venture over to the **Gun Barrel Steak & Game House** (733–3287) at 862 West Broadway. Compared with the rest of Wyoming, Jackson restaurant prices run moderate-to-expensive . . . to *very* expensive at gourmet treats like the **Snake River Grill** (733–0557), across from the Town Square on Broadway.

western
wyomingtrivia

Jackson Hole is the broad, flat expanse of land enclosed by the Teton Mountains on the west; the Yellowstone Plateau on the north; and the Gros Ventre, Hoback, and Snake River Ranges on the east and south. Jackson—without the "Hole"—is the town occupying the southern end of Jackson Hole.

Behind the Wort Hotel at the corner of Glenwood and Deloney is the **Jackson Hole Historical Society & Museum,** with its extensive collection of early Jackson-area photographs, Native American beaded items, fur trade artifacts, and an interesting exhibit of lodgepole furniture from the old Moosehead Ranch. The museum is open from Memorial Day through late September, seven days a week. The historical society also offers walking tours of Jackson on Tuesday, Thursday, Friday, and some Saturdays, beginning at 10:00 A.M. For more information call 733–2414 or visit www .jack sonholehistory.org.

western
wyomingtrivia

In 1895 a minor skirmish between white settlers and Bannock Indians near Battle Mountain south of Jackson resulted in two casualties. However, by the time the news reached the East Coast, it had grown substantially in severity. A New York City newspaper reported: ALL RESIDENTS IN JACKSON HOLE, WYOMING, MASSACRED.

Jackson Hole, as the greater valley stretching away northward from the town of Jackson is known, hosts a number of exceptional events during the year. The **Grand Teton Music Festival** takes place in Teton Village from late June or early July through mid- or late August. Musicians from the leading orchestras, symphonies, and conservatories across the nation journey to Jackson to perform in more than forty orchestral and chamber music concerts, all conducted at the acoustically acclaimed Walk Festival Hall. For a schedule of performance dates and information, call 733–1128 or visit www.gtmf.org.

Later in the year the ***Fall Arts Festival*** showcases the area's rich artistic traditions and talents with a variety of exhibits, workshops, and demonstrations. The festival continues for ten days, during which Jackson galleries exhibit the works of regionally and nationally acclaimed artists. Special events include quilting demonstrations, a Western art symposium, a dance festival, and a miniature art show and sale. For dates and a complete list of activities, contact the Jackson Hole Chamber of Commerce by calling 733–3316 or via the Internet at www.jacksonholechamber.com.

Don't miss the photo opportunities offered by the four-cornered, elk-antler entranceways to the Town Square, which is especially beautiful when adorned with Christmas lights during the holiday season. And, speaking of antlers, the ***National Elk Refuge*** sprawls away beginning at the north edge of Jackson. Several thousand elk migrate here for the winter and linger until spring, when they gradually head back to their mountain territory. Boy Scout troops of the Jackson area gather the shed antlers each spring and sell them at an auction in the Jackson Town Square the third Saturday in May, usually raising more than a $100,000. Eighty percent of the funds raised goes back to purchasing pelletized alfalfa feed for the wintering elk. For information on winter sleigh-drawn tours of the National Elk Refuge, call 733–9212.

western wyomingtrivia

A pair of employees at the National Elk Refuge in Jackson Hole recently built the refuge's new 6,400-square-foot headquarters. They completed the job for an estimated one-third of what it would have cost had the refuge employed a private contracting firm.

The sleigh rides begin just across the highway from the heralded, 51,000-square-foot ***National Museum of Wildlife Art,*** open since 1994. The museum's native rock exterior reflects the surrounding countryside, helping the immense building blend into its setting so well that some passersby fail to notice it. The museum's collection comprises hundreds of artworks in a variety of media, including painting, sculpture, and photography. More than one hundred artists are featured, including John James Audubon, Antoine-Louise Barye, Albert Bierstadt, Carl Runguis, Charlie Russell, and Thomas Moran. Indoor exhibits span more than 200 years of wildlife art, and there's also a wonderful outdoor sculpture garden. The facilities include an auditorium, meeting rooms, and the Rising Sage Cafe. The National Museum of Wildlife Art is located off Highway 26/89/191 about 3 miles north of the Jackson Town Square. For information call 733–5771, or visit www.wildlifeart.org.

Before heading north into Grand Teton National Park, consider taking a detour "over the hill"—the hill being 8,429-foot Teton Pass—to Teton Valley, Idaho. Why mention Idaho in a book about Wyoming? Because traveling via Idaho is the only way to drive into the western reaches of Teton County, Wyoming.

From Driggs, Idaho, go east on Ski Hill Road. In about 6 miles you'll cross State Line Road and roll into beautiful downtown Alta, Wyoming. A superb place to stay in Alta in winter, particularly for families on ski vacations, is the *Teton Teepee Lodge* (353–8176 or www.tetonteepee.com). For a multicourse, Oriental-style dinner that will remain among your most memorable dining experiences (let's just say it's unique), make reservations for a weekend evening at the *Lost Horizon Dinner Club* (353–8226). From Alta it's another 5 steep uphill miles to *Grand Targhee Resort* (353–2300), widely recognized by downhill skiers as one of the country's premier deep-powder ski areas. In summer, chairlift rides to the top of the mountain provide unmatched views of the high Teton peaks, and the resort's summer bluegrass festival in August is well on its way to becoming legendary. Visit www.grandtarghee.com for more information.

If it's winter as you drive back to Jackson, and you happen to have your ice skates along, don't miss the lighted skating rink at *Owen Bircher Park* in Wilson, at the eastern foot of Teton Pass. With laughing kids of all ages decked out in their most colorful winter garb, and snow piled high on the sides of the rink, the scene is a Currier & Ives card come to life.

Now, back in Jackson, head north from town on U.S. Highway 191. (Alternatively, from back in Wilson, you could choose to sneak along the back route, known as the Moose-Wilson Road.) The *Gros Ventre River Ranch,* on the eastern edge of the Bridger-Teton National Forest along the Gros Ventre (pronounced *grow vahnt*) River Road, offers luxurious accommodations with

Abandoned cabin in the Tetons

sweeping views of the Tetons. The ranch can house thirty to forty guests in its heated log cabins and lodges. A short drive takes you to the site of the giant 1925 Gros Ventre Slide, which swept down Sheep Mountain and across the Gros Ventre River, creating the mile-long lake you see today. The waters burst through their natural earthen dam in 1927 and demolished ranches downstream, as well as the town of Kelly (since rebuilt in another location).

The Gros Ventre River Ranch takes guests by the week or for a three-day minimum. Rates vary by season and type of accommodation. Summer season runs from late May through early October. For information call 733–4138, write P.O. Box 151, Moose 83012, or visit www.grosventreriverranch.com.

If you're looking for a unique western experience while in the Tetons or surrounding areas, consider joining up with one of several operations that provide summer wagon train rides or, in winter, sled-dog tours. Contact the **Bar-T-Five Covered Wagon Cookout and Wild West Show** in Jackson at 733–5386 or **Grand Teton Covered Wagon Cookouts** at the Box K Ranch in the Buffalo Valley at 543–2407. If there's snow on the ground, and you'd like to give mushing a try, call **Jackson Hole Iditarod Sled Dog Tours** at 733–7388.

Back on the main highway heading north, you'll drive through the heart of **Grand Teton National Park** (GTNP), established on a smaller scale as a national monument in 1929 and now encompassing almost 500 square miles. One of the youngest mountain ranges on the North American continent, the Tetons rise to nearly 14,000 feet and tower 7,000 feet above the valley meadows below. The absence of foothills makes the Tetons' lofty peaks appear all the more impressive.

Like Yellowstone National Park to the north, Grand Teton offers plenty of hiking opportunities, with more than 250 miles of trails winding through mellow meadows and up steep mountain

western wyomingtrivia

James Stevenson and Nathaniel P. Langford, members of the 1872 Hayden Survey, reported that they reached the summit of the Grand Teton on July 29 of that summer. William O. Owen, who climbed the Grand in 1898 with three others, went to his grave claiming that his was the first ascent.

drainages. Several trails start at picturesque glacial Jenny Lake, with the pack of peaks known as the Cathedral Group providing an awesome backdrop. For trail conditions, backcountry permits, and information on how to remain bear aware, call 739–3300 or go to www.nps.gov/grte. (Entrance fees to GTNP are $20 per car for a seven-day pass, which will also get you into Yellowstone. Alternatively, you can purchase a $50 pass good for a full year at *all* national parks and monuments.)

Young Mountains

Geologically speaking, the jagged, abrupt Tetons are in their infancy. Look across Jackson Hole to the east, and you'll see rising, in dramatic contrast to the faulted, bereft-of-foothills Tetons, the Gros Ventre Mountains, a classic—and much older— folded range, embraced by rolling foothills.

Why are the Tetons so strikingly steep and composed of bare rock? At less than ten million years old, they are the youngest and least eroded of all the Rocky Mountains. Most of the activity along the young Teton Fault, which follows the eastern base of the mountains, has happened within the last five million years. The Tetons and Jackson Hole are both tilted blocks of the earth's crust. As the Teton block moves upward along the fault line, the Jackson Hole block moves down. This explains why the highest peaks of the relatively small range rise immediately along the east front rather than in the middle of the range, as is common with older, more eroded mountains.

The Tetons surely would be a magnificent sight to see even if they hadn't undergone a final sculpting. But "finish work" did occur here and throughout the region in very recent geologic times. Periodically during the last two million years, glaciers covered Yellowstone and much of Grand Teton National Park and Jackson Hole, then retreated. In the mountains the icefields left behind ragged horns, shimmering lakes, and steep cirques at the head of deep U-shaped valleys. On the slopes and in the valleys below, they deposited boulders and laid down the gravels and rock debris of terminal moraines and lateral moraines. They also dug out future lake bottoms, fashioned the depressions called kettles, and dammed rivers with the soils and rocks they deposited.

Be sure to stop at the ***Chapel of the Transfiguration*** near Moose. The log chapel was constructed in 1925 and is still in use for church services and weddings. The plate glass window behind the altar frames a most inspiring view of the Grand Teton, the tallest peak in the park at 13,770 feet, and the second highest in all of Wyoming. (Only Gannett Peak in the Wind Rivers is higher, by just 34 feet.) The park offers a number of ranger-led activities, such as a "fire-and-ice cruise" that includes a discussion of how forest fires and glaciers have shaped the area landscape; Native American art and culture discussions; and wildflower hikes and programs for budding naturalists. Inquire at the visitor centers for dates and times of programs. By all means don't miss the ***Indian Arts Museum*** at the Colter Bay Visitors Center, with its extensive, one-man collection of Native American clothing and art. Exhibits include an 1850s Crow shield, ceremonial pipes, dozens of beaded moccasins, and fine examples of prehistoric basketry. Under lock and key here and viewable on request is the controversial Colter Stone (see "John Cotter" box). The visitor centers in the park are typically open from mid-May through Labor Day.

Yellowstone National Park

The country's first national park, Yellowstone was created on March 1, 1872, with President Ulysses S. Grant signing the "Organic Act" legislation. The park encompasses some two million-plus acres, less than 5 percent of which is roaded or otherwise developed. The balance remains wilderness, containing more than sixty species of mammals, 200 types of birds, and a half-dozen species of game fish. In addition, the park boasts twelve tree species and dozens of types of wildflowers. The lowest elevation is 5,314 feet at the north entrance, and the highest spot is Eagle Peak Summit at 11,358 feet. The park's regular season is from early May through the beginning of November; the winter season is from early December through early March. For information call 344–7381 or visit www.nps.gov/yell.

western wyomingtrivia

Probably due to underlying heat and magma, the ground beneath LeHardy Rapids, located in Yellowstone National Park about 3 miles north of Fishing Bridge, has bulged upward 3 feet in the last seventy-five years.

Staying off the beaten path in Yellowstone National Park can be quite a trick, because there are only a few designated roads to get you through. One tactic is to completely avoid the peak tourist season and visit in spring or fall when the beaten track becomes less traveled, or postpone your Yellowstone adventure until the winter season. The park takes on an altogether different appearance under a deep mantle of snow, so even if you've been there dozens of times during the summer, Yellowstone will seem like a new place.

In winter Yellowstone's heartland is accessible only by ten-passenger enclosed and heated snowcoaches, snowmobiles (whose future in the park is uncertain), cross-country skis, and showshoes. Warming huts throughout the park provide shelter for a brief rest (or possibly for a bivouac in serious weather conditions). Overnight accommodations in winter are available at Old Faithful and at **Mammoth Hot Springs** at the north edge of the park. Rooms cost $156 at the new **Old Faithful Snow Lodge;** and range from $80 to $119 at the Snow Lodge Cabins. At Mammoth, which can be reached by car in winter, there is a variety of accommodations, ranging in price from $70 to $281. For reservations and more information on rates, call 344–7311.

John Colter

During the winter of 1807–08 John Colter, lately of the Lewis and Clark Expedition, made a roundabout, 500-mile trek through the primeval heart of northwest Wyoming. Employed by Manuel Lisa, a young Spaniard from New Orleans who'd established a trading post at the confluence of the Yellowstone and Big Horn Rivers, Colter was surveying the country for its trapping potential, while also trying to convince Native Americans to travel to and trade at Lisa's Fort Remon.

Colter left no known maps, but it's believed that from Fort Remon he crested the Pryor Mountains, then followed the Clark's Fork River into the rugged Absaroka Range. From Dead Indian Hill he traveled down to the Shoshone River, near present-day Cody, where he encountered the stinking springs that became known as "Colter's Hell." From Togwotee (TOE-guh-tee) Pass he dropped into the northern end of Jackson Hole. At the opposite end of the uninhabited valley, he's thought to have forded the Snake River before pressing over Teton Pass into Teton Valley. This portion of the trek is supported by the only known physical evidence remaining of Colter's adventure: the controversial "Colter Stone," a rhyolite slab etched on one side with the year "1808" and on the opposite side with the name "John Colter." The rock was discovered in 1931 by Teton Valley resident William Beard. (The Colter Stone can be seen today, on request, at the Indian Arts Museum at Colter Bay in Grand Teton National Park.)

After returning to Jackson Hole, Colter traveled north along the west bank of the Snake River until wading across above Jackson Lake. Finally, in what must have been the dead of snow-smothered winter, he traversed the future Yellowstone National Park en route back to Lisa's fort. There he made little of his remarkable journey, leaving much, including the exact route taken, to speculation. Still, there's no disputing that John Colter accomplished one of the greatest backpacking trips ever.

No matter what your activities or modes of travel, you'll have an unforgettable experience, for the phrase "winter wonderland" might well have been coined to describe Yellowstone. The geysers that are so spectacular in summer are perhaps even more so in winter; with snow-covered branches and glistening ice surrounding newly erupted geysers, the landscape takes on a fairy tale appearance. Buffalo and elk plowing through the deep snows are likewise a stunning sight. For snowmobilers the 370-mile Continental Divide Snowmobile Trail from West Yellowstone to the Lander area offers a host of loop and point-to-point possibilities. (For a map of the Continental Divide Trail and the latest information on restrictions on snowmobile use within Yellowstone Park, call the Wyoming State Trails Program office at 777–7477. New restrictions on snowmobile use in the park have taken effect.)

If traveling Yellowstone during the peak season is your only option, don't despair. Some of the following sights and strategies will keep you away from the major crowds and provide wonderful Yellowstone memories.

To earn an up-close view of the aftermath of the 1988 fires, walk the 1-mile *Duck Lake Trail,* which begins near the large mudpot in the parking lot of the West Thumb Geyser Basin. Locals in the know stay at the *Lake Yellowstone Hotel,* with its grand pillared entryway and rocking chair views of Yellowstone Lake. It's a gorgeous structure that's listed on the National Register of Historic Places. Room rates range from $120 to $423. For information on and reservations at these and other accommodations in the park, call 344–7311 or visit the Web site: http://travelyellowstone.com.

Another intriguing stop is the *Fishing Bridge Visitor Center* on the north end of Yellowstone Lake. The exhibits here, centering on Yellowstone's birds and mammals, will help you more readily identify the wildlife you see during your subsequent park travels. The center, open from 8:00 A.M. to 7:00 P.M. in summer, also covers lake geology within Yellowstone. A National Historic Landmark, the center was built in 1929–30.

western wyomingtrivia

On William Clark's *A Map of Lewis and Clark's Track Across the Western Portion of North America From the Mississippi to the Pacific,* Yellowstone Lake was called Lake Eustis. Clark named it for Secretary of War William Eustis.

Fishing Cone

Yellowstone's bubbling, aromatic West Thumb Geyser Basin is the site of Fishing Cone, a geyser with a most peculiar history. The cone rises from the shallow, near-to-shore waters of Yellowstone Lake, looking rather like a crater on the surface of the moon. A member of 1870s Washburn Expedition, whose members visited the site, told folks back home about his experience of catching a fish in the lake then inadvertently dropping it into this cone-shaped geyser. On pulling it out, the fish was well done!

Word spread, and by 1903 prospective visitors were reading in national publications that a trip to Yellowstone was incomplete without the hook-and-cook experience. The practice became so popular—practically a "must," rather like witnessing the great falls of the upper Yellowstone River—that National Park Service personnel eventually banned fishing in the area in order to protect overly enthusiastic bait-and-boilers from cooking themselves.

The Crowds

You'll have a much better time at the peak of the season in Yellowstone if you remember that people, too, are worth watching. Humans aren't new to the Yellowstone Plateau; occupancy, after all, goes back at least twelve thousand years. One reason Wyoming locals like the park so much is that they find there a human variety their home state lacks. While you're waiting for Old Faithful to spout with four hundred other tourists on the boardwalk circle, stroll the perimeter, eavesdrop, and count the languages. One day in mid-July we're pretty sure we counted seven. A friend reported ten, but she can tell Mandarin from Cantonese.

And if you like to hike, avoiding crowds is easy on most of the 1,200 miles or more of hiking trails in Yellowstone. Reportedly 95 percent of park visitors wander no more than 400 feet from their cars. So, even when you find yourself in the Hayden Valley stuck behind three RVs stopped to admire two nearby bison bulls, remember that once you get out of the car and on a trail, there's a good chance you'll see no people all afternoon. Pick up a guide to Yellowstone's hiking trails at one of the park's visitor centers or at one of the stores located throughout the park. (Check out the burled lodgepole pine logs used in the porch construction and the sign above the entrance of the original *Hamilton Store* near the Old Faithful Inn.)

All overnight hikes and some day hikes into restricted areas require backcountry use permits. Apply at a park ranger station or visitor center up to fortyeight hours before beginning your hike. Know your hiking capabilities and limitations: As a general rule plan on one hour for every 2 miles and add an hour for every 1,000 feet you ascend. Check out the topography on a map in advance so you know the difficulty of your proposed hike. Be prepared: Carry a trail map, compass, matches, insect repellent, first-aid kit, knife, bear pepper spray, sunscreen, and rain gear at a minimum.

For starters in the Canyon-Tower area, try the relatively tame *Tower Falls Trail*, which leads to the base of the falls. Or *Uncle Tom's Trail*, a strenuous walk dropping some 500 feet in a series of 300 stairs and paved inclines to the base of the Lower Falls. The *North Rim Trail* offers several views along its route, including that of the Artist Point Road Bridge, Crystal Falls, and Upper and Lower Falls. All are listed in the pamphlet, *Canyon*, available at park visitor centers.

Anyone who has visited Yellowstone even once will have a favorite spot, and all are magnificent. But, largely because it is less heavily visited than other parts, the favorite of many locals is the northeast corner, particularly the area around Tower Junction, where the Lamar River flows down from the east to join the Yellowstone. Leave time to fish the confluence of the two rivers and explore the little-used hiking trails around it. And if you don't mind rustic, stay at what may be the park's least expensive lodging option outside of campgrounds—the **_Roughrider Cabins at Roosevelt Lodge._** Sparsely furnished, supplied with woodstoves to dispel the evening chill, they cost only $56 per night and sleep up to six people. Bathrooms and private showers are in a separate bathhouse nearby. Then you can eat well at the lodge and afterwards find a rocking chair, put your feet up on the rail, and watch the sunset from the best porch in the Rocky Mountains. This was Teddy Roosevelt's favorite part of the park, and it may be yours, as well.

The Wolf

The reintroduction of wolves into Yellowstone's Lamar Valley in the mid-1990s has resulted in additional thousands of people flocking to the park to have a look. The wolf has, in many ways, supplanted the bear as the animal to see while in Yellowstone. (This is largely because, since park rangers began discouraging the human feeding of bears in the 1970s, seeing one has become a much less common occurrence.) Winter is the opportune time to see these controversial canids without the disturbance of crowds.

The endangered gray wolf hadn't been seen in Yellowstone for more than sixty years until its reintroduction during the winter of 1994–95. For the most part the wolves kept to the Lamar Valley during the summer of 1995 and caused considerable "wolf jams," as tourists strained their necks to get a peek. The wolves have since moved out into Pelican Valley and other park—and nonpark—locations, breaking into several identifiable packs.

The mature gray wolf (Canis lupus) is approximately three times larger than the coyote (Canis latrans). To determine whether it's a wolf or a coyote you're looking at, consider the following facts. The wolf is full-bodied, while the coyote is more slender or delicate in stature. The wolf will reach an average height of 26–34 inches versus only 16–22 inches for the coyote. This adds up to a weight of 70–120 pounds for a mature wolf and just 27–33 pounds for a coyote. The ears of the wolf are rounded and relatively short, and its muzzle is large and broad. In comparison the coyote's ears are long and pointed, its muzzle long and narrow. Incidentally, by no means are all gray wolves gray; their coats can range from snow white to coal black.

The sight of a wolf shadowing through the woods or trotting through a snowy meadow, or the sound of Canis lupus howling at the winter moon, can stir primeval feelings within even the most "civilized" man or woman. Check with the park about recent wolf sightings, and take a pair of binoculars or a zoom lens to get a close-up view in case you do encounter a wolf.

Petrified tree, Yellowstone

To get even farther away from the crowds, you can expand your hiking ventures beyond the Yellowstone backcountry into the Greater Yellowstone area—to the nearby Absaroka-Beartooth Wilderness, one of the highest alpine areas in the nation, or into the Shoshone National Forest east of the park.

Yellowstone's volcanic past and present are dramatically evidenced by its geysers and hot springs, mudpots, and fumaroles. The park contains the largest and most varied concentration of geothermal features in the world. Overall, some 10,000 known thermal features gurgle, burp, steam, and explode here, including nearly 200 geysers. Some geysers erupt almost continually, while others may lie dormant for months or years. The world's largest geyser, *Steamboat Geyser,* sometimes shoots water and steam more than 300 feet in the air, and its eruptions can last up to twelve hours. Steamboat Geyser is located in the Norris Geyser Basin in the Back Basin segment. Geyser gazers log geyser performance carefully and report their results on an excellent Web site, full of the latest spout times and volumes, as well as great background information. Check out www.geyser study.org, and then follow the links to Yellowstone. Or for an up-to-the-minute view of Old Faithful, visit www.nps.gov/yell/oldfaithfulcam.htm.

The *Museum of the National Park Ranger* at Norris is bypassed by the majority of park visitors. It's particularly interesting, however, with its displays tracing the history of the park ranger profession from soldiers to today's specialists. And the porch fronting the shimmering Gibbon River is an unusually enticing spot to relax on a warm summer afternoon.

At Mammoth Hot Springs, stop at the U.S. Engineer's Office for a glimpse at an unusual piece of architecture. Designed by the Minneapolis firm of Reed and Stem in 1906, the building is known affectionately as The Pagoda, owing to its Asian appearance.

To leave the park head out the northeast corner via the Lamar Valley, aiming for Cody via *Chief Joseph Scenic Highway.* The highway was officially dedicated on September 12, 1995, celebrating the completion of a twenty-seven-year, multiagency effort to build and improve one of the most spectacular alpine highways of the West. The finishing of the Chief Joseph closed the last pavement gap in Wyoming's state highway system.

Places to Stay in Bridger-Yellowstone Country

AFTON

Mountain Inn,
83542 Highway 89,
Route 1;
(307) 885–3156

Silver Stream Lodge
(seasonal),
95329 Highway 89;
(307) 883–2440

ALPINE

Alpen Haus,
junction of Highways 89
and 26;
(307) 654–7545 or
(800) 343–6755

**Best Western Flying
Saddle Lodge,**
Highway 89 and 26;
(307) 654–7561

COKEVILLE

Valley Hi Motel,
Highway 30 North;
(307) 279–3251

JACKSON

Elk Refuge Inn,
U.S. Highway 89 North;
(307) 733–3582 or
(800) 544–3582

Motel 6,
600 South U.S. Highway 89;
(307) 733–1620

Painted Buffalo Inn,
400 West Broadway;
(307) 733–4340 or
(800) 288–3866

Rusty Parrot Lodge,
175 North Jackson;
(307) 733–2000 or
(800) 458–2004

Spring Creek Resort,
atop East Gros Ventre
Butte;
(307) 733–8833

Super 8 Motel,
750 U.S. Highway 89 South;
(307) 733–6833 or
(800) 800–8000

KEMMERER

Antler Motel,
419 Coral Street;
(307) 877–4461

PINEDALE

**Lakeside Lodge Resort
Marina** (seasonal),
on Fremont Lake;
(307) 367–2221

Pine Creek Inn,
650 West Pine;
(307) 367–2191

Wagon Wheel Motel,
407 South Pine;
(307) 367–2871

TETON VILLAGE

Best Western Inn
at Jackson Hole;
(307) 733–2311 or
(800) 842–7666

Crystal Springs Inn,
3285 West McCollister Drive;
(307) 733–4423

Places to Eat in Bridger-Yellowstone Country

AFTON

Homestead Restaurant,
South Highway 89;
(307) 885–5558

Timberline Steak House,
355 Washington;
(307) 885–9892

ALPINE

Brentoven's Restaurant,
1 Colonial Lane;
(307) 654–7556

Kringle's Cafe;
161 Highway 89;
(307) 654–7536

COKEVILLE

**Country Market
Restaurant,**
10501 U.S. Highway 30;
(307) 279–3060

JACKSON

Billy's Burgers,
adjacent to Cadillac Grille
across from Town Square;
(307) 733–3279

Bubba's Bar-B-Que,
515 West Broadway;
(307) 733–2288

**Million Dollar
Cowboy Steakhouse,**
across from Town
Square on Cache;
(307) 733–4790

Snake River Brewing Co.,
265 South Millward;
(307) 739–BEER (2337)

KEMMERER

Log Cabin Restaurant,
1433 Central Avenue;
(307) 877–3458

Polar King Drive-In,
315 U.S. Highway 189;
(307) 877–9448

PINEDALE

**Corral Bar
& Calamity Jane's,**
30 West Pine;
(307) 367–2469

McGregor's Pub,
21 Franklin Avenue North;
(307) 367–4443

**Moose Creek Trading
Company,**
44 West Pine;
(307) 367–4616

TETON VILLAGE

**The Alpenhof Lodge
Dining Room,**
north end of Teton Village;
(307) 733–3462

**Mangy Moose Saloon
& Restaurant,**
south end of Teton
Village;
(307) 733–4913

WILSON

Pearl Street Bagels,
5400 West Highway 22;
(307) 739–1261

Northern Wyoming: Devils Tower–Buffalo Bill Country

Northern Wyoming is a land of jarring contrasts. Verdant, storm-attracting mountains like the Absarokas (*Ab-SORE-uh-kuhs*) and rim dry valleys such as the Big Horn Basin, a baked expanse of badlands and irrigated farmlands, where fewer than 7 inches of precipitation fall in a typical year. The extreme northeast corner, best known as home to Devils Tower National Monument, actually includes a western extension of South Dakota's alluring Black Hills. This area holds a terrain unlike that found anywhere else in the state, where numerous plant and animal species common to the Midwest and the West rarely found together commingle.

From Cody, the eastern gateway to Yellowstone National Park and one of many Wyoming namesakes of William F. "Buffalo Bill" Cody, this route takes you to the warm-water wonders of Thermopolis. From there you'll travel north through Big Horn Basin towns like Worland and Greybull, then over the high Big Horns to Sheridan and Buffalo. Finally, from Gillette you'll head to Devils Tower before turning south toward Sundance and Newcastle.

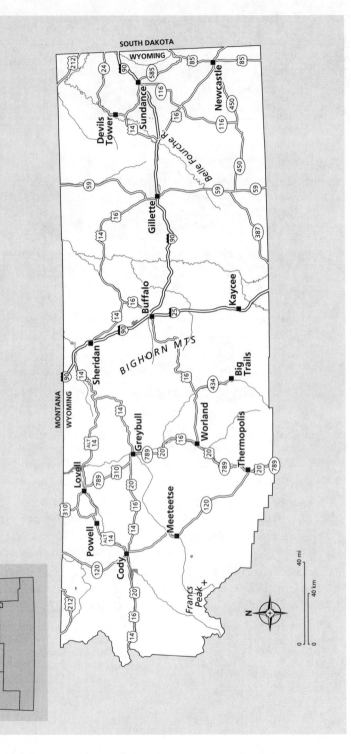

Park County

One way to travel to Cody from Yellowstone is through the spectacular Wapiti Valley, as the canyon of the North Fork of the Shoshone River is called. President Theodore Roosevelt called the Wapiti (rhymes with "hoppity") Valley between Cody and Yellowstone "the most scenic 50 miles in America" (or "in the world," depending on which account one reads). The road drops through the Shoshone National Forest, the first national forest in the country, created by President Benjamin Harrison on March 30, 1891. Wapiti Valley holds lazy streams and fast-moving rivers, sheer desert cliffs of colorful rock formations and heavily timbered north-facing slopes, and large populations of wildlife, from airborne eagles and peregrine falcons to grounded bear and elk.

To see this rough-hewn stretch of the West as it was meant to be seen—aboard the back of a horse, that is—stop in at one of several resorts and dude ranches lining the way. *Absaroka Mountain Lodge* (587–3963 or www.ab sarokamtlodge.com), for instance, which you'll find situated about 12 miles east of the entrance to Yellowstone.

BEST ATTRACTIONS IN DEVILS TOWER–BUFFALO BILL COUNTRY

Bradford Brinton Museum,
Big Horn;
(307) 672–3173

Buffalo Bill Historical Center,
Cody;
(307) 587–4771

Charles J. Belden Museum,
Meeteetse;
(307) 868–2264

Devils Tower National Monument,
(307) 467–5283

Fort Phil Kearney,
outside Story;
(307) 684–7629

Hot Springs State Park,
Thermopolis;
(307) 864–3765

King's Ropes and Saddlery,
Sheridan;
(307) 672–2702

**Medicine Lodge Creek
State Archaeological Site,**
outside Hyattville;
(307) 469–2234

Old Trail Town,
Cody;
(307) 587–5302

Tensleep Preserve,
outside Tensleep;
(307) 366–2671

Wind River Canyon,
south of Thermopolis

William F. Cody was an early promoter of building a dam to impound waters that would be used to irrigate the potentially fertile lands around Cody. The **Buffalo Bill Dam** was completed in 1910 at a cost of nearly $1 million. The view of the Shoshone Canyon is tremendous from the glass-walled visitor center or from the open walkway on top of the dam. The dam is located 6 miles west of Cody on the Yellowstone Highway (U.S. Highway 14/16/20). The visitor center is open 8:00 A.M. to 8:00 P.M. daily May through September. For information call 527–6076 or visit www.bbdvc.org.

The reservoir created by the dam and the shorelines surrounding the lake are within the boundaries of **Buffalo Bill State Park,** with its excellent trout fishing, camping, hiking, and water sports. Aided by the Wyoming winds that are so common, the spot is growing in popularity as a destination for savvy windsurfers. The park entrance fee is $2.00 ($4.00 nonresidents), and camping is an additional $6.00 ($12.00 for nonresidents) per vehicle. For information call 587–9227.

The Shoshone River Canyon offers ample opportunity for thrilling rafting excursions. **Wyoming River Trips** is Cody's oldest and most experienced river-rafting company, with a number of trip options to choose from through the boating season. For rates and schedules call 587–6661 or (800) 586–6661, or visit www.wyomingrivertrips.com.

Alternatively, if you took the advice at the end of the last chapter and lingered in the northeast corner of Yellowstone Park, your most direct route to Cody leads out through the park's northeast entrance near Cooke City, Montana, then down the **Chief Joseph Scenic Highway** through Sunlight Basin. It's a road you'll never forget, more spectacular by far than the Wapiti Valley route. (Teddy Roosevelt never saw this road.)

The road has just recently been widened and turnouts have been constructed, allowing visitors to take advantage of the many photo opportunities along the way. On parts of the scenic highway, you'll trace the route taken by Chief Joseph and his 800 fellow Nez Perce Indians as they fled the U.S. Army in 1877. If it happens to be late September when you're traveling the route, the displays of oranges, yellows, and reds put on by autumn-burnt aspen and smaller shrubs are out of this world, providing explosions of color that contrast magnificently with the drab brown hillsides. At Sunlight Creek the highway crosses the highest bridge in Wyoming, 280 feet above the creek. Stop at the side of the road after crossing the bridge and walk back to enjoy the heart-stopping view of the canyon below.

Farther up the road pull off at Dead Indian Summit for a panoramic view encompassing the North Absaroka Wilderness, Sunlight Basin, the lofty Precambrian heights of the Beartooth Plateau to the north, and Yellowstone National

BEST ANNUAL EVENTS IN DEVILS TOWER–BUFFALO BILL COUNTRY

Meeteetse Ice Fishing Derby,
Sunshine Reservoir; January;
(307) 868–2454

Annual Cowboy Songs and Range Ballads,
Cody; April;
(307) 578–4028

Plains Indian Powwow,
Cody; June;
(307) 587–4771

Ralston Rendezvous & Mule Days,
Ralston; June;
(307) 754–4320

Cody Stampede Rodeo,
Cody; Fourth of July;
(307) 587–5155

Sheepherder Rodeo & Dog Trials,
Kaycee; July;
(307) 738–2444

Hyattville Old-Timers Picnic,
Hyattville;
(307) 469–2234

Gift of the Waters Pageant,
Thermopolis; August;
(307) 864–3192

Deke Latham Memorial PRCA Rodeo,
Kaycee; Labor Day Weekend;
(307) 738–2444

Park to the west. Look down on the road you followed to get to this point: It seems to disappear, consumed by the medley of lush valley lands, colorful rock upthrusts, and snow-topped mountains. The Chief Joseph Scenic Highway meets State Highway 120 at a point approximately 17 miles northwest of Cody.

Cody, population 8,835, offers good restaurants, comfortable lodging, and a variety of attractions to persuade you to stay for a day or two. Topping the list is the *Buffalo Bill Historical Center,* 587–4771. Really it's five museums in one: the Buffalo Bill Museum, focusing on the famed scout and showman's private and public lives; the Whitney Gallery of Western Art, which shows masterworks of classic and contemporary Western art; the Cody Firearms Museum, a comprehensive collection of American and European guns, some of which date to the sixteenth century; the Plains Indian Museum, one of the world's best collections of Plains Indian art and artifacts, including the traditions of the Blackfeet, Shoshone, Crow, Sioux, Cheyenne, Arapaho, Kiowa, Comanche, and Pawnee people; and the new Draper Museum of Natural History, which integrates the humanities with natural sciences to interpret the Yellowstone ecosystem and its connections with the surrounding intermountain basins. If you can spare a day, it's worth it.

Then you might want another day for the town of Cody itself. If so, consider bunking at the **Cody Guest Houses.** Here you'll find a variety of accommodations to choose from, including the charming Annie Oakley and Buffalo Bill western cottages; the luxurious, three-bedroom Victorian House; and the three-bedroom Ranch in the Rockies. Rates range from $99 for a two-person cottage to $450 for the entire Victorian House.

A three-year restoration transformed the 1906 Victorian House into a real showpiece. The home's original front door, with its leaded stained glass, opens into another era. Artistic hand-stenciling graces walls framed by renovated woodwork, and the works of local artists are featured in the gallery. Other rooms and amenities include a formal parlor and living room, dining room, den with television and stereo, spa, patio and barbecue, fireplace, and laundry facilities.

Each guest house has a kitchen, and all can be rented by the day or by the week. The Cody Guest Houses office is located at 1525 Beck Avenue. For information on weekly rates or for reservations, call 587–6000 or (800) 587–6560, or visit www.codyguesthouses.com.

Start your exploration of Cody at **The Irma,** the historic hotel built of native wood and limestone by Buffalo Bill Cody in 1902 and named after the famous westerner's youngest daughter, Irma Louise. The dark old dining room, which originally served as the hotel bar and billiards room, retains its turn-of-the-century western feel: A fancy antique cash register sits at the check-out counter; the walls are covered with wildlife paintings and big-game mounts; an elk-antler chandelier hangs from the tin-covered ceiling; and small molded bison heads embellish the sides of the dining-booth benches. The ornate, French-produced cherrywood back bar was shipped in 1900 to Buffalo Bill from Queen Victoria of England, as a gift of thanks for Cody and his Wild West Show's royal performance. The Irma, listed on the National Register of Historic Places, still operates as a hotel, with renovated rooms furnished in turn-of-the-century motif. Each room is named after a Cody-area settler and goes for $117 to $142 nightly. Motel rooms in the annex cost $77 to $102 per night. The Irma is located at 1192 Sheridan Avenue. For information call 587–4221 or (800) 745–IRMA, or visit www.irmahotel.com.

The original Buffalo Bill Museum opened in 1927 in the log structure that now houses the ***Cody Chamber of Commerce.*** The concept of the museum dates back even farther, to 1917, when, shortly after Buffalo Bill's death, some Cody residents created the Buffalo Bill Memorial Association. Its mission: to "build, construct, and maintain an historical monument of memorial stature in honor of and to perpetuate the memory of our late lamented fellow townsman Hon. William F. Cody. " The impressive ***Cody Mural,*** found in the LDS Church at Seventeenth Street and Wyoming Avenue, covers the entire domed ceiling of the chapel foyer and depicts significant church events of the period between 1827 and 1893. Summer tours are offered Monday through Saturday, 8:00 A.M. to 8:00 P.M., and Sunday from 3:00 to 8:00 P.M. For information call 587–3290.

Serious carnivores won't want to leave Cody without sampling a mouthwatering steak at ***Cassie's Supper Club,*** a historic landmark that was originally opened in the 1920s and operated as a house of ill repute by its owner, Cassie Waters. In addition to top-notch steaks, the club features a variety of chicken, seafood, and pasta dishes. Prices are moderate-to-expensive. After you eat, you can stomp your feet to live country music in the saloon with West the Band on Friday and Saturday evenings. Cassie's is located at 214 Yellowstone Avenue. For reservations or information call 527–5500 or go to www.cassies.com.

Old Trail Town, on the western outskirts of Cody, takes you back to the frontier days, with the reconstruction/relocation of more than twenty historic buildings of the late 1800s. Check out the bullet holes in the door of the Rivers Saloon from Meeteetse, then stop in at the cabin that was used by Butch Cassidy and gang in the Hole in the Wall country, southwest of Kaycee. Before you hightail it out of town, visit the adjacent cemetery and final resting place for the likes of mountain man John "Liver-Eatin' " Johnston and buffalo hunter Jim White. Old Trail Town, located at 1831 DeMaris Drive, is open daily from

Old Trail Town, Cody

8:00 A.M. to 8:00 P.M., mid-May through mid-September. The cost of admission is $5.00 for those age twelve and older ($4.00 for seniors), free for those under age twelve. For additional information call 587–5302.

Before heading south toward Meeteetse and leaving Park County, consider swinging up to Powell, population 5,373. Take Highway 14A northeast from Cody to get there. Named after the legendary Colorado River explorer Maj. John Wesley Powell, the town is home to the **Homesteader Museum,** which honors the folks who settled the surrounding valley. Located at the corner of Clark and First Streets in a historic log building built in 1932 by local American Legionnaires, the museum preserves the heritage of the area via photographs, artifacts, early tools, and farm machinery. The museum, located at 133 South Clark Street, is open Tuesday through Friday, 11:00 A.M. to 5:00 P.M., Saturday from 11:00 A.M. to 3:00 P.M. For more information call 754–9481.

On the return trip to Cody, stop at the **Heart Mountain Relocation Center Monument,** located about 12 miles northeast of Cody on Highway 14A. On-site information explains the relocation camp, where some 11,000 American citizens of Japanese ancestry—two-thirds of them American born—were confined for nearly three years during World War II, making it the third-largest "city" in Wyoming at the time. The Heart Mountain Relocation Center was one of ten camps built to house collectively more than 100,000 Japanese Americans. People were held in detention here even if they had family members serving in the U.S. armed forces. This camp was closed in November 1945, and all that remains today are a few foundations. A portion of the center is listed on the National Register of Historic Places.

En route to Meeteetse, at a point approximately 12 miles outside Cody, pull over to the **Halfway House Stage Stop.** Located halfway between Corbett Crossing and Stinking Water Creek, the stage stop was in use as late as 1908 before automobiles started storming through.

For a settlement supporting a population of fewer than 400, Meeteetse—home of the Pitchfork Ranch, one of the oldest cattle empires in the West—offers a surprising variety of sites. The town's curious name derives from the Crow Indian word for "meeting place of the chiefs." Stop in for a cool one at the more than one-hundred-year-old **Outlaw Parlor Cafe & Cowboy Bar** (868–2585), located at 1936 State Street, and take a gander at the hand-carved Italian rose and cherrywood bar. The Meeteetse Social Club meets regularly at the saloon on weekends for an old-fashioned get-together, with card playing and socializing.

Two free museums also compete for your attention: the **Meeteetse Bank Museum,** 1033 Park Avenue in an old bank building, and the **Charles J. Belden Museum,** at 1947 State Street. The latter features Charles Belden's world-famous Western and ranch photographs, mostly from the 1930s, many of which appeared in *National Geographic* and other magazines. From May through September, the museums are open from 10:00 A.M. to 4:00 P.M. Monday through Saturday; closed Sunday. In October the museums close Wednesday as well; then from November through April they are open Monday, Tuesday, Thursday, and Friday. For more information call the Belden Museum, 868–2264, or the Bank Museum at 868–2423.

The famous Pitchfork Ranch was founded 18 miles up the Greybull River, southwest of Meeteetse, in 1878. Belden married the daughter of the owner and became ranch manager. Many of his photographs of the ranch, which were only recently sold out of the Belden family, and of other places in the West are classics that bring back to life the spirit of the western way. As Belden used to say, "If the picture doesn't tell a story, it's not worth taking." His definitely were worth taking.

Meeteetse goes all out for its three-day Labor Day weekend celebrations. Activities include a rodeo, an old-time parade, a western barbecue, the Absaroka Challenge trail runs, and an arts and crafts fair. Meeteetse may no longer have six stage lines running through, or seven bars and eleven brothels, but it still knows how to have a good time, Wild West style. For information call the Meeteetse Visitor Information Center at 868–2454, check out its Web site www.meeteetsewy.com, or write to Box 238, Meeteetse 82433.

For good grub and a delightful overnight stay, try the ***Broken Spoke Cafe and Bed & Breakfast,*** located at 1943 State Street, next door to the Charles J. Belden Museum. The building was built in 1894 and renovated a century later, in 1994. The cafe features specials and delicious homemade pies every day. Servings are plentiful, and the prices inexpensive-to-moderate. The bed-and-

Life in Meeteetse

Locals tell a story about when the old bank was still operating. Late one Friday afternoon in early July, business was so slow and the day so perfect that the bank manager was overwhelmed by temptation. He reached for his fishing pole in the corner by his desk, stepped quietly out the backdoor and went down to the sparkling Greybull River, just yards away. Spring runoff had subsided a day or two earlier; the water was clear as window glass. He tied on a dry fly and wet the line. Meanwhile, a state bank inspector arrived all the way from Cheyenne and found the front door open and the bank empty. Furious, and thinking he'd teach the manager a lesson, he reached over the counter and pushed the alarm button. A minute later the waitress from the Outlaw Bar showed up, with two beers on a tray.

breakfast, located upstairs, wears a western motif. There are two separate rooms; the larger one includes two bunk beds and a queen-size bed. Room rates are extremely reasonable: $30 for one person, $40 for two, $45 for three, or $50 for four. A $5.00 breakfast is included in the cost of a room. For information or reservations call 868–2110 or e-mail ringo@tctwest.net.

northern
wyomingtrivia

The *Wyoming Bicycle Guidance Map,* produced by the Wyoming Department of Transportation, can be obtained by contacting the Bicycle Coordinator, P.O. Box 1708, Cheyenne 82003–1708. The map rates roads as to their suitability for safe cycling, featuring information such as pavement widths, traffic volumes, and prevailing winds.

On the outskirts of Meeteetse, the *Amelia Earhart Monument* marks the famous aviator's fondness for this area. Earhart was in the process of having a log cabin built on the nearby upper Wood River when she disappeared over the Pacific Ocean in 1937. The partially completed walls of the structure can still be seen near the site of the abandoned Double D Dude Ranch, located approximately 2 miles beyond the Brown Mountain Campground (25 miles southwest of town on the Wood River Road). Beyond the campground a four-wheel-drive vehicle or travel on foot is required. To inquire about road conditions and for more specific directions, stop in at the Shoshone National Forest headquarters at 808 Meadow Lane in Cody, or call 527–6241. Here you can also learn about the area's many other campgrounds and trailheads for staging hiking and horseback-riding adventures.

Hot Springs County

The turn onto the back road leading to some of Wyoming's best-preserved petroglyphs lies about 30 miles outside Meeteetse on the way to Thermopolis. For precise directions to and entrance information regarding the *Legend Rock Petroglyph Site,* contact the Hot Springs State Park Headquarters on Park Street in Thermopolis, or call 864–2176. Legend Rock is a lengthy expanse of sandstone cliffs whose face is embellished with dozens of unique petroglyphs. The oldest works date back some 2,000 years. You can drive to within about 100 yards of the cliff face at the site, where you'll also find a restroom and picnic tables. *Note:* Please do your part to help to preserve the petroglyphs for the enjoyment and education of future generations by refraining from touching or otherwise disturbing them.

Most visitors' favorite is the petroglyph depicting a rabbit with big ears, drawn in a style reminiscent of the figures created by the Mimbres culture, which thrived in New Mexico about a thousand years ago. It's reportedly the only known rabbit rock art in Wyoming. Other intriguing figures include that of Kokopelli, the well-known hump-backed flute player of the American Southwest. Unlike the rabbit and Kokopelli, the bird petroglyph here is a figure common in Wyoming rock art and is typically termed the *Ghost Dance Style Bird*.

According to an Arapaho elder, Paul Moss, the turtle petroglyph is the "Creation Panel." In Arapaho legend the turtle went down to the bottom of the ocean and brought up on his back the mud with which the continents were formed. In Native American teachings the turtle represents the oldest symbol for earth.

Also nearby: a unique working cattle ranch known as the ***High Island Ranch & Cattle Company.*** The ranch comprises a lower lodge situated on the high plains at 6,000 feet above sea level and an upper lodge in the Owl Creek Mountains (a fair share of which were scorched over in the big wildfires of 2000) at an elevation of around 9,000 feet. In all, 130,000 acres await investigation, so don't worry about running into crowds out here. Located approximately 35 miles from the main camp, the mountain lodge at Rock Creek offers excellent trout fishing within a stone fly's throw of the front porch. A number of options are available for your stay. For example: After bunking at the lower ranch on Sunday, on Monday you'll join other guests in riding to the upper camp, then come back down on Friday. As you ride between prairie rangelands and the high elevations of the Owl Creek Mountains, you'll witness the not-to-be-forgotten sights of the 12,800-foot Washakie Needles and a 75-foot-high waterfall. Also keep your eyes open for wild elk and ancient tepee rings.

northern wyomingtrivia

Nomadic Indian tribes living at least part-time in Wyoming in historic times included the Arapaho, Arikara, Bannock, Blackfeet, Cheyenne, Crow, Gros Ventre, Kiowa, Nez Perce, Sioux, Shoshone, and Ute.

In addition to personalized individual outings, riding options at the ranch include an honest-to-goodness 1800s-style cattle drive in late August and cattle roundup weeks held periodically throughout the summer. It's high adventure as you move those dogies along, then sleep beneath the stars to the spine-tingling sound of a coyote serenade. Whether you choose to relax or to work the ranch from predawn to sundown, pick your week and grab a saddle. You'll need to bring an assortment of gear to participate in the trail rides (call for information), as well as your appetite for adventure. Weekly rates run from $1,395 to $1,695, depending on the package chosen. For information, reservations, and directions, call 867–2374 or visit www.highislandranch.com. The regular ranch season runs from mid-May through mid-September. (If hunting is your bag, inquire about the ranch's guided big-game hunts, which usually take place from September through November.)

Both Hot Springs County and Thermopolis, population 3,247, take their names from the world's largest natural hot springs, located at Thermopolis. The Thermopolis *anticline*—a fold in the earth's surface, with rock strata sloping downward on both sides of a common crest—is the largest of several folds along the southern shoulder of the Big Horn Basin. Fractures within the anticline provide an avenue for rainwater and snowmelt to seep down into the hot subterranean depths before it rises again to the surface as hot springs.

Driving into **Hot Springs State Park** in summer is a feast for the senses. A rainbow of aromatic flower gardens lines the way, and the entrance is embellished with a large calcified monolith called Tepee Fountain. An 1896 treaty signed by the Shoshone chief Washakie and the Arapaho chief Sharp Nose gave the healing waters of the hot springs to the white man, with the condition that the Native people would always have free access to a portion of the springs. Thus the state bathhouse is open to anyone at no charge. And if you neglected to bring your own towel or swimsuit, the items can be rented for a small fee.

Submerge yourself into the soothing hot mineral waters, maintained at a steady temperature of 104 degrees Fahrenheit. Facilities include private lockers, showers, and inside and outdoor hot mineral pools. As you soak in the hot waters outside, you can often watch the park's bison herd wander along roads that wind to the top of the colorful bluffs embracing Thermopolis. The bathhouse is open Monday through Saturday from 8:00 A.M. to 5:30 P.M., and on Sunday from noon to 5:30 P.M. It's closed Thanksgiving and Christmas only. The park is located at 220 Park Street. For more information call 864–2176.

Privately owned hot springs in the vicinity offer a few more amenities, such as water slides, large outdoor swimming pools, saunas, Jacuzzis, and game arcades. The **Star Plunge** is open daily from 9:00 A.M. to 9:00 P.M., except from December 1–20. An all-day pass goes for $8.00. For information call 864–3771. Also nearby is **Hellie's Tepee Pools,** under the big dome, with similar prices, hours, and facilities, open every day of the year except Christmas. For more information call 864–9250 or e-mail info@tepeepools.com.

Don't miss other activities in the state park, such as strolling across the replica of a 1916 swinging bridge, which spans the Big Horn River and offers a great view of Mineral Terrace; taking advantage of the pleasantly shaded picnic facilities; and motoring along the high-climbing Buffalo Pasture Road to get a look at the park's primary buffalo herd. For a map outlining the buffalo grazing areas, pick up a Hot Springs State Park brochure at the headquarters near the park's entrance.

Every summer in early August, Hot Springs State Park, in conjunction with local Native Americans, hosts the ***Gift of the Waters Pageant,*** commemorating the signing of the treaty that transferred ownership of the hot springs. The pageant offers outstanding opportunities to see Native Americans in full ceremonial clothing, watch and hear their all-consuming dancing and drumming, and learn about tribal legends. For information on the pageant, call the Thermopolis Chamber of Commerce at 864–3192.

A relatively new Thermopolis attraction with ties to ancient history is ***The Wyoming Dinosaur Center.*** To find the museum (110 Carter Ranch Road) simply follow the green dinosaur tracks painted on the town streets to the big metal building on the east side of the river. You can watch dinosaur bone preparation in the laboratory and at nearby excavation locations. The 16,000-square-foot center is dedicated to keeping Wyoming's dinosaurs in Wyoming and features excellent, full-sized casts of a number of dinosaur skeletons, including *Tyrannosaurus Rex* and *Triceratops,* as well as an original bone mount of a plant-eating *Camarasaurus* excavated nearby. Since the early 1990s, Ed Cole and other paleontologists have made a number of discoveries in the mountains east of Thermopolis, one of which is among the largest dinosaur finds in the Rocky Mountains. Some of Cole's findings are displayed at the center. The entrance fee for adults is $6.00 and for children $3.50; the museum and excavation site tour package costs $12.00 for adults and $8.00 for kids. The center

northern
wyomingtrivia

Between 1897 and 1908, bounties were paid on 10,819 gray wolves in Wyoming.

The rare black-footed ferret dines almost exclusively on prairie dogs.

also offers the chance to dig dinosaurs for a full day on the Warm Springs Ranch, as part of its ongoing research into dinosaur climate and habitat around Thermopolis 140 million years ago. To dig for a day costs $125 per person, or $300 for a family of three. Hours at the center are 8:00 A.M. to 8:00 P.M. daily in summer, and 9:00 A.M. to 5:00 P.M. the rest of the year. For more information call 864–2997 or (800) 455–DINO, visit the Web site at www.wyodino.org, or e-mail the museum at wdinoc@wyodino.org.

The ***Hot Springs County Museum and Cultural Center,*** at 700 Broadway, has rightfully earned its reputation as one of the best small-town museums in the state. Among its exhibits of western and local lore are stagecoaches, a cherrywood bar from the famous Hole in the Wall Saloon, a display on the coal industry, Native American artifacts, and a frontier town replete with newspaper office, dentist's office, and general store. The $4.00 entrance fee ($2.00

for kids and seniors) is a deal. The museum is open in summer from 9:00 A.M. to 8:00 P.M. Monday through Saturday; Sunday from 1:00 to 6:00 P.M. Winter hours are 9:00 A.M. to 5:00 P.M. Tuesday through Saturday. For information call 864–5183 or visit www.trib.com/~history.

For winter travelers Thermopolis sponsors *Cutting Horse Competitions* from November through March. For information call the chamber of commerce at 864–3192 or visit www.thermopolis.com.

Getting hungry? Your best bet in Thermopolis, winter or summer, is the *Ballyhoo Restaurant and Lounge,* 1025 Shoshoni Street, the main drag on the south end of town. Good steaks, seafood, drinks, salad bar, and friendly service rule the day. In summer, sit out on the deck overlooking the Big Horn River. You might see mule deer in the Russian olive trees along the bank or a muskrat in the water. For information call 864–9210.

The countryside spreading away from Thermopolis provides sightseeing options in every direction. A drive south up the *Wind River Canyon,* for instance, offers up-close views of the bowels of the earth that are rivaled in few places. As you motor along next to towering cliffs, the raging Wind River churns white, roiling and frothing along on its way to becoming the Big Horn River. Signs along the length of the canyon interpret the geological formations you're looking at. Rocks in the canyon span eons of geologic time, from sixty-six-million-year-old Cretaceous formations to Precambrian layers more than two billion years old. A number of turnouts offer fantastic photo and picnic ops. Don't miss the precariously placed train tracks on the side of the canyon opposite the highway. In 1995 a massive rock slide obliterated sections of the track. The Chicago, Burlington and Quincy Railroad first went through the canyon in 1911, followed by the state highway in 1925. It's approximately a 60-mile round-trip from Thermopolis to Boysen State Park on Highway 20 via the Wind River Canyon.

To experience the Wind River up close and wet, consider a trip with *Wind River Canyon Whitewater,* operating out of an office in Thermopolis at 907 Shoshone. The season runs approximately from Memorial Day to Labor Day. For information visit www.windrivercanyonraft.com or call 864–9343; call 486–2253 during the off-season.

Outlaw Trail, Inc., a nonprofit community group out of Thermopolis, organizes a once-a-year 100-mile trail ride for a hundred riders. Reservations are on a first-come, first-served basis. The trip, seven days and six nights in July or August, caters primarily to experienced riders; each participant is responsible for caring for his or her own horse and tack. You'll follow the legendary Outlaw Trail of Butch Cassidy to Hole in the Wall country; no doubt you'll hear tales both historic and modern, and both factual and fictional, as you sit around the campfire with your companions. For information on the guided trip, call 864–2287 or (888) 362–7433, or write Outlaw Trail, Inc., Box 1046, Thermopolis 82443. Internet users can visit www.rideoutlawtrail.com or e-mail the organizers at outlaw@trib.com.

Washakie County

The Big Horn Basin, stretching away from the west slope of the Big Horn Mountains, is blessed with fertile soils and a long growing season. Worland, population 5,250, on the banks of the Big Horn River, is an agricultural community; sugar beets are the primary cash crop. The Holly Sugar plant here provides a strong base for the area's economy. Worland was founded in 1903, rather late for a Wyoming town, and named after one of the first pioneers to homestead in the area. Charlie "Dad" Worland ran a makeshift saloon and stage station. In 1906, the Chicago, Burlington and Quincy Railroad arrived, and a year later the 50-mile-plus Big Horn Irrigation Canal was completed, bringing water to the desiccated desert and transforming Worland into an agricultural and trade center.

Artist Peter Toth chose Worland as the Wyoming location for his ***Trail of the Whispering Giants*** monument. Toth spent nearly two decades traveling the country and carving towering wooden Native American sculptures in each of the fifty states. He finished the Worland statue in September 1980. The massive carvings were made as a gift to each state; Toth accepted no payments. To receive its statue each state was required to donate a permanent pedestal and maintain the sculpture. The Hungarian refugee began his unusual quest in February 1972 in La Jolla, California, where he built his first Native American monument, and finished his final work in May 1988 in Haleiwa, Hawaii. Wyoming's *Trail of the Whispering Giants* monument sits on the southwest corner of the Washakie County Courthouse lawn.

The ***Washakie County Museum and Cultural Center*** operates out of an old Mormon church, located at 1115 Obie Sue Avenue. Inside you will find a re-creation of the A. G. Rupp General Store, the Soapy Dale Peak Lodge (a Sheepeater Indian mountain shelter), and an exhibit of early 1900s black-and-white photographs by Rico Stine, which depict the town and surrounding areas. The museum is open in summer from 9:00 A.M. to 5:00 P.M. Monday through Saturday, and in winter from 10:00 A.M. to 5:00 P.M. Monday through Friday, Saturday 10:00 A.M. to 4:00 P.M. There is no entrance fee, but donations are welcome. Call 347–4102 for more information.

Antone's Supper Club (347–9924), 3 miles east of town at 973 Highway 16, is popular with Worland residents.

By heading north from Worland on Highway 433, you'll trace a portion of the historic *Bridger Trail.* Frequent conflicts with Native Americans along the Bozeman Trail east of the Big Horn Mountains in the 1860s created the need for an alternative route to the southwestern Montana goldfields. Scout and explorer Jim Bridger blazed a new trail for the miners, crossing the Big Horn Basin near present-day Worland. East of Worland, 25 miles on the other side of some of the baddest badlands you'll ever lay eyes on, is the quaint cowtown of Ten Sleep. If you go there, on the eastern outskirts of Worland, you'll find a marker commemorating the *Colby Site,* where Dr. George Frison of the University of Wyoming unearthed the remains of a woolly mammoth and Paleo Indian stone tools. Excavations took place primarily from 1973 through 1978.

The name of the town of Ten Sleep, population 304, is said to have come from the Sioux Indians, who had a large camp along the North Platte River near present-day Casper. They measured distances by the number of days, or "sleeps," it took to get from one place to another. It was ten sleeps from the North Platte River camp to the present-day site of Ten Sleep; likewise it was another ten sleeps from there to a certain area of Yellowstone.

The *Ten Sleep Pioneer Museum* (366–2759) is located on the east edge of town in the Ten Sleep Public Park, a pleasant place for a picnic on a hot summer day. The museum is open Memorial Day through Labor Day from noon to 6:00 P.M. The Pioneer Museum highlights history and memorabilia from the Spring Creek Raid, one of many battles that erupted between cattlemen and sheep ranchers in the West.

To preserve "their" range, cattlemen set up boundaries, or "dead lines" (so-called because if sheep crossed the line they and their owners could soon be dead), beyond which sheep were forbidden. In late March 1909, a French sheepman named Joe Allemand—in the company of his nephew Jules Lazier and Joe Emge, a cattleman turned sheepman—departed Worland with 5,000 head of sheep and set out toward Spring Creek, south of Ten Sleep. On April 2, 1909, seven masked men raided the sheepherders' camp, killing all three men and a number of their sheep. Five of the raiders were sent to prison for their deeds, while the other two plea-bargained for their freedom. The killings created a public uproar and virtually ended the range war between cattlemen and sheepmen. A monument marking the site of the tragedy is located on the east side of Highway 434 about 6½ miles south of Ten Sleep.

A bit hard to find but well worth the search is the Nature Conservancy's *Tensleep Preserve,* set aside to protect a unique medley of canyon, upland, meadow, and forest environments. One hundred bird species are at home on the preserve, as are mountain lion, elk, black bear, beaver, and the rare spotted bat. Fishing and hiking are among the recreational pursuits possible at the preserve, which is open to visitors for weekend and five-day conservation programs June through August. Accommodations are in tent cabins, with dining facilities in the preserve's new lodge. The Wyoming chapter of the Nature Conservancy owns and manages this preserve, as well as two others in the state, to help conserve rare plants and animals and the lands and water they need to survive. For information on Tensleep Preserve programs and to obtain directions for finding it, call 366–2671 or visit www.tncwyoming.org.

Leaving Ten Sleep via U.S. Highway 16 East puts you on one segment of the ***Big Horn Scenic Byways.*** The road climbs through stunning Ten Sleep Canyon, one of the scenic marvels of the West, before crossing the crest of the Big Horns at Powder River Pass, elevation 9,666 feet. Numerous Forest Service campgrounds line the road. The Cloud Peak Wilderness to the north offers trips for hikers and horseback riders, while certain nonwilderness trails of the surrounding Bighorn National Forest are great for mountain biking. The highway eventually drops out of the Big Horns and into the town of Buffalo—but we'll get to that town later, after traveling in a longer, roundabout manner to get there.

Big Horn County

From Ten Sleep drive north on a primitive dirt road for 18 miles to Hyattville. (Inquire at the Ten Sleep Mercantile for directions to the turn.) The fascinating ***Medicine Lodge State Archaeological Site,*** one of the most significant prehistoric sites in the Rockies, is found 6 miles northeast of Hyattville off Cold Springs Road. Medicine Lodge Creek runs through the lush meadows and groves of tall cottonwoods, offering outstanding picnicking, camping, and fishing opportunities. The site's plentiful food, shelter, and water have attracted humans for some 10,000 years.

The excavations have been filled in for preservation and safety reasons, but prehistoric petroglyphs and pictographs remain on the walls of brilliantly colored sandstone. Interpretive displays at the cliffs and in the nearby log cabin visitor center provide glimpses of the sixty cultures that camped at the site through the centuries. Stretching away from the archaeological site is the 12,100-acre Medicine Lodge Wildlife Habitat Management Area, a refuge for an extensive elk herd and numerous other types of wildlife (there's also an elk habitat visitor center near the archaeological site). A self-guiding pamphlet leads to various petroglyphs along the cliff walls, while the *Medicine Lodge Nature Trail* brochure highlights the area's natural history. The Medicine Lodge

The Medicine Lodge Creek Site

The summer after graduating from the University of Wyoming in 1973, I was fortunate to be hired by Dr. George Frison as a member of the crew that would excavate the Medicine Lodge Creek archaeological site. The site, nestled in the sandstone Big Horn foothills outside Hyattville, proved to be one of the most productive and important archaeological finds ever located in the Rocky Mountains. Today, the site—and what we unearthed there—provide the centerpiece of a stellar Wyoming state park.

Most people associate archaeological excavations with exacting equipment like fine-mesh wire screens, whisk brooms, trowels, and even dental picks. Indeed all of those tools were employed at Medicine Lodge Creek. However, as I recall, the lion's share of our work that summer involved far cruder methods of excavation—shovels, iron bars, backhoes, even dynamite—because often we had to break through thick sandstone slabs that over the years had fallen off the overhanging cliffs. By the time excavations were completed in the mid-1970s, crews had identified some five dozen levels of occupation going down more than 20 feet below the ground surface. The age of the cultures ranged from historic Crow (1800s) to Paleo Indians dating back more than 9,000 years ago.

Several crew members that summer, including me, holed up in the rustic old farmhouse adjacent to the site, which has since been renovated and turned into the park manager's residence. Today's park, where top-notch camping, fishing, and canyon hiking can also be enjoyed, would be a beautiful place to visit even if it didn't encompass such fascinating and important archaeological findings. But that it does.

State Archaeological Site grounds are open from May 1 through early November, and the visitor center is open from May 1 to Labor Day. Camping costs $6.00 per vehicle, $12.00 for nonresidents. For information call 469–2234.

There's a wonderful backcountry scenic byway that will bring you out around Shell; it's recommended only if you have the four-wheel-drive vehicle that it demands. Inquire about road conditions and directions at the archaeological site visitor center. Once you reach Shell, you'll see the **Shell Stone Schoolhouse,** which is listed on the National Register of Historic Places. Built in 1903, it was the first community building in the region utilizing building materials other than logs. It was in use until the early 1950s. One of the world's most complete *Allosauruses* ("Big Al") was excavated near Shell, and since 1934 paleontologists have unearthed twelve large *Sauropods* in the area. The dinosaur beds, located 10 miles north of Shell on Bureau of Land Management lands, are open to the public.

From Shell head east for another segment of the **Big Horn Scenic Byways,** this one leading through the gorge of Shell Canyon. Watch for the statuesque red Chimney Rock near the west entrance to Shell Canyon. You'll travel briefly into Sheridan County, but a left at Burgess Junction onto Highway 14A heading west will take you back into Big Horn County.

Alternatively, from Hyattville follow paved roads west to Manderson, then take U.S. Highway 20/16 north to Greybull, population 1,815. Greybull, too, is home to some of the world's richest dinosaur beds. The town is located at the confluence of the Big Horn and Greybull rivers and Shell and Dry creeks. It was established in 1909 as a stop along the Chicago, Burlington and Quincy Railroad and derives its name from a legendary albino bison that was sacred to Native Americans.

Area sites include Sheep Mountain, 1,000-foot-high ridge extending for some 15 miles northeast of Greybull. According to geologists, it's a textbook example of a *doubly plunging anticline.* Signs depicting a red devil will lead you to Devil's Kitchen, where fossils and other unusual rock finds are common. Ask for directions at the Greybull Chamber of Commerce on Highway 16, or call 765–2100.

Fossils, petrified wood, Native American relics, and semiprecious stones form the nucleus of the excellent ***Greybull Museum,*** found at 325 Greybull Avenue. The museum is open year-round. From June 1 through Labor Day, it's

An Unlikely Dessert

During the summer I worked at the Medicine Lodge Creek Site outside Hyattville, I was befriended by a gregarious Big Horn Basin cattleman (whose name I won't divulge here). I recall walking with him early one warm August evening in one of his pastures after enjoying supper with him and his family. That's when my typically carefree buddy got all fired up and began ranting about "them *%!& environmentalists."

His soliloquy centered on the fact that certain individuals were lodging complaints about the grazing of private cattle on the public lands of the Bighorn National Forest. He uttered many choice words en route to the lecture's culmination, when my friend, red-faced and waving his arms wildly in the dry air, yelled, "They even complain about my cows crapping in the streams . . . why, look," he bellowed, bending down to pick up large chunk of a dried cowpie, which he proceeded to stuff into his mouth. Then he started chewing like a madman. What he said next, with his mouth crammed full, sounded like, "It annuthn brt!," but I think he meant, "It ain't nothin' but dirt!"

After calming down and realizing what he'd done in his moment of raging indignation, my friend spent the next five minutes spitting and sputtering and looking more than a little bit sheepish.

The Medicine Chest

Native Americans in the Rockies have traditionally traveled to mountain peaks to pray and seek divine intervention from the powerful spirits there. The Medicine Wheel, a National Historic Landmark, is a sacred aboriginal site where Native Americans still perform religious ceremonies. Located at the top of Medicine Mountain at an elevation of nearly 10,000 feet, the wheel consists of twenty-eight spokes radiating from a central hub. The wheel is 80 feet in diameter, and the hub and spokes are made from unhewed rock pieces. Six additional mounds, or cairns, are spaced unevenly around the rim. Each mound has an opening that faces a different direction, and the wheel rim has a break in its eastern edge.

The origin and meaning of the wheel are matters of debate. Some archaeologists maintain that it resembles the Mexican calendar stone, while others believe it was used for astrological purposes other than marking the passage of time. In any event, meditating on the Medicine Wheel can be a powerful and mystical experience. Although they had no direct connection to the creation of Medicine Wheel, Chief Joseph of the Nez Perce fasted at the site, and Shoshone chief Washakie visited the spot to seek guidance in leading his nation. The Medicine Wheel reflects a symbol that is at the very heart of Native American being: the circle. Consider these words from the Lakota Sioux Black Elk, in his book *Black Elk Speaks:* "Everything the power of the world does is done in a circle. The sky is round, the earth is round, and so are all the stars. . . . The life of a man is in a circle from childhood to childhood, and so it is in everything where power moves."

Medicine Wheel National Historic Landmark is administered by the U.S. Forest Service. The site provides breathtaking vistas of the Big Horn Basin, the Wind River Range, and the Absaroka and Pryor ranges. The site is located off Highway 14A, 3 miles north on Forest Service Road 12. The turn is found about 30 miles west of Burgess Junction, or 27 miles east of Lovell. Vehicles pulling trailers are not recommended on the narrow dirt road leading to the parking area. From the parking area it's about a 1½-mile walk to the Medicine Wheel. Please respect the site and do not disturb any of the cultural artifacts while in the area. For information call 548–6541.

open Monday through Saturday from 10:00 A.M. to 8:00 P.M.; Labor Day to November 1, it's open from 1:00 to 5:00 P.M. Monday through Friday; and the rest of the year Monday, Wednesday, and Friday from 1:00 to 4:00 P.M. For more information call 765–2444.

At the Greybull Airport examples of World War II's mighty bombers and transport aircraft make up the ***Museum of Flight and Aerial Firefighting*** (765–4322). You'll learn, among other things, about the first aerial fire reconnaissance, which took place in 1919 in California. Before the advent of the radio, messages were relayed to the ground via notes dropped by parachute or transported by carrier pigeon. You'll also see five of the remaining flying PB4Y-2s used against the Japanese in the South Pacific theater during World War II.

Surrounded by mountains on three sides—the high Absaroka and Beartooth ranges to the west, the rugged Pryor Mountains to the north, and the Big Horns to the east—Lovell, population 2,281, began life as the area's largest ranch. The ML Ranch, founded by Anthony L. Mason and Henry Clay Lovell in 1880, ran some 25,000 head of cattle. Lovell the town got going in about 1900 and was incorporated in 1906, with ranching and sugar beets providing economic stability.

Lovell is known as the Rose City of Wyoming; rose-filled planters and gardens grace the streets, parks, and private yards. The nearby, 120,000-acre **Bighorn Canyon National Recreation Area** encompasses a variety of empty landscapes, from badlands and steep-sided gorges to high prairie laced with trails. The Yellowtail Dam in Montana, dedicated in 1968, created 71-mile-long Bighorn Lake, now a prime boating and camping area. Stop at the solar-heated Bighorn Canyon NRA Visitor Center at the east edge of Lovell for maps of the area and directions to various and varied attractions. The visitor center regularly runs an orientation film on Bighorn Canyon's history, natural features, and available activities. For information call 548–2251 or visit www.nps.gov/bica.

North of Lovell on Highway 37, you can visit the nation's first wild horse preserve, the remote, 47,000-acre **Pryor Mountains Wild Horse Range.** The mustangs running the range here possess the distinctive dun color and dorsal and zebra stripes typical of horses with Spanish ancestry—genetic features not commonly found among wild horse bands in this country. (If you're interested, you can even, look into adopting a horse through the Bureau of Land Management's wild horse management program.) Call the BLM in Billings, Montana, at (406) 896–5013 for more information.

A short loop tour out of Lovell takes you through the small towns of Byron, Deaver, Frannie, and Cowley, which have a combined population of about 1,500. Five miles east of Lovell on Highway 14A, there's an information marker describing the 37-mile **Sidon Irrigation Canal,** completed by Mormon pioneers in 1895. The story goes that work on the project was halted by a large boulder that was in the way. According to legend, prayer and divine intervention caused the rock to split, allowing the canal work to resume. The split rock became known as Prayer Rock. Three miles east of the canal marker is the oilfield community of Byron, which contains a number of attractive old log structures. The area has produced more than 117 million barrels of oil and 13 million cubic feet of gas since 1918.

Taking Highway 114 north you next arrive at Deaver and the **Deaver Reservoir,** which teems with bluegills and crappies. Six miles north on

Highway 310/789, just 2 miles south of the Montana state line, is Frannie, population 209, "The Biggest Little Town in Wyoming." If you've nothing better to do, you can stand in the middle of Frannie and have one foot in Big Horn County and the other in Park County. The town of Cowley, several miles east of Deaver, holds a host of historic sandstone buildings worthy of a look. It's also home to a number of artesian wells, with 98 percent-pure water. Stop for a refreshing sip before heading back east.

Sheridan County

The Big Horn Scenic Byways are especially stunning when decked out in their colorful autumn foliage. Travel on Highway 14 is open year-round, with occasional closures due to weather in winter. Highway 14A is open from approximately mid-May through mid-November. Elevations on the three byways range from 4,800 feet to more than 9,600 feet. On a clear day you'll be able to see Devils Tower rising far to the east. As you descend, the switchbacks on Highway 14 lead you past signed geologic formations, including the Amsden, Chugwater, Gros Ventre, and Tensleep formations. Up high you're guaranteed to see an abundance of wildflowers and wildlife in summer: More than 265 species of birds make the Big Horns their home, and bighorn sheep, mule deer, elk, and moose often strut their stuff adjacent to the byways.

Highway 14 drops eastward out of the Big Horns into Dayton and nearby Ranchester. Near Dayton you'll pass the ***Sawyers Battlefield.*** Here Col. J. A. Sawyers's men battled Indians for thirteen straight days in 1865 before General Connor's troops came to the rescue. On Main Street you'll see the ***cabin of Hans Kleiber,*** a famous artist/naturalist. (A number of his paintings are displayed at the Bradford Brinton Memorial, which we'll visit in Big Horn later.) Another interesting site is the ***Dayton Bell Tower,*** located in the city park. It was built in 1910 and used by residents as an observation point during World War II. In 1911 Dayton became the first community in Wyoming to elect a woman mayor, and Susan Wissler was the first woman mayor in America to serve two consecutive terms. She also operated a millinery and dry goods store and taught in the local school. In Ranchester you'll find the ***Connor Battlefield*** interpreted in the city park, located along the Tongue River bottomlands. The site marks a major military engagement of the Powder River Expedition in 1865, when Gen. Patrick E. Connor's forces attacked and destroyed Arapaho Chief Black Bear's village of 250 lodges. Today the battlefield is a peaceful place to picnic or take a hike. (Cross over the river on the cable footbridge to find additional hiking paths.)

The Big Horn Mountains and the Bighorn National Forest dominate the western horizon as you travel through the Sheridan area. John D. Loucks plotted Sheridan in 1882, naming it after his Civil War commanding officer, Gen. Philip Sheridan. The Burlington and Missouri River Railroad came to town ten

The Sheridan Inn

Built in 1893, the *Sheridan Inn* was financed by the Burlington and Missouri River Railroad. William F. Cody led the Grand March from the dining room at the inn's opening on June 23 of that year. The W. F. Cody Hotel Company, of which Buffalo Bill was part owner, managed the inn from 1894 to 1902. When in town, Buffalo Bill was known to sit on the porch of the Sheridan Inn and audition acts for the upcoming season of his Wild West Show.

Hand-hewn beams span the entire dining area. The ornate bar in the inn's Buffalo Bill Saloon came from England by boat, by rail to Gillette, and by ox-drawn wagon the rest of the way to Sheridan. The lobby's counter, stone fireplace, and cigar case are all original. The inn had electric lights when it opened and was touted as the finest establishment between Chicago and San Francisco. Its two rooms with bathtubs were the first of their kind in the area. Room and board could be had for the pricey sum of $2.50 per day. Famous visitors at the hotel have included Calamity Jane, Ernest Hemingway, General John Pershing, Will Rogers, Charlie Russell, and Presidents Hoover, Taft, and Teddy Roosevelt.

Architect Thomas Kimball modeled the inn after a hunting lodge he had visited in Scotland. The Sheridan Inn, featuring 14-foot-wide porches encircling the entire building, was highlighted in *Ripley's Believe It or Not* as "The House of 69 Gables." The inn was designated a National Historic Landmark in 1964. It ceased to operate as a hotel in 1965; it is now in the process of being restored under the direction of the Sheridan Heritage Center Board. The inn is located at 856 Broadway. You can learn more about it on the Internet at www.sheridaninn.com.

Sheridan Inn

years later. To the credit of its citizens, Sheridan has managed to keep most of its downtown buildings intact, and the entire Main Street district has been designated a National Historic Landmark. It boasts the largest collection of original buildings from the late 1800s and early 1900s in all of Wyoming.

The mansion of senator, governor, and rancher John B. Kendrick, known as the "Sagebrush Senator," offers a great diversion where you can wile away several hours. Kendrick served as governor of Wyoming from 1915 to 1917 and as a U.S. senator from 1917 until his death in 1933. The Kendrick ranches of northern Wyoming and southern Montana encompassed more than 200,000 acres. Now called the *Trail End State Historic Site,* Kendrick's 1913 Sheridan home, nearly 14,000 square feet in size, is an example of Flemish-Revival architecture, a rarity in the West. The house contained a number of devices innovative for the time, including an intercom system that functioned throughout the house, a dumbwaiter that moved between floors, and a stationary vacuum system with a motor in the basement, which helped ease the staff's workload.

A self-guided tour booklet leads you through the mansion, where you'll see beautiful stained-glass windows, a white Italian marble fireplace, French silk damask wall coverings, and sprawling Oriental rugs. Machine-tooled woodwork and a hand-painted ceiling embellish the grand foyer. Also noteworthy is a log cabin at the site that served as the first post office, store, law office, and bank in the city of Sheridan. The grounds are beautifully bedecked with flower beds, and a plant identification list is available. The Trail End State Historic Site, located at 400 East Clarendon Avenue, is open to the public for self-guided tours from March through mid-December. From June through August, the facility is open from 9:00 A.M. to 6:00 P.M. During the rest of its months of operation, it's open from 1:00 to 4:00 P.M., except Memorial Day and Labor Day weekends, when extended hours are observed. The site is closed from mid-December through February. Guided tours for groups may be arranged by calling 674–4589. You can also learn more on the Internet at www.trailend.org.

Don King (not the one with the big hair), founder of *King's Ropes and Saddlery,* started handcrafting saddles and tooling saddle leather more than fifty years ago. He passed along the operation to the next generation, but Don's handiwork is still much in evidence in the combination store-museum at 184 North Main Street in Sheridan. Some of the younger fellas have picked up a thing or two from the old pro over the years, and their creations are displayed, too. Whether you need only to outfit yourself in a King's baseball cap—the unofficial Wyoming state hat (the official one being the cowboy hat, of course)—or are looking to saddle up, King's is the place for quality ropes, saddles, and accessories. The museum collection includes an array of spurs, chaps, and saddles. Hours are 8:00 A.M. to 5:00 P.M., Monday through Saturday. For information call 672–2702.

For an intimate atmosphere and some of the best food in Wyoming, try *Oliver's Bar and Grill* at 57 North Main Street. The menu features a Mediterranean cuisine, with grilled rack of lamb and fresh fish and fresh pasta specials—and always something new and delicious for dessert. Prices are moderate-to-expensive. The restaurant is open for lunch and dinner every day except Sunday. Reservations are recommended; call 672–2838. For a traditional Wyoming flavor, visit *The Mint,* 151 North Main Street. This famous watering hole provides an authentic taste of the West, with plenty of Charles Belden photographs, stuffed critters, cattle brands, and working cowboys wetting their whistles after a day on the range. Call 674–9696.

Traveling south from Sheridan, forsake I–90 for the more picturesque U.S. Highway 87, and then take Highway 335 to Big Horn. This area is home to one of the oldest polo clubs in the United States: the Big Horn Equestrian Center, located on Bird Farm Road south of Big Horn. The center schedules polo matches every Sunday afternoon from May to September. It also sponsors steeplechase races, dressage competitions, steer-roping events, and soccer tournaments. Not surprisingly there's a strong British influence in the area; many of the early ranches here were begun by titled English families. Queen Elizabeth has even visited the Malcolm Wallop family, owners of the equestrian center, on occasion.

The *Big Horn Store* is a general store evocative of a simpler time. Built in 1882, it's one of the oldest businesses in northern Wyoming. The *Bradford Brinton Memorial,* located at 239 Brinton Road in Big Horn, is also an informative and worthwhile stop. The property, listed on the National Register of Historic Places, lies on the internationally recognized Quarter Circle A Ranch. William and Malcolm Moncreiffe established the original homestead in 1892, and Bradford Brinton purchased the property in 1923. Brinton raised thoroughbred horses on the ranch. He also enlarged the house to its present size of twenty rooms. Tours are available of the two-story, white neo-Colonial ranch house.

Brinton loved the West, and it shows in his significant collection of more than 600 original oils, watercolors, and sketches by American artists. Many well-known Western artists were among his friends and ranch visitors. The collection of art displayed includes works by John J. Audubon, Edward M. Borein, E. W. Gollings, Will James, Hans Kleiber, Frederic Remington, and others. Artwork can be found in both the gallery and the ranch homestead.

In addition to paintings, the gallery showcases an excellent array of Native American crafts and clothing items, such as a painted steerhide dance shield, baby cradleboards, a Cree saddle cushion, Sioux ceremonial dress, and a Nez Perce buckskin shirt. Other attractions include a Jefferson Peace Medal dated 1861, which was a gift to a Native American chief, and an Abraham Lincoln letter dated 1848.

Original art found in the homestead includes a Charles M. Russell bronze sculpture, *The Bucker and the Buckeroo;* Frederic Remington's watercolor, *Harnessing the Mules;* and a hallway frieze created by Brinton's friend Ed Borein, one of the most prolific Western artists of all time. The Bradford Brinton Memorial collection holds more than 175 pieces by this master alone.

Among the memorial's distinguished visitors have been Queen Elizabeth II, Prince Philip, and James Michener. Brinton died in 1936 and left the house and ranch to his sister, Helen, whose will created the Bradford Brinton Memorial, which opened in 1961. The memorial is open daily from 9:30 A.M. to 5:00 P.M., late May through Labor Day. Each year the memorial sponsors a special Christmas holiday art exhibit featuring a single artist. For information on regular and special exhibits, call 672–3173 or e-mail kls_bbm@vcn.com, or visit www.bradfordbrintonmemorial.com.

Spahn's Big Horn Bed & Breakfast is found 6 miles beyond Big Horn on Highway 335. Drive until the pavement ends, then proceed another ½ mile on gravel to the sign marking the B&B. Turn left there and follow the road as it winds ¾ mile into the timber. Ron and Bobbie Spahn built the log home from scratch using little modern equipment; the result is one beautiful home and bed-and-breakfast, with a gorgeous view of the valley and surrounding mountains to boot. It's a hypnotic setting, with the breeze blowing through the surrounding pines and, season permitting, snow settling softly on the ground outside. Ron has also cut a number of cross-country skiing and hiking trails through the surrounding woods. Your hosts know the area well and can direct you to any number of scenic attractions. Rates range from $100 to $140 per night, depending on accommodations and season. For information and reservations call 674–8150 or visit the Web site www.bighorn-wyoming.com.

Return to Highway 87 through Big Horn and head south through a region teeming with the tragic history of the Indian Wars. The first site you'll encounter, located about 13 miles down the road, is Massacre Hill, which marks the site of the 1866 Fetterman Fight. The impressive, 20-foot-high **Fetterman Massacre Monument** sits atop the hill, overlooking the battlefield.

Capt. William J. Fetterman, who cut his battle teeth during the Civil War, knew little about fighting Indians, but boasted that with one hundred men he could "ride down the whole Sioux Nation." The skirmish here was precipitated by the government's construction of Fort Phil Kearny, which was in direct violation of a treaty with the Sioux. Led by Red Cloud and Crazy Horse, a band of

Arapaho, Cheyenne, and Sioux retaliated on December 21, 1866, leading Captain Fetterman and eighty-one officers and men into an ambush after they had been sent to rescue a train of firewood wagons under attack. A small band of Indians, led by Crazy Horse, lured the soldiers over a hill and out of sight of the fort. There, hundreds of Indians fell on them. There were no white survivors. The Indians called it the Battle of the Hundred Slain. Evidence indicates that Fetterman and one of his officers chose to die by their own hands.

The shooting started around noon and ended about a half hour later. The massacre created fears that the Indians would subsequently attack Fort Phil Kearny, so post commander Col. Henry B. Carrington sent two civilians to Fort Laramie for help, John "Portugee" Phillips and Daniel Dixon. They probably changed horses twice on the 236-mile ride through four days and nights of blizzards and iron cold; Phillips rode the last 40 miles alone and arrived at Fort Laramie about 10:00 P.M. on Christmas night. Reinforcements finally reached Fort Phil Kearny in mid-January, 1867; the Indians never did attack the fort directly.

A number of interpretive plaques at the battlefield bring the bloody scene back to life and lead you to ponder the decisions Fetterman made during the conflict. Fetterman imprudently ignored the basic rules of Indian fighting, and his was the worst loss suffered by the army in western battles until the Custer fight on the Little Big Horn River a decade later, not far away in southern Montana.

The August following the Fetterman Massacre, in 1867, Indians again attacked, this time against a detail of twenty-eight soldiers and four civilians on a woodcutting mission under the command of Capt. James Powell. The **_Wagon Box Fight_** owes its name to the fact that soldiers defended themselves for more than three hours by removing the wheels from their wagons and arranging the fourteen wagon boxes into a circular barricade. With their improvised fort and newly issued Springfield breech-loading rifles—which could fire up to twenty rounds per minute—the soldiers staved off the Indians, even though the natives far outnumbered the soldiers. Three white men were killed and two wounded; Indian casualty estimates range from a few dozen to several hundred.

The Wagon Box Monument is located near the town of Story. Directional signs lead to the battle site.

Johnson County

Now we turn to Fort Phil Kearny. The fort was established in July 1866 as a command post for the 18th Infantry, whose job it was to protect travelers tackling the Bozeman Trail, which led from the Platte River to goldfields in southwestern Montana. Named after a popular Union general killed in the Civil War, the fort was constructed of logs cut in and hauled from the Big Horn

Mountains. More than 4,000 logs were used to erect the stockade, one of the few palisade fortifications in the West.

After the Union Pacific Railroad laid its tracks far enough west to allow travelers to bypass the Bozeman Trail by traveling to Montana through Idaho, the forts built to protect Bozeman Trail travelers were no longer necessary. Gen. Ulysses S. Grant ordered the closing of Fort Phil Kearny after the Treaty of 1868 was concluded. As a result of the treaty, the area belonged exclusively to Native Americans (for the time being), a fact some of them underscored by burning the fort to the ground not long after its abandonment.

The *Fort Phil Kearny State Historic Site's* museum is open from 8:00 A.M. to 6:00 P.M. daily from May 15 through September 30. The rest of the year, the museum is open from noon to 4:00 P.M. There is a $1.00 gate fee for Wyoming residents eighteen and older; $2.00 fee for nonresidents. The fort grounds, which contain a number of historic interpretive signs and markers, are open year-round from dawn to dusk. Taking place in mid-June at the fort are Bozeman Trail Days, with activities that include both Anglo and Native American interpretations of the Wagon Box Fight and Fetterman Massacre, archaeological tours, and living-history programs. To find Fort Phil Kearny, from Story take Highway 193 southeast about 5 miles to the road leading to the post. For further information call 684–7629 or visit www.philkearny.vcn.com.

Father Pierre Jean DeSmet (known as "Black Robe" to Native Americans) left his mark on Wyoming as the first Catholic missionary in the territory. DeSmet passed Independence Rock, and near Daniel in 1840 he celebrated the first Roman Catholic mass in the region. In 1851 he also "discovered" *Lake DeSmet,* which is located 8 miles northwest of Buffalo off I–25. (Ask a local about the dragon of Lake DeSmet, which reportedly devours young maidens.) You can take advantage of picnic and camping sites at the lake, and you'll also find an 18-foot-high Father DeSmet Monument overlooking it from the west shore.

Buffalo, population 3,900, is an attractive town perched on the east slope foothills of the Big Horn Range. The community surrounds a historic Main Street that's worth a few hours' browsing time, and crowded with tempting choices for the shopper. One favorite is *Margo's Pottery and Fine Crafts* at 1 North Main Street, where you'll find fine ceramics by Margo Brown and a host of other artists. Ask for a self-guided Main Street Walking Tour brochure at the chamber of commerce, found at 55 North Main Street. The tour includes a rundown of more than twenty buildings, many of which feature historic self-portraits in their front windows or on mounted plaques. For information call 684–5544 or (800) 227–5122.

A good place to start touring Buffalo is the old *Occidental Hotel.* Located at 10 North Main Street, the hotel is listed on the National Register of Historic

Places. The original 1880 hotel was a log structure, but that was replaced in 1910 by the current brick building. At one time the hotel occupied the entire block. In recent years guest rooms have again become available; seven of them to be precise, ranging from $100 to $135 per night. A barbershop still operates in the original barbershop location, and the lobby, filled with period furniture, photos, and artifacts, is a self-guided museum. For supper try the new Virginian

The Johnson County War

Johnson County was not only the scene of some of the most vicious fighting between whites and Indians in the West, but it also hosted the infamous 1892 Johnson County War. The fight—during which men were killed, cattle rustled, and homesteads burned—pitted owners of large ranches against homesteaders (also called nesters) and small-scale ranchers.

Absentee cattle barons from Cheyenne put out the word in Texas that they were hiring gunslingers at $5.00 per day, with a $50 bonus for every man killed in Johnson County. On April 6, 1892, a train carrying twenty-six hired guns from Texas and another couple of dozen Wyoming men departed from Cheyenne. They were led by Maj. Frank Wolcott, a former Union army officer now an officer of the Wyoming Stock Growers Association, which was ruled by the big cattle outfits.

Carrying a "dead list" of seventy known and suspected rustlers and sympathizers, including Johnson County sheriff Red Angus, the invaders first stopped at the KC Ranch at present Kaycee and ambushed two men on their list, Nick Ray and Nate Champion. The battle lasted hours. Ray died early in the battle, but Champion fought on until the gunmen torched the cabin and shot him as he fled the conflagration.

Wolcott and his army then moved 30 miles north to the TA Ranch, where they holed up and awaited the arrival of Sheriff Angus. An informant had told them that Angus had gathered an armed force and was moving in their direction. At daylight the invaders found themselves surrounded by 200 well-armed and enraged Buffalo-area ranchers and nesters. A three-day siege followed, with heavy firing from both sides. But only one man was killed; one of the Texans accidentally shot himself in the foot and later died of gangrene.

Peace was finally restored after Governor Barber cabled President Harrison for federal assistance. The president sent troops from nearby Fort McKinney to quell the uprising, and the cavalry arrived as Sheriff Angus and his men were preparing to attack the ranch house with dynamite. The cavalry escorted the invading gunmen and their leaders to Fort McKinney and later returned them to Cheyenne. None of the perpetrators was prosecuted; instead, the men were set free because Johnson County could not afford to pay for the trials.

Although the invaders got off without so much as a day in jail, the Johnson County War marked the end of their unchallenged power in the state.

Restaurant; for a drink try the old Occidental Saloon, which includes the original tin ceiling and back bar. Ask to see the bullet hole in the bar drawer. There's also a 1944 wall mural of the Hole in the Wall, where Butch Cassidy's gang hid out, reportedly painted by a down-and-out saloon customer to pay off his bar tab. Call 684–0451 or visit www.occidentalwyoming.com for more information.

Look for the *Johnson County Cattle War Commemorative Bronzes* on South Main Street near its intersection with Angus Street. The three-quarters life-size sculptures by artist D. Michael Thomas, *Ridin' for the Brand* and *Living on the Edge,* depict the deadly face-offs between the cattle barons' men and the homesteaders.

The *Johnson County–Jim Gatchell Museum,* located at the corner of Main and Fort Streets in Buffalo, is a rare find. Pioneer druggist Jim Gatchell's Western and Native American collections form the nucleus of the museum's holdings. The displays of prehistoric artifacts constitute one of the major collections in Wyoming. The Johnson County War exhibit offers a detailed description of the fighting and events leading up to it; a ring belonging to the slain Nate Champion is among the cattle war memorabilia. Particularly intriguing are a new Bozeman Trail exhibit—the Cattle War, Wagon Box Fight, and 1880s Buffalo Main Street dioramas—and bugler Adolph Metzger's crushed bugle, testifying to the final moments of the Fetterman Massacre. The museum is located in the 1909 Carnegie Library Building, not to be overlooked itself, with its Neoclassical architectural features. The museum is open daily 9:00 A.M. to 6:00 P.M. from mid-April through late November; call 684–9331 or visit www .jimgatchell.com for more information.

After visiting the museum, stroll down to *Seney's Drugs,* located at 38 South Main Street, and belly up to the soda fountain, a favorite Buffalo gathering spot for generations. Seney's malted milks and milk shakes were once recommended by Duncan Hines in his newspaper column. The 1895 building at 84–89 South Main Street features an unusual white cast-iron facade on the second floor.

Take a look at the mural on the side of the building at 51 South Main Street. It proclaims Buffalo as more than a one-horse town. A variety of businesses have operated out of this structure through the decades, including a butcher shop, grocery store, jewelry store, and city electric building. Today it houses the *Hitching Post Art Gallery,* representing the work of local and nonlocal Wyoming artists, with an array of unique wildlife and Western limited editions, woodcarvings, pottery, baskets, beadwork, sterling silver jewelry, and bronzes. For information call 684–9473.

Spend an hour or two at *Washington Park* pitching horseshoes, enjoying a walk, or having a picnic. If it's a hot day, and especially if you're traveling with children, make time for a plunge in the ***Buffalo Public Pool*** in the park. It's very cold, it's free—and it's huge, one of the nicest pools you'll find anywhere. If the kids get hungry, you can buy hot dogs, nachos, snacks, and cotton candy on the spot. The park is located at the intersection of Burritt Avenue and Angus Street. While in town, consider bunking down in one of the cozy log cabins at ***Mountain View Motel & Campground,*** located at 585 Fort Street. Reservations can be made by calling 684–2881 or e-mailing jgampetr@wyoming.com.

Day trips out of Buffalo provide a range of activities and sights. You can pick up a copy of the *Scenic Tours of Johnson County* brochure at the chamber of commerce for a comprehensive listing with descriptions (or at home you can visit www.buffalowyoming.com), but here are some to consider for starters: Begin with a half-day tour of ***Crazy Woman Canyon*** on Highway 16, directly west toward the Big Horn Mountains. Crazy Woman Canyon Road is well marked where it branches off to the left about 25 miles out of town. On the drive you'll encounter rugged mountainous terrain, so make sure your brakes are working and leave your travel trailer behind. You'll drive through the resplendent canyon, gawking at high cliffs and giant boulders that have tumbled down from above. To return to Buffalo continue along the gravel road that took you through the canyon until you reach Highway 196. Turn left and you'll be back in town after 10 miles.

You can go back sixty million years in just a few hours by driving to the ***Dry Creek Petrified Tree.*** Head east 7 miles from Buffalo on I–90 to the Red Hills exit. Then drive north on Tipperary Road for 5 miles, and turn left onto a graveled access road to the petrified tree and surrounding stumps. There is a parking area, picnic table, and a self-guiding loop trail. The cypress trees, when they were composed of wood rather than mineral, grew when the climate here was not unlike that of today's Okefenokee Swamp in Georgia.

Meet up with the ghost of Butch Cassidy at the ***Outlaw Cave,*** which requires a rugged full day's journey to find. The cave is located on public land

Crazy Woman

At least two stories—one about a white woman, one about a Native American, both full of loneliness—claim to be the source of the name of the creek and its canyon. In the first, Crow warriors killed a white whiskey trader but left his young widow to wander up and down the stream, demented. In the second, an Indian woman was the sole survivor of an attack on her camp and family and lived alone in a little wickiup until her death. Afterward, she could still be seen on moonlit nights, leaping from rock to rock along the creek.

The Clear Creek Trail System

The Clear Creek Trail System, a project still under development, stretches through the heart of downtown Buffalo, then runs along the south side of Clear Creek through the city park. After joining the Green Belt, the trail traverses the lands of the Wyoming State Veterans' Home for 2.65 miles. Another stretch reaches from Clear Creek up toward the Big Horn Mountains. Some portions of the trail, 8 miles-plus and growing, are hard surfaced, while others are gravel or dirt. Points of interest for walkers, cyclists, and others using the trail include the old *Occidental Hotel,* which played a role in Owen Wister's novel, *The Virginian,* and the *Johnson County–Jim Gatchell Museum.* Following the Clear Creek Trail is a great way to get acquainted with this historic, quintessentially western town.

with access via Bureau of Land Management roads. (The BLM and local landowners have recently worked out a route that allows public access to the site.) First drive south to Kaycee on I–25, then head about 0.9 mile west on Highway 190 to the Barnum Road junction. Follow Barnum Road 17 miles to Barnum, a T-junction where the road turns to dirt near a sign for the Middle Fork Management Area of the Powder River. Take a left at this sign onto the gravel-and-dirt road designated as the Bar C Road. Most of the road is hard surfaced in dry weather; however, the upper portion requires a vehicle with high clearance and preferably four-wheel drive—or you can mountain bike the final section of the trip. After traveling 8½ miles from the Middle Fork sign, you'll encounter the Outlaw Cave turnoff. From this point it's approximately 2 miles to where you leave your car and hike about a mile down the side of the canyon to the river. At the bottom, the cave is on the far side, so bring a walking stick and your creek-fording shoes if you want a closer look. Whether you cross the river or not, the fishing's excellent. At the top of the trail, where you left your car, is a nice Bureau of Land Management campground with splendid views up and down the canyon. The campground has no water, however, so be sure to bring your own. The scenery is arresting, with panoramas encompassing brilliant red canyon walls. The infamous Hole in the Wall is located farther south. For directions, call the BLM office in Buffalo, 684–1100, visit www.wy.blm .gov/bfo, or e-mail buffalo_wymail@blm.gov. (For information on visiting the Hole in the Wall country by another means—namely, horseback—see the information on Outlaw Trail, Inc., listed under Thermopolis.)

In Kaycee visit *Hoofprints of the Past,* as the Southern Johnson County Museum is officially known. Indian artifacts are on display, along with the old Mayoworth Post Office, the old Kaycee jailhouse, and information on the

Johnson County War. The museum (738–2381) is open daily from Memorial Day through October.

Before leaving the Kaycee area, you'll want to study the KILLING OF CHAMPION AND RAY information sign located just south of town on the east side of old Highway 89. The story details the Johnson County Cattle War battle at the KC Ranch.

To continue on to Campbell County, you can drive east from Buffalo on I–90 or take the longer but more intriguing backroad route along U.S. Highway 14/16 through Clearmont and Spotted Horse.

Campbell County

Stop for a quick photo at **Spotted Horse,** which was named after a Cheyenne chief. The whole town is wrapped up in a combination bar, cafe, and gas station. It's located on Highway 14/16 not long after you leave Sheridan County and enter Campbell County.

When you've taken advantage of the photo op, continue through the wide-open spaces separating Spotted Horse and Gillette and some of the most productive and scenic ranch country in Wyoming. A few miles east of Spotted Horse is the northerly turn to Recluse, established in 1918 as a post office; in fact, the town earned its name owing to the great distance between area ranches and the post office. The **Recluse Branch Library** of the Campbell County Public Library system is most interesting. Located in the Recluse Community Hall, it consists of a wall cupboard that is opened on request to permit patrons to peruse the collection. The library was first organized in 1927 as The Pleasant Hour Club, then in 1934 moved into the Community Hall, a log building constructed with logs cut and hauled by area residents.

On to Gillette, namesake of railroad surveyor Edward Gillette, who laid out the track for the Burlington and Missouri River Railroad between Gillette and Sheridan (from which point it continues north to Montana). Edward Gillette was credited with saving the railroad the added expense of 5 miles of track and thirty bridges in the Campbell County area by routing the railroad through the spot where the town of Gillette grew up. The town was incorporated in 1891, a year after the track was laid.

Gillette's economic well-being centers around coal and, more recently, a new boom in drilling for methane gas trapped in underground coal beds. The mineral coal production has made Gillette the state's fourth-largest town, with a population of nearly 20,000—representing more than half of Campbell County's 30,000 people. The mineral wealth has bought the city some mighty fine cultural facilities. The **Campbell County Public Library,** for instance, houses an extensive collection of books on Wyoming and an impressive array of art by well-known artists. You can also visit the city's planetarium and the Cam-Plex Heritage Center, which includes convention facilities and a 960-seat theater. Call 682–0552 for more information on these and other area attractions.

The Campbell County Public Library, at 2101 South 4-J Road, features the **Sheepherders' Monument,** with its beautiful bronze sculpture and an original "stone johnny" (sheepherder's stone marker) brought in from a nearby ranch. The Campbell County Public Library is open Monday through Thursday 9:00 A.M. to 9:00 P.M., Friday and Saturday 9:00 A.M. to 5:00 P.M., and Sunday 1:00 to 5:00 P.M. The phone number is 687–0009.

A real treat in town is the **Campbell County Rockpile Museum,** located at 900 West Second Street. Here you'll find a fine collection of pioneer vehicles, including a chuck wagon, sheep wagon, and horse-drawn hearse. Black horses pulling the hearse signaled that a man was to be buried, while gray horses indicated that a woman or child had died. Also on display are hand-tooled saddlery, branding irons, a collection of Wyoming's ubiquitous barbed wire, and prehistoric Native American artifacts. Outside there's a one-room schoolhouse, where in winter students were warmed by a woodstove—and by running as fast as possible to the outhouse when necessary. You'll also learn more about the

northern
wyomingtrivia

The town of Banner was named for the flaglike brand of a local rancher out of whose dining room the town's first post office was run.

area's railroading and coal mining legacies. The museum is open June 1 through August 31 on Monday through Saturday, 9:00 A.M. to 8:00 P.M., and on Sunday, 12:30 to 6:30 P.M. During the rest of the year, the hours are 9:00 A.M. to 5:00 P.M., Monday through Saturday. For additional details call 682–5723.

If you're interested in touring a local mine, call the Gillette Convention and Visitors Bureau at 686–0040 or (800) 544–6136 to make arrangements. The

Wyodak Mine, which opened in 1922, is the oldest operating coal mine in the Powder River Basin; it still produces nearly three million tons of coal annually, approximately half of which is burned at the adjacent **Wyodak Power Plant,** off I–90 about 5 miles east of town. You can tour the 330-megawatt power plant, which burns coal to generate steam used to produce electricity. Power plant tours are conducted weekdays, except Thursday, between 9:00 A.M. and 3:00 P.M. To schedule a tour, call the plant at 686–1248, ext. 0.

A variety of dining experiences await back in town. For Chinese-American cooking try the **Hong Kong Restaurant** (682–5829), 1612 West Second Street; for homemade specialties try **Bailey's Bar & Grill** (686–7678), 301 South Gillette Avenue; and for Mexican food visit **Casa Del Rey** (682–4738), 409 West Second Street. Food prices are moderate at all three restaurants.

Nature lovers shouldn't miss **McManamen Park,** with its excellent birding opportunities. The park is designed to attract waterfowl, and benches and viewing blinds are available for up-close bird-watching. McManamen Park is located between Brooks and Gurley Streets along Warlow Drive on the north side of Gillette.

As evidenced aplenty in and around Gillette, Campbell County is indeed coal country. The Powder River Coal Basin contains an estimated one trillion short tons of coal reserves. Behemoth draglines load 240-ton trucks with coal from the Black Thunder Coal Mine near Wyoming's newest community, Wright, population 1,372. Wright lies at the northwest corner of the massive **Thunder Basin National Grassland.** In all, the grasslands cover some two million acres set aside by the federal government for primarily soil conservation and plant and wildlife preservation. To reach this, the heart of the nation's largest deposit of low-sulphur coal, drive 40 miles south from Gillette on Highway 59. There are seventeen coal mines in the area, some of which provide tours. For information call the Thunder Basin Coal Company at 939–1300.

Although the town was founded only in 1976 and incorporated in 1985, it has already assembled a respectable museum. The **Wright Centennial Museum** boasts an interesting collection covering not only coal mining, but also incorporating World War I memorabilia and pioneer farm implements. Outside the museum sits a seventy-ton truck that was retired in 1990. The museum, located at 104 Ranch Court, is free and open mid-May through mid-October from 10:00 A.M. to 5:00 P.M. on weekdays, 10:00 A.M. to 3:00 P.M. on Saturday; closed Sunday. For information call 464–1222.

Tours are also offered at the **Durham Buffalo Ranch,** with more than 3,000 head, one of the largest private buffalo herds in existence. The buffalo (*Bison bison*), or American bison, is a favorite of Wyomingites; the beast is prominently featured on the state flag and serves as the official state mammal.

Weighing a ton or more, the bison is the largest North American land mammal. At one time there were more than seventy-five million of these big critters roaming the prairies and high plains. In a sad saga familiar to most Americans, millions were slaughtered for hides in the late 1800s. Hunters like Buffalo Bill Cody earned their reputations shooting thousands of bison to supply railroad crews with meat. By the time Congress passed the first federal protection legislation for buffalo in 1894, their numbers had dwindled to less than 1,000 individuals in all of North America. The disappearance of the buffalo helped to destroy the traditional ways of life of Native Americans on the Great Plains, who had relied on the animal for food, clothing, shelter, cooking utensils, tools, weapons, and fuel.

Today the buffalo is enjoying a comeback, with more than 70,000 of them scattered across the country in herds ranging in size from several hundred to several thousand. The animal is no longer endangered, so don't hesitate to sample a buffalo steak or burger if your curiosity is piqued. Buffalo meat is lean, healthy, and downright tasty. (To have some cut and wrapped—a quarter, half, or whole bison—you can call Marion Scott at 682–3994.) The Durham Buffalo Ranch, located on Highway 59 about 8 miles north of Wright, encompasses more than 55,000 acres. Group tours can be arranged by making advance reservations; call 939–1271.

Crook County

Proceed easterly from Gillette to Moorcroft, population 838, located on the banks of the Belle Fourche (pronounced *bell foosb*) River. Drovers on the Texas Cattle Trail moved thousands of cattle through the Moorcroft area in the 1880s and 1890s, and the town also served as a major railhead for cattle shipped from the large ranch spreads in this region. In fact, in 1891 Moorcroft ranked as the leading cattle shipping point in the country. ***The Texas Trail Museum*** in downtown Moorcroft captures the essence of those cattle-driving days and the rich legacy of the area's ranching past. The museum is located at 220 South Big Horn. It is open daily from 1:00 to 4:00 P.M., May through September.

As you drive from Moorcroft toward Devils Tower on U.S. Highway 14, you'll notice Keyhole Reservoir on your right. From ***Keyhole State Park*** you can peer at the astounding formation of Devils Tower, rising beyond your crackling campfire. Keyhole State Park's 14,000 acres of surface water provide plenty of boating, fishing, and swimming opportunities. The reservoir and surrounding wetlands are also a mecca for more than 200 species of birds. Be on the lookout for bald eagles, common yellowthroat, osprey, wild turkeys, and white pelicans. At park headquarters you can obtain a complete bird list.

Entrance fee is $2.00 for in-staters ($4.00 for nonresidents) and the fees for camping are $6.00 and $12.00, respectively.

The park was named after the "keyhole brand" used by the nearby McKean Ranch. The park entrance is situated on the south side of the reservoir and is accessible from Highway 113. From Memorial Day through Labor Day, you can walk the park's 6.2-mile official Volksmarch trail. A full-service marina and motel is located on Headquarters Road, adjacent to the lakeshore. For information call 756–3596.

Continue winding along U.S. Highway 14 to reach Devils Tower Junction. Turn north there onto State Highway 24, and soon you'll arrive at the access road leading to *Devils Tower National Monument.* The first documented white men to take in the stunning view of the tower were members of Capt. W. F. Raynolds's 1859 Yellowstone expedition, and Col. Richard I. Dodge led a U.S. Geologic Survey expedition to the unique formation in 1875. Appreciating its unique attributes, President Theodore Roosevelt designated Devils Tower as the nation's first national monument in 1906.

Devils Tower is a magnificent sight, rising an abrupt 865 feet. The top spreads out to a 180-by-300-foot oval. A paved 1¼-mile walking path surrounds the base of the big rock's perimeter. Nearby, a large prairie dog town will keep you and the kids occupied, as the furry critters vie for your attention with a variety of amusing antics.

The Legend of Devils Tower

Most geologists believe Devils Tower is the remaining "throat" or rock core of an ancient volcano, exposed after millions of years of erosion. Hot magma rising from inside the earth formed the tower's long vertical columns as it cooled and contracted. The top is 5,117 feet above sea level and about 1,280 feet above the nearby Belle Fourche River. The rocks and boulders at its base are broken pieces of columns shed from the core.

The geologist's outlook is a pragmatic one. The area's Native Americans have their own ideas. The most popular of the Mateo Tipi, or Bear Lodge, Indian legends involves the story of a bear chasing seven Indian girls. To escape, the girls jumped up on a rock several feet high and prayed, "Rock, save us." Hearing the pleas of the girls, the rock began to elongate itself upward, pushing them higher and higher into the air, out of reach of the bear. The bear clawed at the sides of the rock, which continued to grow until it reached the sky, and the claw marks are there to this day. As for the Indian girls, they became the seven stars making up the constellation Pleiades. (In Greek mythology these seven stars are the daughters of Atlas.)

The unique geological phenomenon of Devils Tower made it to the big screen in Hollywood's production of *Close Encounters of the Third Kind*. Devils Tower has also drawn a lot of attention due to the large number of rock climbers scaling its sheer sides. (Recently climbing limitations have been enacted, and in June a voluntary ban is imposed by the National Park Service, honoring requests from Native Americans who consider the tower sacred.) Wyoming rancher William Rogers was the first to reach the top of the formation

Close Encounters of the Gravitational Kind

After sitting in the entrance station of Devils Tower National Monument for most of the summer of 1978, patiently accepting fees and orienting visitors, I'd heard it asked way too often, "What's it like on top?" (The only more common query was, "Where are the aliens parked?"—because the summer I spent working as a ranger at Devils Tower happened to be the one immediately after the release of the wildly popular movie *Close Encounters of the Third Kind*.)

"Oh, it's grassy, flat, a couple hundred feet across," I'd respond time and again. "Birds and small mammals and even some snakes live up there." But I felt slightly deceitful every time I recited the description because I'd never seen the top of Devils Tower with my own eyes. By late in the summer, I decided it was time to change that.

Fellow ranger Hollis Marriott, an expert rock climber, offered to lead me and another neophyte climber to the top of the tower. Until then I'd done absolutely no technical climbing. I'd never tried rappelling, either, but even off a modest cliff, but Hollis assured me I'd do fine. She proposed to lead us up the Durrance route, the easiest of several-dozen routes to the top of the tower. But *easiest* is a relative term, as I was reminded on that day.

I was in pretty respectable aerobic shape from running that summer, but my lack of specific climbing strength and skills required me to use far more energy than necessary. Climbing Devils Tower ended up being one of the toughest things I'd ever done, and also the scariest. My legs and arms shook almost uncontrollably at times from a combination of fear and fatigue. From the top—which indeed was grassy, flat, and a couple of hundred feet across—in order to get back down, I had to step off into a void, seeing nothing below me but air for some 500 feet down (the approximate height of a fifty-story building). The nothingness ended harshly in a jumble of rocks and boulders. I had to place great faith in the climbing rope, the carabiners, and my climb leader to do their jobs properly, which they all did.

To say I was happy to get back to horizontal ground is a world-class understatement. But after that I spoke with a new authority—and with a knowing twinkle in my eye, I'm sure—when asked, "What's it like on top?"

on July 4, 1893, using wooden pegs that he pounded into crevices in the rock face. More modern rock-climbing techniques were not employed to climb the tower until 1936, when Fritz Wiessner and other members of the American Alpine Club made the ascent.

Try to be at the tower around sunset for a spectacular sight, one that resists description. It simply must be seen to be believed.

Devils Tower National Monument is open year-round; however, the campground and visitor center are open on a seasonal basis. The campground is open from mid-April through early October, depending

Devils Tower

on the weather. The visitor center, which includes a bookstore, is open from 8:00 A.M. to 7:00 P.M. in the summer, from 8:30 A.M. to 4:30 P.M. in spring, and 9:00 A.M. to 5:00 P.M. in the fall; closed from late November through early April. Park entry costs $10.00 per vehicle; camping is $12.00 per night. Inquire at the visitor center about special programs and interpretive presentations. The center is located 10 miles south of Hulett on Highway 24, then west 3 miles on a paved park road. For information call 467–5283.

Crook County was named after the famous Indian fighter, Gen. George Crook. Another less-skilled and less-fortunate Indian fighter, Gen. George A. Custer, traveled through Crook County as he led the first government expedition searching for gold in the Black Hills of South Dakota and Wyoming. You can still make out remnants of Custer's exploratory trail, which was carved in July 1874 by a hundred wagons and a force of 1,000 troops, engineers, geologists, and miners crossing the terrain. For the most part the 1876 Black Hills gold rush was confined to the South Dakota side of the border, but a few abandoned glory holes are located in the Aladdin area of Wyoming. A Custer Expedition interpretive sign is found about 3 miles west of Aladdin on the south side of Highway 24.

The Black Hills of Wyoming deliver a treasure of a sort other than gold. The route along the Bear Lodge Mountains, as you wend between Devils Tower and Aladdin on Highway 24, dishes up a veritable mother lode of lofty sandstone cliffs, red hills, wildflower-filled meadows, creeks and ponds, and clusters of ponderosa pine, juniper, and scrub oak. Along the way you can picnic at the Bearlodge Campground west of Aladdin or at any of several other campgrounds in the Black Hills National Forest.

The name of the town of Aladdin, population 15, was taken from the character in *Arabian Nights* who rubbed the lamp and released two genies. The name was chosen by the California capitalist who laid out the town as a rail stop for the Burlington and Missouri Valley Railroad.

Although there may or may not be any genies here, Aladdin will cast a small-town spell on any visitor who chooses to spend an hour or two at the ***Aladdin General Store.*** In addition to serving the local area with groceries and hardware, the store operates as the post office and community center, where issues of the day are discussed. The general store also encompasses a little museum. The structure housing the Aladdin General Store was built by Bill Robinson in 1896 as a saloon, and today the building is listed on the National Register of Historic Places—as is a mine tipple from the late 1880s that's located 2½ miles east of town. It is one of the few remaining tipples in Wyoming.

In Aladdin's Antique Attic, which is part of the general store, you'll discover antique furniture, blankets, rugs, books, and Western art. So, grab a book and a refreshment and kick back on the front porch. The Aladdin General Store is open daily in summer Monday through Saturday from 8:00 A.M. until 7:00 P.M. and on Sunday from 9:00 A.M. to 6:00 P.M. For information call 896–2226 or visit www.aladdinwy.com.

The largest community in Crook County is Sundance, population 1,161. You can get to Sundance from Aladdin by following State Highway 111 south, then I–90 southwest; or, alternatively, by returning to Devils Tower Junction and driving southeast on U.S. Highway 114. The town boasts a number of attractions, including the ***Crook County Museum and Art Gallery,*** where you can see the original furniture from the courtroom where the Sundance Kid was tried and convicted of horse thieving. He had made the fateful mistake of stealing a slow horse. The misadventure cost the Kid, then known as Harry Longabough, eighteen months in jail.

The museum also displays cowboy gear, branding irons, a re-creation of a prehistoric buffalo jump, and Native American artifacts. The art gallery displays works by Crook County artists and photographers. Summer hours are 8:00 A.M. to 8:00 P.M., Monday through Friday. Off-season hours are 8:00 A.M. to 5:00 P.M., Monday through Friday. The museum and art gallery are located on the lower level of the Crook County Courthouse, at 309 Cleveland Street. For information call 283–3666.

The town sits below Sundance Mountain—whose Sioux name is *Wi Wacippi Paha,* meaning "Temple of the Sioux"—where Sioux Indians once performed sacred sun dances. The religious ceremony represented the triumph of good over evil and marked the beginning of life. The sun dance ritual lasted from several days to weeks, and many Native Americans traveled to *Wi Wacippi Paha* to take part in the ceremony.

Weston County

Newcastle, population 3,065, lies along the Cheyenne–Black Hills Stage Route, only 10 miles from the South Dakota border. The town, founded as a coal-mining and -shipping center, was named after the better-known Newcastle-upon-Tyne, the great English coal port. (Burlington Northern trains coming from the massive coal mines in the Thunder Basin rumble through Wyoming's version, demonstrating that you can at least haul coal through, if not to, Newcastle.)

One Newcastle attraction is actually outside of town, at the ghost town site of **Cambria.** Cambria once was a thriving Burlington and Missouri River Railroad coal town, with a population of 1,500 people comprising some two dozen nationalities. From the 1880s through 1928, Cambria supplied the nation with thirteen million tons of coal.

Three miles farther north at 23726 Highway 85 in Newcastle, you arrive at the **Flying V Cambria Inn** (746–2096 or w3.trib.com/~flyingv). Cambria's Flying V Casino opened in 1928, just months before the mines closed for good. It now houses a bed-and-breakfast and a restaurant in a beautiful, hilly setting. The Tudor castle-like structure is listed on the National Register of Historic Places. The restaurant specializes in Italian food, seafood, and steaks, and serves dinner only. It's open from June through December. Dinner and lodging prices are moderate.

Back in Newcastle the **Anna Miller Museum** features an abundant collection of material about, and artifacts from, the international melting pot of Cambria. The museum is housed in one of the last-constructed Army National Guard cavalry stables, built in the 1930s and now listed on the National Register of Historic Places. Here you can browse through collections of fossils, 1890 firefighting equipment, and various means of horse-drawn transportation, as well as through the country store and pioneer doctor's office. Outside you can visit the 1890–1930 Green Mountain Schoolhouse and the early 1900s Novak Miller Cabin. The museum is open year-round, Monday through Friday from 9:00 A.M. to 5:00 P.M. It's located at Delaware and Washington Park, off Highway 16. For information call 746–4188.

On the north side of Main Street, east of the railroad tracks, there's a sign marking the site of the hanging of Diamond L. Slim Clifton. Clifton was lynched in 1903 after the murder of his neighbors, Louella and John Church. An angry mob stormed the jail and took Clifton from the sheriff at gunpoint. He was hanged from the railroad bridge, which has since been removed.

For a bite to eat before leaving Weston County for Niobrara County, consider stopping at the ***Old Mill Inn,*** located at 500 West Main Street. As its name indicates, the structure once operated as the town flour mill. Hours are 5:00 A.M. to 10:00 P.M. daily. For information call 746–2711.

Places to Stay in Devils Tower– Buffalo Bill Country

BIG HORN

Bozeman Trail Bed & Breakfast,
304 Highway 335;
(307) 672–2381 or
(877) 672–2381

BUFFALO

Blue Gables Motel,
662 North Main Street;
(307) 684–2574 or
(800) 684–2574

Comfort Inn,
65 Highway 16 East;
(307) 684–9564 or
(800) 228–5150

EconoLodge,
333 Hart;
(307) 684–2219 or
(800) 55–ECONO

Wyoming Motel,
610 East Hart;
(307) 684–5505 or
(800) 666–5505

CODY

Best Western Sunset,
1601 Eighth Street;
(307) 587–4265

The Burl Inn,
1213 17th Street;
(307) 587–2084 or
(800) 388–2084

Econolodge Moose Creek Inn,
1015 Sheridan Avenue;
(307) 587–2221

Holiday Inn,
1701 Sheridan Avenue;
(307) 587–5555 or
(800) 527–5544

Skyline Motor Inn,
1919 17th Street;
(307) 587–4201 or
(800) 843–8809

GILLETTE

Arrowhead Motel,
202 Emerson;
(307) 686–0909

Clarion Inn,
2009 South Douglas Highway;
(307) 686–3000

Quality Inn,
1004 East Highway 14/16;
(307) 682–2616

GREYBULL

Greybull Motel,
300 North 6th Street;
(307) 765–2628

Yellowstone Motel,
247 Greybull Avenue;
(307) 765–4456

HYATTVILLE

Paintrock Inn (seasonal);
(307) 469–2335

KAYCEE

Cassidy Inn Motel,
346 Nolan Avenue;
(307) 738–2250

LOVELL

Super 8 Motel,
595 East Main;
(307) 548–2725

Western Motel (seasonal),
180 West Main;
(307) 548–2781

MEETEETSE

Oasis Motel,
1702 State Street;
(307) 868–2551

Vision Quest Motel,
2207 State Street;
(307) 868–2512

MOORCROFT

Cozy Motel,
219 West Converse;
(307) 756–3486

Moorcourt Motel,
420 North Yellowstone
Avenue;
(307) 756–3411

NEWCASTLE

Fountain Motor Inn,
2 Fountain Plaza;
(307) 746–4426 or
(800) 882–8858

Sundowner Inn,
451 West Main Street;
(307) 746–2796

POWELL

Best Western Kings Inn,
777 East 2nd Street;
(307) 754–5117

Park Motel,
737 East 2nd Street;
(307) 754–2233 or
(800) 506–7378

SHERIDAN

**Best Western Sheridan
Center Motor Inn,**
612 North Main Street;
(307) 674–7421 or
(800) 528–1234

Guest House Motel,
2007 North Main Street;
(307) 674–7496 or
(800) 226–9405

Mill Inn,
2161 Coffeen Avenue;
(307) 672–6401

SUNDANCE

Bear Lodge Motel,
218 Cleveland Street;
(307) 283–1611

Sundance Mountain Inn,
26 Highway 585;
(307) 283–3737

TEN SLEEP

Flagstaff Motel (seasonal);
(307) 366–2745

Log Cabin Motel;
(307) 366–2320

THERMOPOLIS

Coachman Inn,
112 Highway 20 South;
(307) 864–3141

Holiday Inn,
Hot Springs State Park;
(307) 864–3131 or
(800) HOLIDAY (465–4329)

Super 8 Hot Springs Motel,
166 Highway 20 South;
(307) 864–5515

WORLAND

Super 8,
2500 Big Horn Avenue;
(307) 347–9236

Town House Motor Inn,
119 North 10th;
(307) 347–2426

Places to Eat
in Devils Tower–
Buffalo Bill Country

BUFFALO

Dash Inn,
620 East Hart;
(307) 684–7930

Winchester Steak House,
117 Highway 16 East;
(307) 684–8636

CODY

Franca's Italian Dining
(3-star AAA),
1421 Rumsey Avenue;
(307) 587–5354

Irma Hotel & Restaurant,
1192 Sheridan Avenue;
(307) 587–4221

**Olive Glenn Golf
& Country Club**
(must golf to eat),
802 Meadow Lane;
(307) 587–5688

Royal Palace Restaurant,
103 Yellowstone Avenue;
(307) 587–5751

**Sarsaparillas Saloon–
Buffalo Bill Village,**
1701 Sheridan Avenue;
(307) 587–5544

GILLETTE

Granny's Kitchen,
West Highway 14–16;
(307) 687–1200

Mona's Cafe,
403 El Camino Drive;
(307) 686–6506

**Prime Rib Restaurant
& Wine Bar,**
1205 South Douglas
Highway;
(307) 682–2944

GREYBULL

Lisa's Fine Foods,
200 Greybull Avenue;
(307) 765–4765

MJ's Cafe,
333 North Second Street;
(307) 765–9228

HYATTVILLE

Paintrock Inn;
(307) 469–2335

KAYCEE

The Invasion;
(307) 738–2211

LOVELL

Big Horn Restaurant,
605 East Main;
(307) 548–6811

Scoop Drive-In,
384 West Main;
(307) 548–7514

MOORCROFT

Donna's Diner,
203 West Converse;
(307) 756–3422

NEWCASTLE

Old Mill Inn,
500 West Main Street;
(307) 746–2711

POWELL

Hansel and Gretel's,
113 South Bent;
(307) 754–2191

Skyline Cafe,
141 East Coulter;
(307) 754–8052

SHERIDAN

Oliver's Bar and Grill,
57 North Main Street;
(307) 672–2838

Silver Spur Cafe,
832 North Main Street;
(307) 673–7330

SUNDANCE

Aro Restaurant,
203 Cleveland Street;
(307) 283–2000

Higbee's Cafe,
101 North Third;
(307) 283–2165

Log Cabin Cafe,
1620 Cleveland Street;
(307) 283–3393

TEN SLEEP

Flagstaff Cafe;
(307) 366–2745

Mountain Man Cafe,
201 2nd Street;
(307) 366–2660

THERMOPOLIS

Ballyhoo Restaurant,
1025 Shoshoni Street;
(307) 864–9210

Holiday Inn,
Hot Springs State Park;
(307) 864–3131 or
(800) HOLIDAY (465–4329)

WORLAND

China Garden,
616 Big Horn Avenue;
(307) 347–6168

Central Wyoming: Oregon Trail– Rendezvous Country

The North Platte River and the towns lining its banks help define the eastern half of this region, where history was made by the tens of thousands of people who, often possessing little more than a dream of a better life, migrated west along the Oregon and Mormon Trails. A slightly later regional history involved the forts, fights, and treaties—and treaties broken—of the Indian wars.

From Lusk, U.S. Highway 18/20 will take you to I–25 and the North Platte River corridor. From the city of Casper, you'll head west through countryside inhabited by pronghorn antelope, cattle, an occasional natural gas well, and little else. The wide open begins closing in west of Riverton, where Lander and Dubois serve as major staging points for adventures in the mountains of the Shoshone and Bridger-Teton National Forests. There you can explore some of the wildest and most spectacular country the contiguous forty-eight states have to offer.

Niobrara County

Lusk, population 1,447, boomed after the cry of "Gold!" was heard in the nearby Black Hills in the late 1800s. A much later upward turn in the area economy was related to the post–World

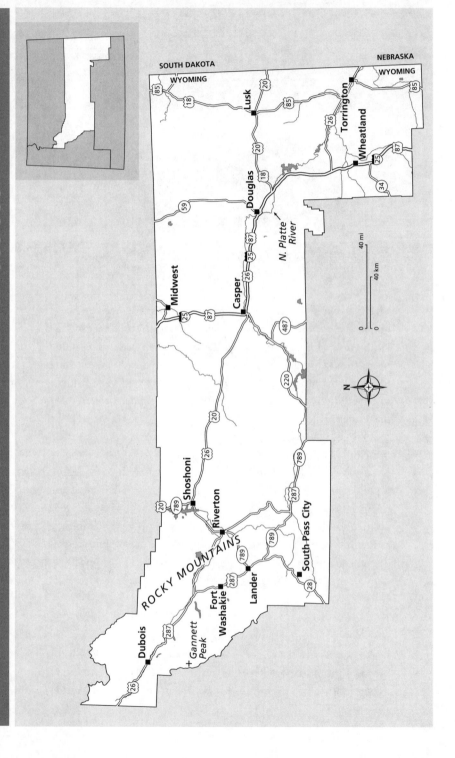

War II oil boom, which eventually went bust after the wells dried up. The town lies at the intersection of U.S. Highway 20, coming out of the east from Nebraska, and U.S. Highway 85, which more or less follows the historic route of the Cheyenne–Black Hills Stage and Express Line. A trip on this line tackled some 300 miles of rough roads and treacherous river crossings through Indian territory.

What better location, then, than Lusk to find the *Stagecoach Museum?* The museum occupies the former National Guard Armory, 322 South Main Street. The transportation section houses more than merely stagecoaches: a fine collection of covered wagons, for instance, including a dray wagon, Lusk's old street sprinkler, and early fire-fighting wagons. The centerpiece is a stagecoach used on the Cheyenne–Black Hills line. Built by Abbott & Downing of Concord, New Hampshire, in the 1860s, the coach features a leather brace suspension system that eliminated the need for metal springs. A similar stagecoach is exhibited at the Smithsonian Institution in Washington, D.C.

You can explore four pioneer rooms and an early doctor's office, stare at the always-popular two-headed calf mount, and inspect the front of an old store moved in from the Silver Cliff townsite. The volunteer-staffed museum is open May through October from 10:00 A.M. to 4:00 P.M., Monday through Friday. For more information call 334–2950.

BEST ATTRACTIONS IN OREGON TRAIL– RENDEZVOUS COUNTRY

Ayres Natural Bridge,
outside Douglas;
(307) 358–3532

**Club El Toro and
Svilar's Bar & Dining Room,**
Hudson;
(307) 332–4627 and 332–4516

Fort Fetterman,
outside Douglas;
(307) 358–2864

Hell's Half Acre,
west of Casper

**National Bighorn Sheep
Interpretive Center,**
Dubois;
(307) 455–3429

**National Historic Trails
Interpretive Center,**
Casper;
(307) 261–7700

Oregon Trail Ruts,
Guernsey;
(307) 777–6323

Sinks Canyon State Park,
Lander;
(307) 332–6333

South Pass City State Historic Site;
(307) 332–3684

Willie Handcart Company site,
south of Atlantic City;
(307) 775–6256

Several miles east of Lusk on Highway 20, you'll find a restored **Redwood Water Tower,** one of only a few still standing in the country. The Fremont, Elkhorn and Missouri Valley Railroad built the tower in 1886 to supply water for its steam engines. When the railroad tracks reached Lusk on July 13, 1886, a gold spike was driven with a silver hammer to commemorate the occasion. A little farther east from the water tower, you can locate a **Texas Trails Marker,** honoring the cowboys who drove thousands of head of cattle from Texas to Montana between 1876 and 1897.

Approximately 13 miles north of Lusk on Highway 18/85, the **Fort Hat Creek** interpretive sign marks the 1875 establishment of an outpost by soldiers from Fort Laramie. Ironically, the soldiers weren't where they thought they were: They located the fort on Sage Creek in Wyoming rather than Hat Creek in Nebraska. The **Hat Creek Monument** and the old fort site are located on private land 2 miles east on a county road, then southwest 1 mile on gravel. (The marker and log building used as a stage station can readily be seen from the road, so please respect the rights of the property owner.)

central wyomingtrivia

One of the first dinosaur fossils discovered in America, a *Triceratops,* or three-horned dinosaur, was found along Lance Creek in Niobrara County.

Fort Hat Creek played a prominent role in the surrender of Crazy Horse. The Sioux warrior sent a messenger to Hat Creek on May 1, 1877, announcing his intention to surrender. The message was then telegraphed to Fort Robinson, in Nebraska. On May 6, Crazy Horse rode up to the Red Cloud Agency, shook hands with General Crook's emissary, and smoked the peace pipe, thus concluding the Great Sioux War. Four months later at Fort Robinson, a military guard bayoneted Crazy Horse in the back, and he died shortly afterward.

A unique Western character, **Mother Featherlegs Shepard,** earned her name and reputation by riding herd on her cattle with her red pantaloons flapping in the breeze like feathers. The roadhouse madam on the Cheyenne–Black Hills Stage Line was murdered by "Dangerous" Dick Davis in 1879. A monument to Mother Featherlegs is located 10 miles southwest of Lusk. Access to the site is by way of a dirt road located just south of the rest area on U.S. Highway 85.

Two architecturally notable buildings that you can't miss in Lusk are the 1919 **Niobrara County Courthouse** and the 1919 Renaissance-Italianate **Niobrara County Library,** the last Carnegie Library in Wyoming still serving its intended purpose. The dilapidated **Yellow Hotel** south of the Chicago

BEST ANNUAL EVENTS IN OREGON TRAIL– RENDEZVOUS COUNTRY

Wild West Winter Carnival,
Riverton; late January/early February;
(307) 856–4801

Wyoming State Winter Fair,
Lander; March;
(307) 332–3892

Chugwater Chili Cook-off,
Chugwater; June;
(800) 972–4454

Jackalope Days & Invitational Arts Show,
Douglas; June;
(307) 358–2950

Frontier Fourth of July,
Fort Laramie;
(307) 837–2221

Balloon Rally,
Riverton; July;
(307) 856–4801

Beartrap Music Festival,
Casper; July;
(307) 266–5252

The Legend of Rawhide,
Lusk; July;
(800) 223–LUSK (5875) or
(307) 334–2950

Gold Rush Days,
South Pass City; late July;
(307) 332–3684

Deer Creek Days,
Glenrock; early August;
(307) 436–9294

Wyoming State Fair,
Douglas; August;
(307) 358–2398

Whiskey Mountain Buckskinners Rendezvous,
Dubois; August;
(307) 455–2556

Cowboy Poetry Gathering
Riverton; September;
(307) 856–4801

2 Shot Goose Hunt,
Torrington; December;
(307) 532–7515 or 532–1638.

Northwestern Railroad Depot has known better days, like when owner Madame Del Burke ran a successful brothel at the hotel. Lusk reportedly owes its early water and electrical systems to her generosity (she apparently financed many of the city bonds for those services).

The annual *Legend of Rawhide* pageant takes place in Lusk in early July. This celebration of Wyoming's Wild West has been continually polished and perfected for nearly half a century. The grisly sounding story revolves around a white man who kills an Indian maiden and is subsequently skinned alive by vengeful Indians. Festivities include two live performances, with a cast of 200, as well as a country-western music concert and barbecue, an art show, a parade, and outdoor pancake breakfasts. For information and dates call (800) 223–LUSK (5875).

Little Wonder He Became a Legend

By the time he reached his twenty-first birthday, years before beginning his celebrated Wild West Show, William F. Cody had done things that most men, even of his day, only dream about. Born near LeClaire in Scott County, Iowa, on February 26, 1846, young Cody moved to the Salt Creek Valley of Kansas with his family. At age eleven he began working as an ox-team driver. In 1859, when he was thirteen, Cody went west to Pikes Peak, Colorado, joining hundreds of older men in the search for gold. Then, in 1860 he became one of the youngest of the Pony Express riders, serving a stint during which he earned quite a reputation, exhausting twenty horses as he accomplished a stretch of 322 miles in twenty-one hours and forty minutes.

At fifteen years of age, still employed by Russell, Majors, and Waddell (proprietors of the short-lived Pony Express) as an assistant wagonmaster, Cody drove a bull train to the Wyoming Territory. After arriving at Fort Laramie, he briefly joined a group of trappers working in the Chugwater River country. During the Civil War he served the Union as a scout in Missouri and along the Santa Fe Trail. Then, in March 1866 Cody married Louisa Federici and tried his hand at domestic living; together the couple managed the Golden Rule Boarding House in Salt Creek Valley.

In 1867, the year Cody turned twenty-one, he was hired by the Goddard brothers to kill buffalo to provide meat for workers on the Kansas Pacific Railroad. During one eight-month period, he reportedly killed 4,280 of the easy-to-shoot beasts, and acquired the nickname "Buffalo Bill" after winning a bison-killing contest with another Bill—Bill Comstock.

Goshen County

The Oregon, Mormon, and California Trails all played a part in Goshen County history. Fort Laramie, a resting and replenishing place for weary emigrants, was also an important stop on the Pony Express route and the Cheyenne–Black Hills Stage Line. But before visiting Fort Laramie, stop in at Torrington, located 57 miles southeast of Lusk on U.S. Highway 85, only 8 miles from the Nebraska border.

Torrington's **Homesteader's Museum** features a Cheyenne–Black Hills stagecoach that was cheered by thousands attending Buffalo Bill's Wild West Show after the turn of the century. The museum is located in the 1926 Union Pacific Depot just south of town, across the road from Torrington's largest employer, the Holly Sugar factory. The depot is a rather ornate structure designed by the noted architectural firm Gilbert Stanley Underwood. Inside you'll find materials from the 4A Ranch, historic photographs of the area, and information and artifacts relating to Wyoming homesteaders. The museum is open from 9:30 A.M. to 4:00 P.M. Monday through Wednesday, 9:30 A.M. to 7:00

P.M. on Thursday and Friday, noon to 6:00 P.M. on Saturday, and noon to 4:00 P.M. on Sunday. Call 532–5666 for information.

Twenty-two miles south of Torrington just off U.S. Highway 85, you'll find a pleasant park known as ***Hawk Springs State Recreation Area.*** The park provides excellent fishing and picnic facilities, but the real draw is the blue heron rookery found at the site. With some time and patience you might spot blue herons, great horned owls, wood ducks, a variety of teal, and a host of other birds. Be sure to bring along a pair of binoculars. Camping fees are just a few dollars per vehicle per night. For information contact the Hawk Springs State Recreation Area at 836–2334.

Traveling west on Highway 26, you'll come to the town of Lingle, situated within 2 miles of the August 19, 1854, ***Grattan Massacre.*** It was the first major confrontation on the Great Plains between U.S. troops and Native Americans. The incident started when Lt. John Grattan went to a Sioux village to arrest a tribal member for killing a steer. A shot was fired, panic ensued, and Grattan and his twenty-eight men were killed. The massacre sparked the tragic Plains Indian Wars and the eventual removal of tribes to reservations in the late 1800s.

Fort Laramie National Historic Site is excellent, complete with many original buildings, interpretive programs, and fort tours. Top-notch facilities notwithstanding, the site retains "off the beaten path" status owing to its location. Fort Laramie is open year-round, but it's in summer that the place really fires up, when park rangers dress in period costumes and transform themselves into the characters that made Fort Laramie such a vibrant part of the story of western expansion, from 1841 until the end of the Indian Wars in 1890.

It began in 1834, when William Sublette erected a trading post at a nearby site. Sublette sold his Fort William in 1836 to the American Fur Company, which later rebuilt the fort a mile up the Laramie River at the eventual site of Fort Laramie. The government purchased the fort in 1841.

There's plenty of history to be absorbed at Fort Laramie today, along with the possibility of encountering a ghost or two inhabiting certain post buildings. Ask your guide to elaborate. ***Old Bedlam,*** located within the fort near the west end of the parade grounds, is the oldest remaining structure in Wyoming. Built in 1849, through the years it served as post headquarters, officers' quarters, and

Fort Laramie

Fort Laramie

Without a doubt Fort Laramie is a must-see for anyone traveling through the region, just as it was for travelers in the mid- to late 1800s. The fort was a gathering spot for Native Americans, trappers, traders, gold seekers, Pony Express riders, and emigrants. By the time Oregon Trail travelers reached Fort Laramie, they had journeyed 650 miles since leaving Independence, Missouri, and they still had some 1,200 miles to go through the deserts and mountains stretching westward before them. Six-mule-team wagons were their preferred method of locomotion, but oxen were often substituted for mules because they were less expensive. A six-mule team commanded around $600, whereas eight oxen could be purchased for around $200. Emigrants typically spent between $800 to $1,200 to properly outfit themselves for the journey.

The dangers were many, such as those recorded by one emigrant:

"We passed Fort Laramie yesterday and obtained several little articles needed in camp. At this camp, an emigrant, who, with his wife, was travelling with another family, murdered the other man and his wife. He then took possession of the man's team and provisions and he and his wife started the return trip to the Missouri River, reporting that they had become discouraged and would go no further. Within a day, the dead bodies of the murdered couple were discovered and the officers at Fort Laramie notified. We heard that they were apprehended, tried at Fort Laramie at the charge of murder, convicted and hanged. We did not learn their names."

living quarters for other post residents. Additional original structures worthy of touring include the bakery, cavalry barracks, commissary, guardhouse, officers' houses, powder magazine, and surgeon's quarters. The visitor center at Fort Laramie is open from 8:00 A.M. to 4:30 P.M. daily year-round (with extended hours in summer), except Thanksgiving, Christmas, and New Year's Day. The fort grounds are open until dusk every day of the year. Fort Laramie National Historic Site is located 3 miles southwest of the town of Fort Laramie off Highway 26. For more information call 837–2221 or visit www.nps.gov/fola.

Platte County

Following U.S. Highway 26 west into Platte County, you'll cross the North Platte River at Guernsey, population 1,147. But before you do that, enjoy a pleasant side trip to the almost ghost towns of *Hartville* and *Sunrise* by turning north about 1 mile east of Guernsey onto State Highway 270. The road winds amid a series of red gorges, rolling rangelands, and pine- and juniper-studded hills. Four miles north along the way is picturesque Hartville, Wyoming's oldest incorporated town still going (even if not going strong). The Hartville Uplift contains one of Wyoming's richest mineral deposits, and prospectors searching for gold, silver, copper, and other minerals in the Eureka Canyon area settled Hartville in the 1870s. After the copper deposits played out in the late 1880s, an iron deposit discovered near the future site of Sunrise kept things moving along. Sunrise was incorporated in 1900, by which time it was a thriving "city" with a population of 750 and, among other amenities, an opera house.

If you're in town any time from May through October, stop in at the **Old Miners' Bar,** the state's oldest house of libation, for a gander at one of the grander back bars ever to inhabit a Wyoming tavern. Crafted in Germany in 1864, it traveled the final miles of its long journey to Hartville by wagon in 1881. The old stone buildings (in particular, the town jail) with their false fronts provide great backdrops for photos. Ask a local for directions to the boothill cemetery, where you're bound to dig up (not literally!) some interesting tidbits of lore.

Sunrise, located a mile east of Hartville on Highway 318, has its own allure. The Colorado Fuel and Iron Corporation employed some 700 workers here at its Chicago Mine, known as Glory Hole. One of the nation's largest open-pit iron ore mines, it has been idle since 1980. Still, you can garner an understanding of the scope of the mining activity that went on here for decades. A few brick houses and the YMCA remain standing in Sunrise.

The Guernsey area offers a lot to history buffs and outdoor enthusiasts. A short drive from town leads to two vivid reminders of days gone by: the **Oregon Trail Ruts** and **Register Cliff.** The cumulative effect of thousands of wagons traversing relatively soft sandstone outcroppings resulted in wagon wheel ruts between 2 to 6 feet deep. The grinding action of wheels rolling across sandstone was exacerbated by the ponderous hooves of countless mules and oxen, wearing away the rock above the banks of the North Platte. Today the deep ruts serve as a profound connection to one of the largest human migrations the world has known. The ruts and associated interpretive signs are located ½ mile southeast of Guernsey, off Highway 26. Simply follow the signs.

Emigrants also carved their names into Register Cliff, located 2 miles southeast of Guernsey. The earliest names date back to 1829. For information on both the Oregon Trail Ruts and Register Cliff, contact Wyoming State Parks and Cultural Resources in Cheyenne, 777–6323.

Guernsey was named after Charles Guernsey, an area rancher, legislator, and early promoter of the Guernsey Dam and Reservoir. He also wrote the popular book *Wyoming Cowboy Days*. **Guernsey State Park** provides ample recreational opportunities and camping facilities. The park encompasses more than 6,200 acres of land and nearly 2,400 acres of water. It features 142 campsites and three day-use areas. The tall bluffs and warm waters make it a favorite

Oregon Trail ruts near Guernsey

with day-trippers and overnight campers alike. The park also features a 6.2-mile **Volksmarch** route, which follows a scenic trail at an elevation of around 4,500 feet, overlooking the dam, reservoir, and down-slope countryside. The trail's difficulty is rated 4.0 on a 5.0-point scale, meaning it's a pretty darn demanding stroll. For more park information call 836–2334.

In the 1930s the Civilian Conservation Corps (CCC) built a number of rock-and-log structures in the state park, and they also constructed much of the park's road system. The young men dubbed one section of road "Mae West Drive" because of its beautiful curves. One of the most impressive rock buildings built by the CCC houses the **Guernsey State Park Museum.** Its large arched rock entrance, native flagstone floors, hand-hewn roof timbers, and wrought-iron fixtures reflect the quality craftsmanship typical of CCC works. The exhibits, which also were fashioned in the 1930s, illustrate the ways in which humans through the ages have adapted and related to the area's natural environment. Museum hours are 10:00 A.M. to 6:00 P.M., seven days a week, May 1 through October 1. For information call 836–2900.

For an uncommonly pleasant drive, weather and time of year permitting, from Guernsey follow the paved road marked Greyrocks Road or Power Plant Road. En route to Wheatland the road traverses some captivating countryside and also wends past the **Greyrocks Reservoir.**

For a restful night make reservations at **The Blackbird Inn** in Wheatland, population 3,548. The 1910 Victorian B&B, operated by April Smith, displays many antique furnishings. Each room suggests a theme, from "Alaska" and "Whale" to "Wyoming." You'll have the opportunity to savor a sit on the inn's front porch, with its swing and wicker furniture, as the brilliant Wyoming sun goes down. Don't think too much about the next morning's breakfast, or you might not get that much sleep after all: fried eggs and spuds, fresh fruit, bagels, muffins, juice, sausage and bacon, hot coffee . . . for openers. The inn is located at 1101 11th Street. Rates range from $65 to $150. For reservations call 322–4540 or visit www.blackbirdinn.com.

According to legend the name of the town of Chugwater (population 192) derives from the racket stampeding buffalo made as they splashed into the water after being driven off nearby bluffs by Native Americans. The Swan Land and Cattle Company called Chugwater its headquarters, even though most of the company's stockholders called Scotland home. It was among the last and most famous of the great ranch spreads of the 1880s. At one time more than 113,000 head of cattle grazed on the company's land. The brutal winter of 1886–87 killed off many of the enterprise's cattle, but the company reorganized and managed to stay in business another fifty years. After the turn of the century, however, the legendary cattle company switched to sheep.

Chugwater is home to another well-known ranch—the **_Diamond Guest Ranch, Inc._**—where weary travelers can spend a day or a week and experience ranch life as it was and is. The ranch was founded by horse breeder George R. Rainsford in 1880; four generations later, it continues as a working ranch, with many of the original buildings still in use. From the ranch proper you can head out on a trail ride, cast for fish while standing in the shade of a broad cottonwood, or just plain old relax. The Diamond Guest Ranch has it all—with good food, to boot. Additional activities and facilities include a Saturday night dance, hayrides, a swimming pool, breakfast cookouts, and horseshoe pits. The Diamond Guest Ranch is open to the public from Memorial Day to Labor Day. You can book a deluxe or ranch room in the historic 1878 ranch house, or camp at one of the many campsites with or without water and electrical hookups. Rooms run from $55 to $75 per night; RV hookups are $20 per night. The ranch is located 14 miles west of Chugwater on Diamond Road. For more information and reservations, call 422–3564 or (800) 932–4222, or on the Internet visit www.diamondgr.com.

central wyomingtrivia

Spanish Diggings is an area of roughly 10 miles by 40 miles located southwest of Lusk. Here prehistoric peoples dug deep holes into high-quality quartzite to acquire the raw materials for fabricating stone tools. The site was named by cowboy A. A. Spaugh, who came across it in 1879 and incorrectly surmised that Spaniards had dug the holes while searching for gold.

On the way out of town, stop on Main Street and treat yourself at the **_Chugwater Soda Fountain,_** one of the oldest fountains in Wyoming, and the purveyor of some truly outstanding ice-cream treats.

Unfortunately, it's now time to tackle a stretch of I–25. Head north for the last stop in Platte County, the town of Glendo, which occupies the site of the

1861 Horseshoe Stage Station of the Hockaday-Ligget Stage Line. John "Portugee" Phillips and Daniel Dixon stopped at the station on their long ride for help through fierce cold from Fort Phil Kearny to Fort Laramie after the Fetterman Massacre in December 1866. Phillips continued on alone from this point. But a westerner who was to become much better known, Buffalo Bill Cody, rode for the Pony Express as a teenager out of the same spot.

The major attraction at Glendo today is the **Glendo State Park,** with its 12,500 acres of remarkably clear reservoir waters, offering fishing, waterskiing, sailing, and power boating. From a pine-shrouded campsite, you can watch the sunlight play off 10,272-foot Laramie Peak in the Medicine Bow National Forest to the southwest. A small buffalo herd grazes near the south side of the reservoir. For park and campsite information, call 735–4433.

Converse County

There's no con in Converse County unless, of course, you consider the jackalope. Long a source of speculation and heated debate, the legendary critter calls Converse County his headquarters. In fact Douglas is the self-proclaimed **Jackalope Capital of the World,** as evidenced by the giant statue of the beast in the middle of town at Jackalope Square. Obviously, Douglas stands at least a hare above other would-be contenders for the honor.

The **Wyoming Pioneer Memorial Museum,** on the Wyoming State Fairgrounds in Douglas, has a great display of venerable saddles. Also on exhibit are the original bar (crafted by Brunswick in England in 1914) from the LaBonte Inn, guns and memorabilia from the infamous Johnson County War, Native American clothing and decorative arts, and a collection of Western art. The free-to-enter museum is open year-round, Monday through Friday from 8:00 A.M. to 5:00 P.M. and, in summer only, on Saturday from 1:00 to 5:00 P.M. For information call 358–9288.

Thirty-two miles south of Douglas on Highway 94, you'll stumble across Esterbrook, a copper-mining town established in 1886 but soon thereafter relegated to has-been status. The main attraction remaining is a rustic log church, the **Esterbrook Chapel,** which is still used for weddings and other special events. Laramie Peak towers above the town, providing a truly inspirational backdrop for the newlyweds. Serious hikers will find the climb up **Laramie Peak** only moderately difficult: a little more than 5 miles and 2,500 feet in elevation gain up a well-maintained, switchbacking trail used by about equal numbers of hikers, joggers, and growling dirt bikers. The trail was built in the 1960s to provide access to radio towers at the top, which, if you're not prepared for it, can seem a little industrial because of the towers and metal buildings. Still,

The Jackalope

Scientifically known as *Pegirus lepuslopus* ineptus, the jackalope's lightning-like speed is partly to blame for the legions who doubt its existence. But for clear evidence, one has only to view the large ruts in the earthscape just south of Douglas to see where today's jackalope's ancient ancestors, the dynalopes and jackasaurs, roamed.

Today's jackalope, a direct descendent of those earlier models, is known after dark to sometimes mimic the singing and yodeling of lone cowboys. Contrary to myth, however, they do not sing in harmony with one another. Although you likely won't spot a jackalope, primarily because of their great speed and intense dislike of humans (unless you spend several days out on the lonesome prairie), you will undoubtedly see their droppings in many places. The pellets appear much like those of a rabbit, only about half again as large. A good jackalope mount is a trophy without equal. Many authorities have argued that the animal is misnamed, and that it should be known as the jackadeer. Its antlers are much more like the antlers of a deer than they are like the horns of a pronghorn antelope; moreover, like a deer, they shed their antlers annually (pronghorns don't shed their horns).

When its comes down to it, you can say just about anything you want about the jackalope and dare others to prove you wrong.

from 10,272 feet the views are splendid. On a clear day you can easily see 100 miles in every direction—southwest to Elk Mountain and the Snowy Range; north to Pumpkin Buttes in Campbell County; and southeast to the coal-fired power plant outside Wheatland. The big blue cone of Laramie Peak was the first real Rocky Mountain the early emigrants saw as they came west up the Oregon Trail. The Laramie Peak hiking trail takes off from the Friend Park campground southwest of Esterbrook; you might choose to camp at the campground and climb the mountain the next day. Call the Douglas Ranger Station of the Medicine Bow National Forest, 358–4690, for directions or a map.

Take Highway 93 for 11 miles northwest out of Douglas to reach ***Fort Fetterman,*** named after Lt. Col. William J. Fetterman, killed by Indians in 1866 near Fort Kearny in the fight that became known as the Fetterman Massacre. Fort Fetterman was built in 1867 to supply troops engaged in subduing Indian uprisings. A major named Dye, who was assigned to build the fort, wrote that the post was "situated on a plateau . . . above the valley of the Platte, being neither so low as to be seriously affected by the rains or snow; nor so high and unprotected as to suffer from the winter winds."

Dye sorely underestimated the potency of Wyoming winds and winters, and difficult work under brutal weather conditions earned the fort the reputation as a "hardship post" by the men stationed there. After the Treaty of 1868, Forts Reno, Phil Kearny, and C. F. Smith were abandoned, leaving Fort Fetterman as the lone army outpost in or near the disputed Indian territory. The fort was abandoned in 1882 after the Native Americans were moved to reservations and no longer posed a threat to travelers and settlers.

The restored Officer's Quarters house a museum interpreting the fort's history. Living history programs are presented during the summer season, which runs from Memorial Day through Labor Day. Visitor center hours are from 9:00 A.M. to 5:00 P.M. daily, while the grounds are open from sunrise to sunset. For information call 684–7629.

Few people, it seems, other than in-the-know locals, find their way to the peaceful sanctuary of *Ayres Natural Bridge.* LaPrele Creek flows under a rock bridge 50 feet high and 150 feet long, formed by eons of erosion. Be careful; the soothing sound of the flowing water can cast a hypnotic spell, and you may inadvertently spend hours at the site. Adding to the natural beauty, the bridge is framed by sheer red sandstone walls, lending the entire scene an amphitheater effect. Elm and cottonwood trees provide shade and put the finishing touches on the picturesque scene.

Meandering LaPrele Creek carved the bridge. Originally, the creek swung a wide loop well to the east of where it runs now. As the creek continued to run through hundreds of millennia, however, it cut more and more deeply into the sandstone before and after flowing through the loop. Finally, the sandstone wall was undercut so much by the water running against it on both sides that the creek took a shortcut right through the rock, abandoning the longer loop but leaving a "bridge" over the shortcut where the river continues to flow today. While many other natural bridges exist around the world, Ayres Natural Bridge is one of few with water still flowing underneath.

To reach the park, follow I–25 for 11 miles northwest of Douglas to exit 151. The bridge is located 4 miles south from there, at the end of County Road 13. The surrounding park is open April 1 through October 31 from 8:00 A.M. to 8:00 P.M. Overnight camping, not to exceed three consecutive nights, is permitted. Note: Pets aren't allowed, and there is no potable water at the site. For information call 358–3532.

With your arrival at Glenrock, population 2,231, you are in oil country, as evidenced by the pumpers on the outskirts of town. Oil was first discovered around 1916, whereupon the town quickly swelled to more than 5,000 residents. A second major strike in 1949 brought another round of prosperity. Today the town's economic viability hinges on another energy source: the Dave Johnston Power Plant, located 6 miles east.

Bridging the Past

Ayres Natural Bridge is one of Wyoming's unspoiled treasures. It's no wonder that emigrants found the site so refreshing. One wrote about his visit:

"Today we camped near the natural bridge and laid by to wash and rest our cattle. We noticed it had become general for the stock to begin to suffer and lag with the increasing roughness of the country. It is more noticeable among the horses than with the cattle. We saw several bands of buffalo today but got no meat. Grass is scarce and seems to be getting more and more scarce the further we go, having been used up by those ahead of us."

Pioneer travelers to the bridge included Robert Stuart in 1812 and Capt. Benjamin Bonneville in 1832. Other early trappers and prospectors plied the lower LaPrele Creek area for fur and gold. A number of subsequent emigrants left marks, carving their names or initials into the red sandstone cliff walls. By 1851 Mormons traversing the emigrant trails had established abundant gardens in the valley with the help of irrigation ditches. Large storehouses preserved surpluses to be shared with other Saints on the westward march to Utah.

Not all area inhabitants found the natural bridge inviting. Ancient Native American stories tell of an evil spirit, the King of Beasts, who was thought to live beneath the bridge. According to legend, a hunting party sought shelter under the arch of the bridge during a terrifying thunderstorm. A lightning bolt struck and killed one of the men. The others fled in terror, later telling their chief how the hills had opened up and the King of Beasts emerged with long, daggerlike teeth and flashing eyes to swallow the young man's life.

In 1881 Alva Ayres, a freighter and bullwhacker, purchased the property encompassing the bridge and used it as headquarters for his shipping business. Two years after his death in 1918, his heirs donated the bridge and fifteen acres of land to Converse County for a park surrounding Ayres Natural Bridge.

Kit Carson guided John C. Fremont's first expedition to the West past the site in 1842. The name Glenrock came about as a pragmatic reference to the large rock resting in the glen at the edge of the townsite. A few of the estimated 350,000 Oregon Trail emigrants who passed by carved their names and the dates into the ***Rock in the Glen.*** It's located in the park on the south side of U.S. Highway 20/87, at the west end of Glenrock. The ***Deer Creek Station*** was built in the 1850s and served as an important stop on the Overland Stage and Pony Express routes and the emigrant trails. Native Americans torched the station in 1866; today all you'll find is a Deer Creek Station historical marker at Fourth and Cedar Streets in Glenrock.

A narrow gorge located a few miles west of present-day Casper forced emigrants traveling on the south bank of the North Platte River to cross to the other side. Often because of the sheer number of people and wagons it took several days to be ferried safely across the river. Some of the more impatient tried to swim across and didn't make it.

An entrepreneur named John Richard (pronounced *re shaw*), along with four other French traders, built the first bridge to span the North Platte River, just above the mouth of Deer Creek, northwest of Glenrock near the eastern edge of present-day Casper, Richard and his partners expected huge profits, but their dreams, along with the wooden toll bridge, were washed down the river during the spring floods of 1852.

central wyomingtrivia

The first commercial ferry operation in the Rocky Mountain West was established in 1847 on the North Platte River near the future site of Casper by Mormon leader Brigham Young.

Plenty of Wyomingites don't even know about the **Paisley Shawl/Hotel Higgins,** located at 416 Birch Street in Glenrock. Reopened in 1980, the restaurant elegantly serves a select and scrumptious menu. Prices are moderate-to-expensive, but worth it. (The restaurant's name relates to a circa 1865 family heirloom shawl made in Paisley, Scotland.) Hours are generally Tuesday through Saturday, 11:00 A.M. to 2:00 P.M. and 6:00 to 9:00 P.M. Call 436–9212 for seasonal hours and menu changes. (The bar is also open Sunday and Monday, but no food is served.)

Hotel Higgins was built in 1916 and reputed to be the "Finest Hotel North of Denver." It is listed on the National Register of Historic Places. The original terrazzo tile remains throughout. In its early days, the hotel hosted celebrated folks like William Jennings Bryan and Governor Robert Carey. The current owner, Beverly Doll, has restored the rooms to their 1900 appearance, and Hotel Higgins now operates as a bed-and-breakfast inn, serving a full champagne breakfast in the enclosed porch area. Each room is uniquely decorated and appointed with a brass, iron, or carved-wood bed. Adjoining rooms are available for families. Rates are $60 for a double and $70 for a suite. For hotel and restaurant information or reservations, call 436–9212 or visit www.hotel higgins.com.

Natrona County

Take the Old Glenrock Highway (U.S. Highway 20/26) west out of Glenrock, avoiding the humdrum and bustle of I–80, and soon you'll pass the entrance to

Edness Kimball Wilkins State Park (located just east of Hat Six Road). Nestled alongside the North Platte River, the park's 315 cottonwood-filled acres provide a shady oasis perfect for an afternoon picnic. You can walk along the tree-lined trails or wade in the swimming pond. Bring your binoculars; there's an abundance of birds and wildlife to observe along the North Platte. Rainbow, brown, and cutthroat trout and channel catfish can be fished in the river here, also. (For more information on fishing in the Platte/Powder drainages, contact Wyoming Game and Fish at 777–4600 or http://gf.state.wy.us.)

Continuing on Highway 20/26 you arrive at Wyoming's oil capital, the great city of Casper. Casper grew up along the banks of the North Platte River, and there it remains. A good way to begin your visit to Casper is to head to the top of the hill north of town, just off I–25, to the resplendent, new ***National Historic Trails Interpretive Center.*** It's a museum operated by the Bureau of Land Management and dedicated to the Oregon, California, and Mormon trails and the Pony Express National Historic Trail. All four trails followed essentially the same route as far as the Continental Divide, and the trails crossed the North Platte at what's now Casper. The museum, at 1501 North Poplar Street, near the red-roofed Casper Events Center, commands a grand view of Casper, Casper Mountain, and the North Platte River. Exhibits use the latest technologies to tell the emigrants' and the express riders' dramatic stories—don't miss the virtual river crossing in a covered wagon or the drafts of cold air around the struggling Martin Handcart Company. The center is open from 8:00 A.M. to 7:00 P.M. daily from April 1 through November 1; in the winter it's open Tuesday through Saturday from 9:00 A.M. to 4:30 P.M. Admission is $6.00 for adults, less for seniors, students, and children; for more information call 261–7700 or go to www.wy.blm.gov/nhtic.

History buffs also won't want to miss ***Fort Caspar,*** at 4001 Fort Caspar Road, near where Wyoming Boulevard now crosses the North Platte River. The fort originally began as a trading post in 1859; in 1861 a company of volunteer cavalry began guarding the post and the bridge nearby, which together became known as Platte Bridge Station. On July 26, 1865, Lt. Caspar Collins and a small detachment, sent to escort a military wagon train, were attacked while crossing the bridge. Collins and four of his twenty men were killed. The three-wagon military train that Collins' detachment was sent to protect was also attacked and destroyed by a party of Arapaho, Cheyenne, and Sioux warriors. After four hours of fighting, twenty-two soldiers lay dead at what become known as the Battle of Red Buttes. You'll see a ***Red Buttes Battle Marker*** located on the north side of Highway 220 at a paved turnout about ½ mile west of Robertson Road. In tribute to Collins, the government officially changed the post's name from Platte Bridge Station to Fort Caspar. (His surname had already been

Beyond Jackson Hole

Just about any skier in the United States can tell you that the Jackson Hole Mountain Resort is located in Wyoming. The somewhat more informed will also know that Grand Targhee Resort is likewise situated in the Cowboy State. Other than that pair of Teton Range ski areas, however, few out-of-staters can name even one additional Wyoming ski area.

Surprisingly, nine additional ski areas, most of them small and family oriented, lie hidden high in the hills and mountains of Wyoming. Here's a list of all eleven, along with the vital stats.

Antelope Butte,
east of Lovell; December to April;
Vertical Drop: 1,000';
(307) 655–9530

Big Horn,
east of Ten Sleep; late November
to April;
Vertical Drop: 800';
(307) 366–2600

Grand Targhee,
Alta; mid-November to April;
Vertical Drop: 2,000';
(307) 353–2300

Hogadon,
Casper Mountain; Thanksgiving
to Easter;
Vertical Drop: 600';
Also has several kilometers of
groomed cross-country trails, some
lighted for night skiing;
(307) 235–8499

Jackson Hole,
Teton Village; December to April;
Vertical Drop: 4,139';
(307) 733–2292

Pine Creek,
east of Cokeville; mid-December
to April;
Vertical Drop: 1,200';
(307) 279–3201

Sleeping Giant,
west of Cody; December to April;
Vertical Drop: 1,200';
(307) 587–4044

Snow King,
Jackson; December to April;
Vertical Drop: 1,571';
(307) 733–5200

Snowshoe Hollow,
Afton; Saturday/holidays;
Small hill with rope tow only;
(307) 886–9831

Snowy Range,
Centennial; December to April;
Vertical Drop: 1,400';
(307) 745–5750

White Pine,
Pinedale; December to April;
Vertical Drop: 1,100';
Also has great cross-country trails;
(307) 367–6606

employed to name Fort Collins, Colorado.) Two years later the government abandoned the fort.

In 1936 the Works Progress Administration (WPA) reconstructed a number of the log buildings, using sketches made by Collins in 1863. An interpretive center/museum opened in 1983. The fort's buildings are open from May 1 through October 1, and closed for the winter. From mid-May through August 31, the museum is open from 8:00 A.M. to 7:00 P.M. Monday through Saturday, and noon to 7:00 P.M. on Sunday. In September, the museum closes at 5:00 P.M. every day. From October 1 through mid-May, you'll find the museum open 8:00 A.M. to 5:00 P.M. Monday through Friday, closed Saturday, and open Sunday from 1:00 to 4:00 P.M. For information on hours, summer festivals, or historic reenactments, call 235–8462.

The *Crimson Dawn Museum* preserves the Casper Mountain homestead of Neal (that's a "she") Forsling. Elizabeth Paxton, as she was known in her maiden days, homesteaded in 1929 on Casper Mountain, having moved west from her childhood home of Independence, Missouri. She soon met and married Jim Forsling who, sadly, froze to death in 1942 while skiing home from town with eighty pounds of supplies on his back. Neal started traveling a lot after that, painting the scenes she saw around the world. She always returned to her beloved homestead, however. Before she died at age 88 in 1977, Neal donated her remaining land to Natrona County to use as a park. Her log cabin now serves as a museum, containing memorabilia from the family's life on the mountain, as well as several of Mrs. Forsling's paintings. The address is 1620 Crimson Dawn Road. It's open mid-June through mid-October from 11:00 A.M. to 7:00 P.M., Saturday through Thursday (closed Friday). Call 235–1303 for directions and further information. (Also on Casper Mountain: *Hogadon,* an "upside-down" ski area whose parking lot is on top of the mountain.)

Casper was incorporated in 1889, and the almost simultaneous discovery of oil in the area cinched the settlement's future. Many of downtown Casper's buildings were built during the 1920s oil boom. A walking tour of downtown is a fine way to spend a few hours in Wyoming's version of the Windy City. You can pick up a self-guided walking tour brochure from the Casper Historic Preservation Commission at Fort Caspar or at the Casper Area Chamber of Commerce office, 500 North Center Street. A couple of the more unusual structures you can investigate include the 1940 *Courthouse,* at 200 North Center Street, built by the WPA and featuring an intricate frieze depicting the heritage of Casper; and the 1921 *Rialto Theater,* located at 102 East Second Street, boasting unique cornices, a classic marquee—and a balcony, if you want to take in the feature.

At 302 South David Street, you'll find a late-Gothic Revival *fire station* with CASPER FIRE STATION 1 spelled out on the frieze above the fire truck entrances. The date of construction, 1921, is listed prominently in the terra-cotta shield at the top of the building's front. The fire station was added to the National Register of Historic Places in November 1993. While still in the down-town area, also have a look at the statue of *Prometheus,* who stole fire from Mount Olympus and gave it to man. It's located in front of the Natrona County Library, 307 East Second Street.

Two blocks away, at 400 East Collins Drive, is the excellent *Nicolaysen Art Museum and Discovery Center.* The structure containing the museum and center is the beautifully refurbished Old Casper Lumber Company building. "The Nic" is a great place to browse, view special exhibits, or purchase unique art items by regional artists. It celebrates art with invitational shows and other special events, while offering kids of all ages hands-on creative experiences with a variety of activities in the Discovery Center. The art museum is open from 10:00 A.M. to 5:00 P.M. Tuesday through Saturday, and noon to 4:00 P.M. on Sunday. There is no admission fee for individuals, though donations are cheerfully accepted. For information on schedules, membership, or the latest shows, call 235–5247 or go to www.thenic.org on the Internet.

central wyomingtrivia

U.S. Geological Survey topographic maps for the entire state can be found on the Internet at the Web site of the Wyoming Geographic Information Advisory Council: http://wgiac2.state.wy.us.

Two side trips out of Casper come highly recommended. First, take High-way 220 southwest of town about 5 miles to the *Goose Egg Inn.* In-the-know locals regularly travel here for the fine steaks and other specialties. Appropri-ately, the address is 10580 Goose Egg Road. It's open 5:30 to 9:30 P.M. Tuesday through Saturday. For reservations call 473–8838.

The surrounding area brims with history. Spreading out along the North Platte River, the renowned Goose Egg Ranch served as a setting for Owen Wis-ter's *The Virginian.* It was founded by the Searight Brothers of Texas, and sub-sequently owned by generations of Governor Carey's family. Later it was renamed the CY Ranch. A portion of the ranch land was platted as part of Casper, and the original 1877 ranch house was torn down in the early 1950s.

From the Goose Egg Ranch make tracks for *Independence Rock,* located 55 miles southwest of Casper on State Highway 220. This, probably the best known of all of the Oregon Trail landmarks —and one of the most poignant— is also known as the "Register of the Desert." The 190-foot-high outcropping contains an estimated 50,000 names inscribed by wagon train and handcart emigrants. It earned the name Independence Rock when explorer William Sublette celebrated the Fourth of July at the rock in 1830. He wrote:

> Most of our company visited the summit of Independence Rock, which was reached with much difficulty but without accident. We found the rock literally covered with the names of emigrants. Some of these names were written with chalk, some were cut with a cold chisel, whilst ohters [sic] were written with tar.

Near Independence Rock, Ella Watson, known in the newspapers of the time as Cattle Kate, scored another first for Wyoming women in 1889, earning the dubious distinction of becoming the first woman hanged in the state. Ella and bar owner Jim Averell appear to have been branding other people's cattle, until they were finally strung up by their neighbors for doing so.

One of the neighboring ranchers who hanged Watson and Averill was Tom Sun, who first came into the country in 1872 and established his ranch headquarters on the Sweetwater a few miles upstream from Independence Rock at **Devil's Gate,** where the river has cut a vertical slot 370 feet high through hard granite.

The meadows through which the Sweetwater meanders here were for a long time a welcome resting place on the Oregon Trail and later a way station for the Pony Express. A trader named Charles "Simonot" Lajeunesse established a post here early in the 1850s (Seminoe Reservoir on the nearby Platte River took his nickname), and it was near Lajeunesse's little store that desperate Mormon pioneers, pulling two-wheeled handcarts, pulled in for shelter in October 1856.

Most members of the handcart companies were converts recruited by Mormon missionaries from the mines, slums, and factories of England and Wales. The first three companies to travel to nine-year-old Salt Lake City in 1856 did about as well as any that traveled by conventional wagons. But two, the Martin and Willie companies, ran into trouble. They started dangerously late in the year, not leaving from the railhead at Iowa City until late July. To make matters worse, their carts were made of green wood and had been coming apart and needing constant repair for hundreds of miles. The emigrants forded the Platte above Casper, at Red Buttes; then, while they and all their

central wyomingtrivia

Bill, Wyoming, north of Douglas on State Highway 59, was named for the four men sharing the first name of Bill, whose homesteads shared a corner at the location.

goods were still soaked, the first blizzard hit. Storm followed storm, until they were strung out in little family groups the entire 60 miles from the river crossing to Devil's Gate. The Willie company made it up the Sweetwater nearly to South Pass before bad weather forced them to stop. About seventy members of the 500-strong Willie company died before the rest were rescued. Edward Martin's company of 576 Mormons pulled in at a place near Devil's Gate now called Martin's Cove, where the dramatic Sweetwater Rocks come down to the prairie and offer shelter from wind and storms and a few juniper trees grow along the prairie edge and provide firewood. The members of Martin's company began dying shortly after they left the Platte. By the time they pulled in at the cove, they were dying by the tens and dozens; about 145 died in all. Survivors were rescued by parties Brigham Young sent from Salt Lake City to look for them. It is the most dramatic story of all the tales of Mormon migration, and to the Mormons, Martin's Cove is holy ground.

Tom Sun's children, grandchildren, and great-grandchildren, meanwhile, continued to ranch at Devil's Gate and part of the family still ranches in the area today. A second branch of the family, however, sold the core of the old ranch to the Mormon Church in 1997—including the 1870s house and barn and a strip of deeded land that runs from the ranch headquarters up the Sweetwater River for several miles.

In recent years the church has transformed the property into the ***Mormon Handcart Visitor Center at Martin's Cove,*** on Highway 220, 62 miles southwest of Casper and 62 miles north of Rawlins. The low, log, L-shaped ranch house is now a museum, with the first room telling the story of the Suns and their ranch; the rest of the building is devoted to the handcart story. Another, new log cabin is devoted to the ranchers and Native Americans of the Sweetwater Valley, and a replica of Lajeunesse's trading post has just been completed. The church has also laid gravel on a broad trail that leads up the Sweetwater to the cove, with historical markers along the way. It's a 4-mile round-trip and well worth the walk, both for history and for the magnificent views of the Sweetwater River, the Sweetwater Rocks, and to the south the Green and Ferris mountains. Handcarts are available to pull for those desiring a more true-to-history experience. The church has taken what was a regular working ranch for 125 years and transformed it into a historic site and religious shrine, open daily from 8:00 A.M. to 7:00 P.M. from mid-May through Labor Day, 9:00 A.M. to 4:00 P.M. the rest of the year. Everything is free; groups are welcome for tours and overnight camping. For more information call 328–2953 or visit www.handcart.com.

The second excursion from Casper before continuing westward involves following I–25 north 21 miles, then State Highway 259 north for 4½ miles. On the right-hand (east) side of the road, you'll see the remnants of the landmark

Miles and Miles of Wyoming

I, along with several companions, once accomplished a feat relatively few can claim: We walked a beeline nearly 200 miles long through the heart of Wyoming.

We'd been dispatched to look for evidence of prehistoric Native American camps along the route of a proposed natural-gas pipeline. From south-southeast to north-northwest we walked, beginning south of Sinclair and winding up near Lost Cabin. We were compelled to walk right up, down, over, or through whatever we happened to encounter. That included historic Whiskey Gap, where a Major Farrell once ordered a contraband barrel of whiskey smashed near the spring where his troops were camped. As the booze poured into the spring and over the ground, soldiers scurried up with cups to save what they could; some lay on the ground and stuck their faces right into the eighty-proof stream. One soldier claimed it was the best spring water he'd ever tasted, and Farrell recorded in his journal that it was fortunate the Indians did not attack that night.

As for our small army, each night we would meet up with the Jeep that carried our mobile camp. At one point, at a crossing of Sage Hen Creek, the Jeep got stuck. Because I was training for marathons at the time, I was elected by the others to trot westward over ridges and through valleys and come-what-may to seek help at a nearby uranium mine we knew to be somewhere in the vicinity.

Along this 200-mile swath of remarkably wild country we also saw pronghorns and coyotes, rattlesnakes and raptors; a couple of our party members even hooked into some monster trout at the point where we forded the Sweetwater River.

Though it might be hard to come up with an excuse to do something like this, I highly recommend it. It's a trip that not only will take you off the beaten path, but way off any kind of paths whatsoever and into the very soul of Wyoming.

whose name is associated with one of the biggest political scandals ever to come out of Washington.

Teapot Rock is clearly visible from the dirt turnout (don't look for a teapot anymore—two tornadoes in the 1920s destroyed the handle and spout). Teapot Rock is located on private property, so please don't trespass for a better look.

The Teapot Dome scandal erupted when President Harding's Secretary of the Interior, Albert Fall, leased the Teapot Dome oil fields to the Mammoth Oil Company, owned by Harry F. Sinclair, without first going through the proper bidding process. Wyoming's Sen. John Kendrick called for a complete investigation in 1922, and, six years later, Fall was convicted of accepting a $100,000 bribe. He spent a year in federal prison.

Continuing on you'll pass the famous Salt Creek Oilfields, one of Wyoming's largest and still pumping. Then you'll arrive at Midwest, population

408. Proceed to the Town Hall, 531 Peake Street, and inquire about the **Salt Creek Museum.** If the museum's not open, they'll give you the key and ask you to lock up when you're finished. It's a delightful and informative little museum that presents the history of Midwest, nearby ghost towns, and the Salt Creek Oilfields. You'll learn, for instance, that the first claim was issued in 1883, oil was first discovered in 1889, and the first oil well was drilled in 1908 at a depth of 1,050 feet. The area's population peaked at around 2,500 in 1929, when the company-owned hotel was capable of feeding 1,200 people per hour and the high school boasted the first lighted football field in the nation. To contact the Midwest Town Hall, open 8:00 A.M. to 5:00 P.M. weekdays (closed at lunch time), call 437–6513.

central wyomingtrivia

The Wyoming State Flag, adopted by the fourteenth legislature in 1917, was designed by Mrs. A. C. Keyes of Casper.

Another excursion out of Casper you might want to consider is one organized and led by the **Historic Trails West.** A number of outings are available, via horseback, Conestoga wagon, and river raft. The tours range from several hours to several days in duration, and food and sleeping equipment are provided. For expedition information and reservations, call 266–4868 or go to www.historictrailswest.com.

About 42 miles west of Casper on Highway 20/26, pull over to gaze out across **Hell's Half Acre,** a starkly beautiful stretch of badlands that provide the raw materials for some unusual Wyoming landscape photos. Native Americans once drove herds of buffalo off the cliffs to their deaths here, and Captain Bonneville's exploratory expedition stopped by in 1833. Alert sci-fi fans will recognize these badlands as the setting for the 1997 bug-and-mayhem flick *Starship Troopers.* Today there's a Hell's Half Acre restaurant/store, where, if it's open, you can stock up on Hell's Half Acre postcards.

Fremont County

If you're running short of funds and would like to try your hand at prospecting, consider making a trip to the Lost Cabin area near Lysite. Turn north at the metropolis of Moneta, population 10, onto Highway 176, the Lysite-Moneta Road. The pavement ends about 8 miles later at Lysite, where you might want to swing into the country store for a snack and to inquire about road conditions before continuing on to Lost Cabin, located 3 miles northeast.

As the story goes, a band of prospectors extracted thousands of dollars worth of gold from a rich lode in the vicinity before Indians attacked and killed all but one or two of the miners, who escaped to the nearest town. Despite repeated attempts after that, the Lost Cabin Mine was never rediscovered. The site of present Lost Cabin is home to ***The Big Tipi,*** as Native Americans called the mansion built in 1900 by Wyoming sheep magnate John B. Okie. Okie outfitted the mansion with elaborately carved fireplace mantles, lavish chandeliers, costly Oriental rugs, and intricate and colorful panels of stained glass. The mansion also incorporates an unusual octagonal tower. Outside, Okie constructed a greenhouse, dance hall, and aviary to house his collection of exotic birds. The mansion is located on private property, but you can't miss seeing it from the road.

Returning to Moneta, take Garden City Road 459 for 21 miles south, then BLM Road 2107 east to ***Castle Gardens,*** one of Wyoming's finest collections of ancient rock carvings. (Inquire at Moneta about road conditions before attempting this journey.) Perhaps the best-known petroglyph is one no longer residing there: the Great Turtle petroglyph, which disappeared from Castle Gardens one day only to mysteriously pop up years later at the Wyoming State Museum. It's still periodically displayed at the museum in Cheyenne. Another mystery surrounding the Great Turtle is, why would a water-loving snapping turtle from the Mississippi or Missouri River country appear in a petroglyph in arid Wyoming?

After hours of exploring the dry wide-open and then driving the 21 miles from Moneta to Shoshoni (population 635), you'll no doubt be ready for a burger and shake at the ***Yellowstone Drug Store,*** 127 Main Street. Over an average summer, the Yellowstone churns some 35,000 rich malts and milk shakes for travelers. Head south one block from the drugstore, passing plenty of abandoned storefronts, and take a right before the railroad tracks to see a

Petroglyphs, Castle Gardens

jail that's more than a century old. Imagine what it must have been like to spend hot summer or frigid winter nights behind those bars, especially considering all the hell-raising that must've been going on: Hard as it is to imagine, during Shoshoni's boom years the town supported nearly two dozen saloons, along with two banks, two mercantile establishments, and several livery and feed stables.

Boysen State Park stretches from the outskirts of Shoshoni into the Wind River Canyon, a singularly spectacular drive described earlier in the book (see Thermopolis). The first white men in the area were those with the 1825 Ashley Fur Party. An earlier dam was built at the mouth of the canyon in 1908 by Asmus Boysen, a native of Copenhagen, Denmark, for whom the reservoir and park are named. The Chicago, Burlington and Quincy Railroad laid tracks through the Wind River Canyon in 1911 and ended up suing Boysen after the tracks were flooded due to the waters impounded by the dam. The railroad won the suit and had Boysen's dam dynamited. The present dam was constructed in 1951, and the state park was designated in 1956. You'll find plenty of day-use and overnight facilities on the 76 miles of often wind-blown shoreline. For information call 876–2796.

Twenty-two miles southwest of Shoshoni on Highway 26/789 is Riverton, home to the September **Cowboy Poetry Gathering,** featuring the region's top rhymin' wranglers. The event happens at Central Wyoming College. For ticket information call the Riverton Chamber of Commerce at 856–4801.

Hudson, population 407, located 14 miles southwest of Riverton, holds a pair of surprises: two of the most celebrated restaurants in Wyoming. **Svilar's Bar & Dining Room** (332–4516), at 173 South Main Street, specializes in melt-in-your-mouth steaks. Across the way, at 132 South Main Street, is **Club El Toro** (332–4627), also featuring fine beef cuts. Prices at both establishments are moderate, and the pair of eateries have an interesting understanding: each is closed on alternate Mondays; that is, on a Monday when Svilar's is closed, El Toro is open, and vice versa. Both are also closed on Sunday.

In the attractive town of Lander, motor or walk along Main Street between Sixth and Seventh Streets to have a look at the enormous stack of antlers marking the Fort Augur Trading Post. For a snack try the **Popo Agie Brewing**

Company (332–7388), located at 148 Main Street or, for great steaks and seafood, an ample soup-and-salad bar, good drinks, and an excellent wine list, head to *The Hitching Rack* at 785 East Main Street on the hill southeast of downtown. For reservations call 332–4322.

On Main Street near the Popo Agie (*po PO zhuh*) River stands a Lander landmark, the 1888 mill built by Eugene Amoretti and used to grind wheat and supply electricity for the town. It's been in continual use as a flour and feed mill since its construction.

Not surprisingly, considering the grand mountains backing the town, a number of outfitters operate out of the Lander area. From mid-June to mid-September, *Allen's Diamond Four Ranch,* a licensed professional outfitter since 1973, offers guided horseback tours by the half day or day and pack trips exploring the Popo Agie Wilderness of the Wind River Range. Pack trips last from four to seven days, and the Allens also guide big-game hunting parties in the fall. For information call 332–2995, or check them out on the Internet at www.diamond4ranch.com.

Lander Llama Company provides a full line of outfitting services and pack trips, employing these ungainly but sure-footed beasts to do the hard work. For information (including details on the company's rentable bunkhouse) and reservations, call 332–5624 or (800) 582–5262 or visit www.land erllama.com.

Lander is also home to the headquarters of the *National Outdoor Leadership School* (NOLS), the foremost school of its kind in the country. NOLS, which was started by the late, legendary mountaineer Paul Petzoldt, offers adventure-travel and leadership-training trips in the nearby Wind Rivers, as well as far-flung Baja California, Alaska, Africa, and elsewhere. For a catalog detailing the school's offerings, drop by the office at 284 Lincoln Street in Lander, or visit www.nols.edu.

Just outside of Lander, at 2343 Baldwin Creek Road, enjoy the best in western hospitality at the *Baldwin Creek Bed & Breakfast.* Nestled against a protective, red-hued bluff, the views from the main house and bunkhouse cabins are outstanding. Each room is furnished in western decor, and the main house features guest quarters and a kitchen complete with plenty of snacks. The food served for breakfast is tasty and plentiful. Overnight rates are $90 to $95 in summer; $70 to $75 the rest of the year. To inquire about weekly rates or to make reservations, call 332–7608 or visit www.wyomingbandb.com.

See the scenes behind the fashioning of bronze carvings and foundry work at *Eagle Bronze, Inc., Foundry & Gallery,* located at 130 Poppy Street on the south edge of town (in the industrial park off U.S. Highway 287). Eagle Bronze performs casting work for many of the West's top artists, and several of the foundry's creations are featured in the on-site gallery and in other places through-out Lander. Eagle Bronze offers foundry tours ($2.00 per person) Monday through Friday in summer. Tours generally start at 10:00 A.M., but call ahead for details, 332–5436.

Sinks Canyon State Park features a magic act performed by the Popo Agie River: It crashes and disappears into a large cavern, known as the Sinks, in the side of a mountain . . . only to reappear ½ mile down canyon as a trout-filled pool called the Rise. A couple of interesting facts about Sinks Canyon: First, more water comes out at the Rise than flows into the Sinks; second, the water flowing out at the Rise is a few degrees warmer than water entering the Sinks. A visitor center near the Sinks presents information on this unusual rock-and-water phenomenon and on area wildlife. The park includes self-guided nature trails, picnic grounds, and campsites. All visitors should walk across the swinging bridge spanning the Popo Agie, and the more ambitious will want to hike the Popo Agie Falls Trail for 1½ miles to a spectacular vista point. The vis-itor center is open daily Memorial Day through Labor Day from 9:00 A.M. to 6:00 P.M., and the center hosts a speakers series through the summer. To reach Sinks Canyon State Park, take State Highway 131 southeast out of Lander for 6 miles. For information call 332–3077.

Season and road conditions permitting, continue south from the Sinks on Highway 131 to the historic mining areas of Atlantic City and South Pass City. Alternatively, you can return to Lander and travel to the area entirely on paved roads. It's approximately 25 miles from Lander via U.S. Highway 287 and State Highway 28, and the roads are well marked. Be sure to stop at the marked viewpoint to look down on stunning Red Canyon as you climb above Lander's bucolic valley setting.

Today *South Pass City State Historic Site* is one of Wyoming's largest and best restored historic sites, with more than thirty structures distributed over thirty-nine acres. Yet South Pass City, where the past is palpable, is often over-looked. Boardwalks and dirt streets lead you to buildings such as the 1890 schoolhouse, the South Pass Hotel (opened as the Idaho House in 1868), the 1890s Carissa Saloon, the Riniker Cabin, and the 1870 Sweetwater County Jail. As you wander in and around the buildings, you'll earn a real sense of what life in an 1890s gold-mining town was all about. For a truly grand old time, come for Gold Rush days in late July for vintage baseball, old-time music, and more. South Pass City State Historic Site is open May 15 through September 30 from 9:00 A.M. to 6:00 P.M. The entrance fee is $1.00 for Wyoming residents eighteen and older; $2.00 for out-of-staters. For further information call 332–3684 or visit www.southpasscity.com.

For a good view of the Oregon Trail as it approached South Pass, drive to the Oregon Trail–Lander Cutoff–South Pass Area interpretive sign located on the south side of Highway 28, approximately 39 miles from Lander. Here you can still see the wagon ruts crossing the desert.

On the way back to Lander, stop at the ***Atlantic City Mercantile,*** located at 100 East Main Street in the semi-ghost town of Atlantic City. The town is reached by driving a few miles northeast on dirt from South Pass City. You'll see the remains of the Duncan Gold Mine along the way. Atlantic City is a delightful place to grab a bite or spend a night. The 105-year-old Merc includes a saloon and steak house, with all sorts of historic paraphernalia and photographs hanging from or nailed to the walls. Browse through the small museum and check out the ornate antique, still-in-use stove in the saloon, and the set of swinging doors attached to the wall of the back room.

The Merc serves up barbecue on Sunday beginning at 11:00 A.M. and ending when it's all gone from May 1 through November 1. Lunch is served Tuesday through Sunday, and the steakhouse is open beginning at 5:00 P.M. Thursday through Sunday. For information call 332–5143.

For bunking down in historic surroundings, you can't do better than the ***Miner's Delight B&B*** at 290 Atlantic Road. The 1895 log hotel lets three rooms and four cabins, some with private and some with shared bath. Accommodations run from $60 to $75 per night, including a full breakfast. For reservations, call proprietors Donna and Ken Ballard at 332–0248.

A United States Steel taconite strip mine (taconite is a low-grade iron ore) rejuvenated the area's economy from 1962 to 1983, but the depleted hills are all that remain of that boom. Times are quiet for now . . . just awaiting the next boom.

An 8-mile side trip south on gravel roads from Atlantic City serves as a haunting reminder why the Oregon-Mormon Trails have been called "the

Atlantic City Mercantile

longest graveyard in America." That evidence is the site of the **Willie Hand-cart Company tragedy,** where in 1856 an estimated sixty-seven Mormon pioneers died—having never laid eyes on their promised land in Utah—after being trapped by an unusually fierce October snowstorm. (See discussion earlier in this chapter.) To find the unsettling spot, turn south at the Miner's Delight Inn and climb the big hill out of town; after 4 miles make a left and proceed another 4 miles. There's camping and a water pump at the site.

From South Pass City–Atlantic City, return to Lander. The area provides countless outdoor recreation opportunities. In addition to the pack trips already mentioned, there's rock climbing in Wild Iris Canyon, with routes ranging from 5.7 to 5.14 in difficulty. In winter, thousands of snow-covered acres of cross-country skiing terrain beckons, and the Continental Divide Snowmobile Trail runs from near Lander all the way to Yellowstone, with hundreds of miles of groomed trails traversing some of the most spectacular country in the world. For information on the trail, call the Bureau of Land Management at 775–6256.

Moving northwest from Lander on U.S. Highway 287, you'll drive through lands of the Wind River Indian Reservation, home to the Eastern Shoshone and the Northern Arapaho tribes. The reservation, which encompasses some two million acres, contains the graves of at least two and maybe three great Native Americans: Shoshone chief Washakie, Arapaho chief Black Coal, and Sacajawea, the Shoshone woman who traveled with the Lewis and Clark Expedition.

As a child, Sacajawea was captured by Minataree Indians and sold to French fur trader Toussaint Charbonneau, who fathered their son, Baptiste. Sacajawea proved invaluable to the Corps of Discovery's leaders, particularly when it came to horse trading with the Shoshone in the Continental Divide country of Montana and Idaho. Sacajawea returned to the Shoshone people late in her life and died in 1884. **Sacajawea's Grave** is located in the southwest corner of the Shoshone Cemetery at Fort Washakie, approximately ½ mile north of the Shoshone-Episcopal Mission sign. (Many scholars, it must be said, argue that Sacajawea died and was buried at Fort Manuel in the Dakotas.)

Chief Washakie allied himself with the white people's government as an intermediary for the Shoshone, in a successful attempt at peaceful coexistence. Washakie was widely recognized as a sage leader, and his strategy of joining the government's forces in battles against other tribes was eventually rewarded with the presentation of large tracts of land in Colorado, Idaho, Utah, and Wyoming. In the end, however, the original reservation lands assigned under the Fort Bridger Treaty of 1863 were whittled down and negotiated away from the Native Americans, until all that remained were the lands of the present Wind River Reservation.

South Pass City

The first white men to cross the Continental Divide at South Pass in 1812 were the fur traders known as the Astorians. The pass was "discovered" again in 1824 by fur trapper Henry Ashley; however, Lt. John Charles Fremont is credited with widely publicizing the South Pass route after his expedition crossed through it in 1842. During the next two and a half decades, more than 350,000 Oregon-Mormon Trail emigrants traveled up the gentle slopes as they headed west to surmount the Continental Divide. South Pass, at a relatively low and accessible elevation of 7,805 feet, was key to making it feasible for the wagon trains even to pass through the Rocky Mountain region.

Thousands of gold-hungry California-bound prospectors passed through in the late 1840s and 1850s. Had they known what lay hidden in the ground of the surrounding area—gold, that is—they may have found little reason to push on.

The first version of South Pass City was an 1850s stage stop and telegraph station, where the Oregon Trail made its final crossing of the Sweetwater River. South Pass City at its present site was built in 1867 after the discovery of gold brought a flood of prospectors to the Sweetwater Mining District. The mining town soon flourished, becoming the site of some 300 buildings. The Carissa Mine began producing gold in 1867; it was last worked in the 1950s.

This once-thriving, rough-and-tumble gold camp gave birth to a women's suffrage bill, introduced to the first territorial legislature assembly in November 1869 by South Pass City representative William Bright. The suffrage bill passed both the council and the house on December 10, 1869, and the governor of Wyoming signed it into law. Soon after, on February 14, 1870, Esther Hobart Morris became the first woman in the United States to hold political office when she was sworn in as justice of the peace at South Pass City. The territorial legislature voted to repeal the suffrage bill in 1871, but Governor Campbell vetoed the action.

The entire town almost pulled up stakes and moved to California in the mid-1960s. Thankfully, a group of concerned Cowboy Staters outbid Knott's Berry Farm, which was trying to buy the town, so South Pass City remained where it grew up a century earlier—in the barren high country at the tail end of the Wind River Range—instead of moving to the coastal lowlands of California. The state of Wyoming subsequently purchased the settlement from its saviors and later designated it the South Pass City State Historic Site.

Chief Washakie died in 1900 on the Wind River Reservation at around the age of 100. Mount Washakie and the Washakie Wilderness were named after the great Shoshone chief, as were Fort Washakie, which was renamed from Fort Brown in 1878, and Washakie Center at the University of Wyoming in Laramie. The post at Fort Washakie was abandoned in 1909, but the town bearing the

Two-Wheeled Solitude

The *Great Divide Mountain Bike Route* is a 2,470-mile off-pavement bicycle touring route stretching along the Continental Divide from Canada to Mexico. As the route's primary architect, I was extremely concerned about what I would and would not find between South Pass City and Rawlins, where the route would necessarily encounter miles of high, dry desert and a corner of the vast Great Divide Basin. Would there be water? Would people end up hating this stretch of the route? Or, like some emigrants who traveled through here, might they even perish? I certainly hoped not.

However, with the invaluable assistance of Bureau of Land Management recreation planner Ray Hanson, an outstanding route (with at least a little water) using existing dirt roads was linked together. Here the Great Divide Route occasionally coincides with more famous, and far older, trails: the Oregon-Mormon, the California, and the Pony Express trails. It also flirts with a border-to-border hiking path, the Continental Divide National Scenic Trail. For 135 miles self-supported cyclists riding through the area see no trees, but they do encounter wild horses, pronghorns, and a historically vital slice of American backcountry visited by very few folks. Some who have ridden the entire route from Canada to Mexico, in fact, swear that this empty stretch of Wyoming was their very favorite part of the entire Great Divide.

For information on mountain biking in the Great Divide Basin and along other parts of the Great Divide Route, you can contact the Montana-based Adventure Cycling Association at (406) 721-1776 or www.adventure cycling.org.

chief's name remains. His grave is found in the old fort cemetery: Take South Fork Road west until you come to the *Chief Washakie Gravesite.*

The Arapahos, historic enemies of the Shoshone, were admitted onto the Shoshone reservation in 1878, supposedly on a temporary basis. Today, however, Arapahos living on the Wind River Reservation outnumber the Shoshone approximately 3,500 to 2,500. During summer months residents of the reservation display their rich and colorful traditions in a variety of ways. Powwows, sun dances, horseback relay races, and rodeos all are open to the public, as are Shoshone and Arapaho cultural centers and certain historic sites. To fish on tribal land, you must first buy a recreation stamp issued by the Shoshone and Arapaho Tribal Fish and Game Department at Fort Washakie. For information call the Lander Chamber of Commerce at 332–3892 or (800) 433–0662.

Eleven miles before arriving in Dubois, turn right (north) onto the gravel East Fork Road (Road 277) for a scenic, 11-mile trip to the *Lazy L & B Ranch.* A wonderful family vacation can be enjoyed at this hundred-year-old cattle and guest ranch now owned by Lee and Bob Naylon. The ranch abuts both the Wind River Reservation and a large elk refuge. You can bed down in log cabins surrounding a central yard or nestled alongside a singing stream. Down-home cooking begins with a breakfast served buffet style and continues with lunch served by the pool or on the trail. Then there's dinner, a real treat after a day filled with hiking, horseback riding, and fly-fishing. The kids eat with the wranglers, while the older folks enjoy quiet dinners and evening entertainment back at the ranch. To close the day you can soak your weary bones in the outdoor heated pool and watch as the setting sun turns the surrounding slopes of the Absaroka Range a brilliant crimson.

The Lazy L & B Ranch, homesteaded in the 1890s by Scottish emigrants, sits at an elevation of 7,200 feet, in a setting of tall cottonwoods beneath high cliffs of red clay. Anglers can fish in stocked ponds or try their luck in the East Fork of the Wind River. Entertainment options include the ranch's own cowboy poet or driving to Dubois for dancing at the Rustic Pine Tavern. For the kids there's a petting zoo with goats, chickens, rabbits, sheep, ducks, geese, and other animals. The corrals are filled with horses and donkeys, with one to match the skill—or lack thereof—of any rider. The main lodge has two cozy fireplaces, a library, and game tables. All-log guest cabins have private baths or showers, electric heat, and sittin' porches. The season runs from the end of May through mid-September. (September is reserved for adults only.) Weekly rates are about $1,225 per adult and $1,125 per child age twelve and under. For information or reservations call 455–2839 or (800) 453–9488, or visit the Web site www.lazyLB.com.

crowheartbutte

After traveling north from Fort Washakie 16 miles on U.S. Highway 287, then northwest on U.S. Highway 26/287 for another 10 miles, you'll spot a large butte to the north. Legend explains that the name, *Crowheart Butte,* derives from an 1866 struggle to the death between Crow and Shoshone chiefs. Victorious, the Shoshone chief celebrated by eating the heart of his vanquished rival (or, say some accounts, by simply displaying the heart on his lance). The Shoshone chief in question was Washakie. Queried years later about the accuracy of the story, he had only this to say, "One cannot always remember what he did when he was young and in the heat of battle."

Jakey's Fork Homestead, 4 miles east of Dubois off Forest Service Road 411 (south of Highway 26/287), offers another unique overnight option. You can sleep in an original homestead, with the cold water of Jakey's Fork flowing just outside your bedroom window, or in the two-room suite of the main house. In the morning you're welcome to explore the homestead, with its sod-roofed buildings, and the surrounding mountains and redrock badlands. Sourdough flapjacks, fruit, and biscuits or Scottish oat scones highlight owner Irene Broderick's breakfast menu.

Nearby Trail Road (Road 257) offers potential views of bighorn sheep, osprey, waterfalls, and petroglyphs. Rates at Jakey's Fork Homestead are $75 to $130 per night. For information and reservations, which are requested, call 455–2769 or visit www.frontierlodging.com.

Within walking distance of the bed-and-breakfast is the **Dubois Fish Hatchery,** in operation since 1930. The Lake of the Woods brood stock, obtained about 30 miles southwest of Dubois, furnishes a major portion of the cutthroat eggs for the entire state. The hatchery also raises graylings and golden, brook, rainbow, and brown trout. Rainbow trout make up approximately 60 percent of the hatchery's annual production. The hatchery's three incubators are capable of handling up to six million eggs at one time. The informative hatchery tour takes you through the entire process, from egg fertilization through fish planting. The fish hatchery is located at Five Fish Hatchery Court. For information call 455–2431.

Dubois, population 962, grew up around a post office established on Horse Creek more than a century ago. Dubois has kept its Old West ambience well intact; in fact, it has even embellished the ambience in recent years. Boardwalks and false-front stores abound. You'll also notice immediately that wild animals are highly regarded by the townspeople: Oversize likenesses of bears, elk, moose, rainbow trout, and other critters decorate store fronts and parking lots.

Be sure and stop at the **National Bighorn Sheep Interpretive Center,** completed in 1993. It contains fascinating exhibits on bighorn sheep biology, habitat protection, and herd management techniques employed at the Whiskey Mountain Wildlife Habitat Management Area (located several miles south of town). Dubois is a natural location for the interpretive center because the area is home to North America's largest population of Rocky Mountain bighorn sheep. The center came about through the cooperative efforts of the U.S. Forest Service,

How You Say It

If you want to sound like a local, put the accent on the first syllable of Dubois and pronounce the "s" at the end; in Wyoming the town rhymes roughly with "NEW toys." The question took on a new wrinkle in 1997 when Phil Dubois came from North Carolina to take over the presidency of the University of Wyoming, the state's only four-year institution of higher learning. He pronounces his name the regular French way: "DoobWAH," even when passing through Dubois, and both he and the citizens of the state take a cheerfully laissez-faire (that's LESSay-FAIR) attitude toward each other's pronunciational peculiarities.

Bureau of Land Management, Wyoming Game and Fish Department, Town of Dubois, and private individuals and nonprofit organizations.

The central exhibit, a 16-foot-tall "sheep mountain," displays full-size bighorns in a simulation of their natural environment. Interpretive scenes ringing the slopes of the mountain depict predator-prey relationships, lambing areas, and dominance battles. Children young and old will be fascinated by the center's great hands-on displays. A gift shop offers nature books, posters and cards, wildlife-theme clothing, prints, sculptures, and antler art crafted by local artisans. For fall and winter travelers, a special treat awaits: You can drive your own four-wheel-drive vehicle or sign up for a guided drive to view wildlife in the Whiskey Mountain area. November is the prime bighorn rutting month. Binoculars and spotting scopes are provided, but participants are responsible for bringing their own lunches. Dress warmly! Tours start at 9:00 A.M. and typically last about four hours. The museum asks for a $25 donation per person for the tour and that you call at least twenty-four hours ahead. The tours begin in mid-November and continue through March.

> ## wyomingtrivia
>
> Wyoming is home to the nation's first national park (Yellowstone), the first national monument (Devils Tower), and the first national forest (the Shoshone).

The National Bighorn Sheep Interpretive Center is located at 907 West Ramshorn, off Highway 26/287. Hours from Memorial Day weekend to Labor Day weekend are 9:00 A.M. to 8:00 P.M. daily, and it's open daily from 9:00 A.M. to 5:00 P.M. the rest of the year. Entrance fees are $2.00 per adult, 75 cents per child age twelve and under, or $5.00 per family. For information on the center or the winter wildlife tours, call 455–3429. Alternatively, you can check out the center's Web site, www.bighorn.org.

Immediately next door, at 909 West Ramshorn, is the ***Wind River Historical Center,*** which focuses on the Shoshone and Arapaho Indians, the area's ranch and frontier life, and the timber industry's historical importance to Dubois. (The town's sawmill shut down in 1987, after which community leaders began putting a greater emphasis on tourism—spawning, among other things, the fine bighorn sheep museum described earlier.) Exhibits include five or six historical buildings that have been moved to the site, including Dubois' first high school and first gas station. The museum is open Monday through Saturday from 9:00 A.M. to 4:00 P.M., Memorial day through the end of September. Admission is $1.00 for adults and 50 cents for children twelve and under. For information call 455–2284 or visit www.windriverhistory.org.

Not far away, at 120 East Ramshorn, **Stewart's Trapline Gallery and Indian Trading Post** stocks a fine collection of original paintings and drawings by former owner Mark R. Stewart. Current owner Kit Stewart also displays an extensive collection of traditional Native American art, representing more than two dozen tribes. You can choose a treasure for your home from a variety of art forms, including beadwork, pottery and basketry, sand paintings, Navajo rugs, kachina dolls, Zuni fetishes, and contemporary Native American silver jewelry. For information call 455–2800.

A number of self-guided driving tours out of Dubois are worth considering. You have your choice of investigating badlands or motoring past a series of three glacial lakes for great fishing, wildlife viewing, and wildflower sniffing. Native American petroglyphs are also accessible for photographing. Pick up the map pamphlet describing "Six Loop Tour Options in the Wind River Country" at the Dubois Chamber of Commerce office, located at 616 West Ramshorn, or call them at 455–2556.

Driving northwest from Dubois on U.S. Highway 26/287, you'll come upon the **Union Pass Monument** about 8 miles out. The monument marks the first road across the Absaroka/Wind River ranges. You can follow the Union Pass Road for a remarkable trip, earning long-range views of the Tetons and close-ups of the Wind Rivers. The road eventually drops out above Pinedale in the Green River drainage. Parts of the route are very rough and poorly marked, so obtain supplies and a good map before striking out on the adventure.

what'sinaname

The 9,210-foot Union Pass was named by Capt. William F. Raynolds when he crossed it in 1860, guided by mountain man Jim Bridger. Raynolds may have chosen the name because the pass unites the West's three great river systems; creeks flow from it down to the Wind, Green, and Snake rivers, tributaries of, respectively, the Missouri, the Colorado, and the Columbia. But he may also have hoped the name would somehow avert the looming Civil War, which began in 1861 and nearly shredded the nation before union was restored.

Back along the main highway, drive another 9 miles and you'll reach the impressive carved **Tie Hack Monument.** Sitting near the site of the first tie camp on the Wind River, the monument commemorates the tie hackers, who cut some 400,000 railroad ties annually between 1914 and 1946. The ties were transported downstream on the Wind River during the spring runoff. The lumberjacks precariously went along for the ride, too, during an annual operation that lasted several wet weeks. Many of the men suffered from an ailment called "squeak heel," caused by having continuously wet feet. Eventually their Achilles tendons would dry out and actually make a squeaking noise when they walked.

Tie hackers had to cut a tie to a precise 7 inches per side in order to pass close inspection. For this they earned 10 cents per tie, or up to $3.00 a day, at a time when their room and board cost $1.50 per day. Each tie hacker cared for his own equipment, which would cost him roughly ten days' pay to acquire. It was said that the Scandinavian tie hackers could plane logs so smooth with their axes that you could run your hand over them and pick up nary a splinter.

Ahead of you lies the beginning of the Wyoming Centennial Scenic Byway, leading to Togwotee (*TOE guh tee*) Pass, elevation 9,658 feet, and the Bridger-Teton National Forest. The route provides yet another way to descend into the incomparable beauty of Jackson Hole. (That area is covered in "Western Wyoming.") The drive up Togwotee Pass alternates between mountain meadows, lodgepole forests, and jagged cliffs. Not long before reaching Togwotee Pass, a right-hand turn will lead roughly 5 miles to the ***Brooks Lake Lodge*** (455–2121; www.brookslake.com), a traditional western lodge-with-cabins enterprise that has been accommodating Yellowstone-bound travelers since the early 1920s. Rates range from $275 to $325 per person per night in summer and include all meals and activities. Come the snow-bound winter, rates begin at $195. It's a fitting and proper place, indeed, to wind up a tour of the great state of Wyoming.

Places to Stay in Oregon Trail–Rendezvous Country

CASPER

Days Inn,
301 East E Street;
(307) 234–1159 or
(800) DAYS–INN
(329–7466)

Holiday Inn,
300 West F Street;
(307) 235–2531

Parkway Plaza Hotel,
123 West E Street;
(307) 235–1777 or
(800) 270–STAY (7829)

Super 8 Lodge,
3838 CY Avenue;
(307) 266–3480 or
(800) 800–8000

DOUGLAS

Alpine Inn,
2310 East Richards;
(307) 358–4780

Best Western Douglas Inn,
1450 Riverbend Drive;
(307) 358–9790 or
(800) 528–1234

Plains Motel,
628 East Richards;
(307) 358–4484

DUBOIS

Bald Mountain Inn,
1349 West Ramshorn;
(307) 455–2844 or
(800) 682–9323

Branding Iron Inn,
401 West Ramshorn;
(307) 455–2893

Lakes' Lodge, Inc.,
1 Fir Road;
(307) 455–2171 or
(877) 455–2171

GLENROCK

All American Inn,
500 West Aspen;
(307) 436–2772

Higgins Hotel,
416 West Birch Street;
(307) 436–9212 (don't let the
exterior scare you off!)

LANDER

**Best Western Inn
at Lander,**
260 Grandview Drive;
(307) 332–2847 or
(800) 528–1234

Holiday Lodge,
210 McFarlane Drive;
(307) 332–2511 or
(800) 624–1974

Pronghorn Lodge,
150 East Main Street;
(307) 332–3940

LUSK

Rawhide Motel,
805 Sourth Main;
(307) 334–2440

Town House Motel,
525 South Main Street;
(307) 334–2376

RIVERTON

Days Inn,
909 West Main;
(307) 856–9677 or
(800) DAYS–INN
(329–7466)

Holiday Inn,
900 East Sunset Boulevard;
(307) 856–8100 or
(800) HOLIDAY (465–4329)

Sundowner Station,
1616 North Federal;
(307) 856–6503 or
(800) 874–1116

TORRINGTON

King's Inn,
1555 Main Street;
(307) 532–4011

Oregon Trail Lodge,
710 East Valley Road;
(307) 532–2101

WHEATLAND

Best Western Torchlight,
1809 North 16th Street;
(307) 322–4070 or
(800) 528–1234

Vimbo's Motel,
203 16th Street;
(307) 322–3842 or
(800) 577–3842

Wyoming Motel,
1101 9th Street;
(307) 322–5383

Places to Eat in Oregon Trail– Rendezvous Country

ATLANTIC CITY

The Dredge Saloon & Cafe
15 North Granier Avenue;
(307) 332–7404

CASPER

**Botticelli Ristorante
Italiano,**
129 West Second Street;
(307) 266–2700

The Cottage,
116 South Lincoln;
(307) 234–1157

Flaming Wok,
601 Southeast Wyoming
Boulevard;
(307) 232–9211

Garden Creek Cafe,
251 South Center Street;
(307) 265–9018

The Goose Egg,
5 miles southwest of Casper
on Highway 220;
(307) 473–8838

Guadalajara Restaurant,
3350 CY Avenue;
(307) 234–4699

Sanfords Grub & Pub,
241 South Center Street;
(307) 234–4555

DOUGLAS

Grasslands,
2341 East Richards Street;
(307) 358–3575

La Bonte Inn,
206 East Walnut Street;
(307) 358–9856

**La Costa Mexican
Restaurant,**
1213 Teton Way;
(307) 358–2449

DUBOIS

Cowboy Cafe,
115 East Ramshorn;
(307) 455–2595

Ramshorn Inn,
202 East Ramshorn;
(307) 455–2400

Rustic Pine Steak House,
121 East Ramshorn;
(307) 455–2772

GLENROCK

Classic Cafe & Pizza,
201 South Fourth Street;
(307) 436–2244

Four Aces,
316 West Birch Street;
(307) 436–9010

LANDER

Highwayman Cafe,
974 Highway 789;
(307) 332–4628

The Hitching Rack,
Highway 287 South;
(307) 332–4322

LUSK

Fireside Inn,
904 South Main Street;
(307) 334–3477

RIVERTON

The Breadboard,
124 East Washington
Avvenue;
(307) 856–7044

China Panda,
300 North Federal;
(307) 856–7666

TORRINGTON

The Bake Haus,
1915 Main Street;
(307) 532–2982

WHEATLAND

Vimbo's Restaurant,
203 16th Street;
(307) 322–3842

Wheatland Inn,
86 16th Street;
(307) 322–9302

Indexes

Entries for Bed-and-Breakfasts, Hotels, Inns, and Lodges, Restaurants appear on pages 169–70.

GENERAL INDEX

BED-AND-BREAKFASTS, HOTELS, INNS, AND LODGES

RESTAURANTS

About the Author

Cowboy State native Michael McCoy lives in Teton Valley, Idaho, 10 miles from the Wyoming border. He is the editor of *Greater Yellowstone: Inside and Out* magazine, and his outdoor and travel writing has appeared in Northwest Airlines' *World Traveler, Men's Journal, Bicycling, Montana,* and other national and regional publications. McCoy holds degrees in anthropology from the University of Wyoming and zoology from the University of Montana, and he serves as field editor for the Montana-based Adventure Cycling Association. He edited *Classic Cowboy Stories* for the Lyons Press and recently contributed to *Ahead of Their Time,* a Wyoming Wilderness Association anthology that celebrates heroes of the wilderness movement in Wyoming. His other Globe Pequot books are *Montana Off the Beaten Path, The Wild West,* and *Journey to the Northern Rockies.*